Ancient Ways for Modern Times

PATHS TO HEALTH AN LONGEVITY

James Shyun, M.S.A.O.M.
Grandmaster of Eight Step Preying Mantis Kung Fu
and Michael A. Cimino, MS

ACMAF Publications
American Chinese Martial Arts Federation Publications
    P.O. Box 5142
    Hacienda Heighs, CA 91745

For information or to order additional books please write to ACMAF Publications or visit our website and on-line store at 8step.com

Copyright ©2004 by James Shyun and Michael A. Cimino

All rights reserved
No part of this book may be reproduced or transmitted in any form or by any means, electronic or mechanical, including photocopying, recording, or by any information storage and retrieval system without permission in writing from the publisher.

ISBN: 1-932583-11-4

Printed in the United States of America

First Printing

Disclaimer:
The nature of health is multi-factorial and one of exposure and individual response to continuous influences. The reader is advised that any health concern should be addressed by a licensed health care professional and that the authors of this book as well the publisher, editors, reviewers, and their agents are not responsible for the use or misuse of any information contained herein. Furthermore, any injury, misinterpretation, unplanned or unintended outcome due to ones own action or that of an action taken by any individual in response to the information contained within this book is not the responsibility of the authors, publisher, editors, reviewers, and their agents. Any use, personal or otherwise, of the information contained within this book is at the sole discretion of the reader understanding that the authors, publisher, editors, reviewers, and their agents hold no responsibility for such use of information contained herein.

Dedications and Acknowledgements

I would like to extend special recognition and offer my gratitude to Grandmaster Wei Hsiao Tang for passing the martial arts and medical knowledge contained within the Eight Step Preying Mantis system to me over twenty years of training and education. Through Grandmaster Wei's dedication, the system has lived on and been made available to the public. I would also like to express my gratitude to my parents for giving me the opportunity to study under Grandmaster Wei, and to my children, Anita and Anthony, and my wife Stephanie for their understanding and support over the years. In addition, I would like to offer my special appreciation to all of the Sifus for supporting the American-Chinese Martial Arts Federation and helping to make these arts available to the public.

Grandmaster James Shyun, M.S.A.O.M.

I would like to thank my parents, my wife, Linda and children, Jesse, Daniel, Hillary, and Colby for their support, patience, and understanding through the long hours of training and education necessary in practicing the martial arts and the many hours spent with Grandmaster Shyun recording the information and preparing the manuscripts necessary to bring this information to book form. I would also like to express my sincere appreciation to Grandmaster Shyun for his teaching and patience throughout this entire process of transcribing the knowledge; preparing, correcting, and editing the manuscripts until the information is presented as accurately as possible.

Michael A. Cimino, M.S., R.Ph.

Contents

Chapter 1
    Introduction 1

Chapter 2
    Shyun Kwong Long 11

Chapter 3
    The Environment .31

Chapter 4
    Diet, Health, and Longevity 70

Chapter 5
    Breathing 108

Chapter 6
    Exercise and Rest 143

Chapter 7
    The Spirit and Religion 177

Chapter 8
    History and Conclusions 189

    References 197

Chapter 1

Introduction

(Health and the Martial Arts)

In ancient times, one of the most basic prerequisites for survival was self-defense. The great kung fu masters of China, with their extensive knowledge base and mastery of the martial arts, excelled in this area. For centuries these masters adhered to an intricate and inter-related set of principles and methods that not only guided the practice of martial arts, but also produced and maintained health, fitness, and longevity. The greatest of these individuals, the grandmasters, were looked upon as counselors, healers, leaders, and protectors of their communities. Those who wished to become students of the martial arts sought after them, and if accepted, served as apprentices. The complete systems encompassed a vast body of knowledge, inclusive of martial arts techniques, breathing exercises (Chi Kung), and a form of Chinese Medicine specific to the martial arts, later termed Abimoxi. The knowledge base within each system was protected as rigorously as military secrets are protected in modern times. As a result, only the most trusted, loyal, and devoted students were entrusted to receive the entire knowledge base contained within each of the many martial art systems. The majority of students, those, who were not necessarily devoted to the art, were never privy to these secrets.

In this century, the emphasis of the martial arts on combat and self-preservation is declining, compared to previous centuries, given the relative advances in law enforcement and societal values. Modern society provides an expansive system of laws and order, intended to protect the individual against harm. Village, town, city, county, state, and national governments are equipped to protect residents and citizens from crimes ranging from vandalism to foreign aggression. Today, while martial arts certainly provide the capacity for self-protection, the emphasis, the greatest value offered by the martial arts to modern society, is rapidly evolving toward health, fitness, and longevity. Proper practice and understanding of this knowledge will hopefully lead to long, active, and vital lives for those who adopt the concepts and principles outlined in this book. Until now, the centuries' old secrets pertaining to health and longevity of one system, Eight Step Preying Mantis Kung Fu, have never been revealed to the general public. Through presentation of key points, in easy-to-understand terms, the reader should gain an appreciation for these alternative methods, which foster health and longevity. The key points include 1) the knowledge base of great kung fu masters that leads to health, fitness, and longevity, 2) perspectives on martial arts training practices considered to promote health and longevity, 3) an example of personal health issues that have been overcome in the life of one of the great Grandmasters, through the methods of Eight Step Preying Mantis Kung Fu, and 4) correlates from modern thinking and western medicine which support some of these principles and methods.

Images of men dressed in pajama-type clothing, donned with knotted black belts, yelling, jumping through the air, kicking, punching, twirling weapons in contorted motions, performing superhuman feats of combat strength come to mind when most people think of martial arts. Movies and television programs capture the sensational aspects of the martial arts to stun and amaze audiences, through special effects and the unique blend of acrobatics, acting, and martial arts abilities. While entertaining, this depiction and presentation of martial arts has little resemblance to true martial arts training. Recently, many parents have come to understand the benefits of improved concentration, discipline, positive attitude, and better school grades among children who attend martial arts classes. For others, martial arts have offered extended benefits in terms of health, fitness, and longevity. These are emphasized in this book.

The Grandmasters of Eight Step Preying Mantis lived well past the eighth decade of life. Aside from the outward and obvious physical abilities, and beyond the disciple and concentration required in the early stages of training, the core elements that contributed to the health and fitness of these individuals allowed for the vitality they experienced through the advanced decades of life. The core elements not only addressed the outwardly visible aspects of health, but also those, which are internal and not as obvious. For example, the effects of exercise on the musculoskeletal system are readily apparent such as muscle tone, strength, and endurance, yet the impact on the cardiovascular system is not as obvious, such as lower blood pressure and resting heart rate. The physical exercises of importance also have a positive health effect on the cartilage and bone, in addition to the muscle. These exercises also train pulmonary system (lungs) in addition to the entire cardiovascular system (heart, large and small blood vessels), such that excessive strain or improper breathing are avoided. This prevents heart and lung damage. Additional elements of training include the time of day at which these exercises are performed. The timing is intended to coincide with the predominant time of chi flow to particular organ systems. The timing addresses the health needs of the central nervous system, the mind and soul, the immune system, the blood element forming system (bone marrow), the gastrointestinal system including the small and large intestine, gall bladder, stomach and liver, other organs such as the spleen and pancreas, the excretory system including the kidneys and urinary bladder, and the reproductive system. Methods attending to body metabolism and energy generation and distribution within the body are also important elements of training. These and other important factors must be addressed to appreciate the health benefits of the Grandmasters of this martial art. Unlike the western concept of exercise, which promotes the visible external aspects of a healthy body and cardiopulmonary endurance (eg. running, weight lifting, rowing, aerobics), the great kung fu masters recognized both the internal aspects of the martial arts, as well as the external. Their understanding avoided several pitfalls of physical exercise, specifically, the expense to the internal organs and other tissues, such as ligaments and joints. Through proper breathing, coordinated with posture and other practices, including internal visualization, the ability to energize the often-neglected internal organs can be achieved. Tai Chi Chuan is an excellent example of an internal martial art, which assists in accomplishing this goal. An entire chapter will be devoted to these forms of exercise, referred to as Moving Chi Kung. These types of health related practices, found in the martial arts, are not widely practiced in western society. In an attempt to be accurate, avoiding misrepresentation of other martial art systems, only that, which is contained within the Systems of Eight Step Preying Mantis and Shyun Style Tai Chi Chuan, as taught by Grandmaster James Shyun, Shyun Kwong Long, will be presented in this book. All reference made in this book to the Chinese martial arts and/or Chinese martial arts health experts should be understood to be made in this context.

  Exercise is one part of a broader set of principles, referred to as the Three Pillars of Longevity. These include proper diet and proper sexual behavior, in addition to proper exercise. It is believed that attending to these three will determine an individual's vitality and longevity. Improper diet is one of the leading causes of disease. One only has to scan the magazine racks, turn on the TV, open a newspaper, or search the vast array of excellent books published on the subject, to recognize the widespread opinions over diet and health in western society. The relationship between diet and health has been recognized among martial arts masters and practitioners of Chinese medicine for thousands of years. The medical writings of the 7th century, Sun Sze-Miao indicated that the best way to treat illness was through a balancing of proper dietary components. Diet has proven to be a method to treat disease over the centuries. In western history, certain fruits, such as limes and oranges, could be used to treat scurvy among sailors, a condition later understood to be due to a deficiency in vitamin C. The potential of foods to balance ying and yang energy, thus serving as a treatment of illness, and moreover, to improve and maintain health, has been appreciated for centuries on an empirical basis. The use of foods to establish health, on a wider scale, is likely to be understood through the rigors of modern science. As has the use of fruits and other foods rich in vitamins been understood to provide benefit in the treatment and prevention of illness due to vitamin deficiencies, the use of diet will likely be understood to treat other illnesses, based on providing a rich and natural source of antioxidants and other life enhancing substances.

It is believed, within this system of Chinese martial arts, Eight Step Preying Mantis, that five basic considerations should be made with regard to diet. These include the amount of food consumed, season, personality and body type, and the application of Yin and Yang theory and the Five Element theory to diet. The amount of food consumed is not necessarily the amount of food required to sustain the body for optimal health. Often, food is used as a source of comfort, leading to excessive consumption to satisfy taste or some other psychological need. Under these circumstances the amount of food consumed can be considerable, leading to the short-term shunting of energy and blood to the digestive processes, thus leaving energy required for other organ systems, deficient. Difficulty breathing due to an overfilled stomach and somnolence following a large meal are readily apparent adverse effects of such behavior. Less visible are the effects on other organs. Chronic behavior of this nature will ultimately lead to excess weight, possibly obesity, and the diseases that often follow, such as diabetes and cardiovascular diseases. From a martial arts perspective, overeating will leave the martial artist vulnerable for similar reasons. Again, the advantage of consuming the proper amount of food not only provides a mechanism to improve health, by preventing such diseases, but also promoting organ function and optimizing the potential for health and longevity.

The type of food consumed, based upon the season of the year, is as important as amount of food consumed. For example, during winter, foods such as meat, whole grains, and even moderate amounts of alcohol, serve to increase Guardian Chi, which bolsters the body's defenses against common winter illnesses. Personality also dictates the optimal foods a person should consume. For example, an individual who is extroverted and have a type A personality, should consume cooling or Yin type foods, thus providing balance to the Yang personality. This brings into play the Yin and Yang Theory with respect to dietary behavior. Foods can correct for Yin or Yang deficiencies, resulting from factors other than personality type, thus improving and maintaining health and internal fitness. Specific foods may address the needs of various organs that can be in a state of deficiency, thus insuring proper balance. For example, sweet food can address certain conditions of the stomach. Western medicine recognizes the value of sweet substances for treating nausea in children. An entire chapter will be devoted to the subject of proper diet and use of foods in promoting health based upon the Yin and Yang and Five Element Theories.

Sex is a very personal topic and one that is often used in a moral or ethical context. The issue of proper sexuality will be discussed here strictly from a health perspective. In Traditional Chinese Medicine it is believed that a persons level of energy, overall health, and vitality are determined through original essence, or Jing Essence, which is derived from an individual's parents, through the joining of DNA from the sperm and ovum. Factors, such as excessive work, stress, and overindulgence in sexual activity, deplete Jing throughout life.

Moderation with respect to sexual activity preserves Jing, and therefore, promotes longevity.

Several related concepts are pertinent from a health perspective. Jing Essence, believed to hold the potential for all genetically derived characteristics of the offspring, DNA, is therefore related to disease. It has been known for years that some diseases are genetically based, such as Down's syndrome. Only recently has DNA testing revealed the presence of genes that may predispose to other illnesses, including certain cancers, via oncogenes. Whether faulty genetic structure occurs at some point following union of sperm and ovum, or is inherited from parental genetic material, is dependent upon the disease. Sickle cell disease is inherited from the parental genetic makeup, for example. It is as conceivable that general characteristics can be influenced by genetic makeup, in a manner similar to disease. Energy level or vitality can, therefore, be included among the many characteristics inherited from either or both parents. One need only consider the number of energetic people encountered and determine the energy level of their parents to make a correlation. Jing Essence, thought to be housed in the kidneys, underlies the foundation of this concept, not only in Chinese Medicine, but also in reference to several recent books (1). Much of a person's resilience and energy can be explained, in part, through understanding of the endocrine system. Hormones produced in the kidneys and adrenal glands, located near the kidney, such as cortisol and erythopoetin, are responsible for resilience to stressful conditions and for maintaining blood cells with oxygen carrying capacity, respectively. It is, therefore, conceivable that similar observations with regard to energy level and the kidneys were made, which are now explained, based on normal hormone production by the kidneys and other glands located near the kidneys. On the one hand, Jing Essence was understood on the basis of general observations over the course of centuries, while the modern understanding, based on specific scientific observations, revealed the role of specific hormones of the endocrine system.

The topics of diet and exercise have briefly been introduced. The environment and our interaction with the environment, breathing methods, rest, and incorporating religious beliefs into one's life represent other important aspects of health and longevity. The types of breathing, incorporated within the martial arts applications, not only lead to an increase in lung capacity, but also assist in exercising of the internal organs. The time of day in which the breathing and related exercises are performed strengthens different organs. The types of exercise include stretching, strengthening, toning, and relaxation. These exercises are performed while coordinating with deep breathing, mental attitude, and focus. One goal of such exercise is to increase internal energy. In general, it is these "internal" aspects of the martial arts, which are consistent with health and longevity. These will be given specific attention in one or more of the following chapters.

It can be appreciated at this point, that numerous factors contribute to fitness, health, avoidance of disease, and longevity. For optimal effectiveness, these factors must be viewed in a holistic manner. That is, one or more factors should not be ignored in preference to others. All are important. They are inter-related, dependent upon one another in some cases, and influence one anther. All are paths to health and longevity, and must be traveled.

Through the accumulated knowledge, resulting from trial and error over centuries, the great kung fu masters have left a legacy, from which modern culture can gain. Over the last three to four centuries of western culture, through the scientific method, various hypotheses, related to health and disease, have been tested. In many cases, the two approaches of trial and error and the scientific method have addressed similar topics. While the approach of each may be different, sufficient consistency exists, supportive of practices associated with improved health and longevity. Despite support from two different paths of knowledge, it would be erroneous to assume that those who participate in the health and fitness practices described in this book will benefit or achieve the same benefit compared to others. Factors, which cannot be controlled for, will play a role in the effectiveness of attempts to improve health and longevity. These factors include, genetic makeup, individual proficiency in technique or understanding, dedication to practice, unknown factors that influence health and longevity, and unanticipated and unpredictable events, which have profound effects on health and longevity, such as accidental trauma, will influence outcome. No claim can be made, as to the impact of the contents of this book on the health, fitness, or longevity of any individual. People interested in participating in this methodology should always seek medical advice, as would normally be the case with any activity that holds the potential to impact health status. The contents of this book outline the knowledge and practices believed to be associated with improved health and longevity. Participation in this knowledge and practice is at the reader's own discretion and choice. It is, of course, hoped that with appropriate participation, outcomes similar to those experienced by the great masters of kung fu will be achieved, and lives benefited.

The information contained in this book is derived from four general sources. These include, the information passed from generation to generation within the Eight Step Preying Mantis System of Kung Fu. In addition, peer reviewed, scientific reports, such as clinical trials, provide much of the supportive information where indicated. Other sources of information pertaining to modern thinking on the subject matter, such as material contained on various websites, is also provided. Finally, information that falls into the realm of "common knowledge," for example, the association between high cholesterol and cardiovascular disease, represents another source of information. References will be provided for peer-reviewed scientific information. Information noted to stem from the Chinese martial arts represents that of the Eight Step Preying Mantis System and Shyun Style Tai Chi Chuan, for reasons mentioned earlier. Information which is derived from "common knowledge" or available through Internet websites will not be referenced, unless unique.

It must be kept in mind, that, the purpose of this book is to present the ancient paths which have led to health and longevity, yet the relevant ideas, thinking, and scientific evidence available in modern times must also be considered. Therefore, the additional information provided, related to modern times, should be viewed in this context, not necessarily as the definitive evidence supporting these ancient practices, but as complimentary. In this regard, the lack of modern scientific evidence will not be viewed as a lack of support for a practice or concept, merely a gap in modern knowledge that may someday be filled.

Chapter 2

Shyun Kwong Long

The sound of bicycle tires rolling over packed soil, sand, and stone that formed the roadway passing in front of Wei Shou Tong's home mixed with familiar voices, breaking the silence of the afternoon's solitude. It had been several days since passerby's traveled this particular path in rural Taiwan.

"Shou Tong!" called out Mr. Chen waving to Wei Shou Tong as he emerged from the side of his house located west of Taipei on the lower slope of the Chung Ho Mountains.

"Welcome" responded Shou Tong. "It has been some time since you visited."

"Yes, please forgive us for not visiting sooner," Mr. Fong said apologetically, as he and Mr. Chen approached their long-time friend.

"Why have you come all this way today?" questioned Wei Shou Tong intuitively, as he noted some urgency in the two men approaching.

"We have been asked by friends to speak with you about their ill son."

"What does this involve?"

"There is a young boy, who is very ill. His family asked, through our friends, to speak with you and determine if you will go to their home and see him - possibly help him?"

"Who is this boy?" Wei Shou Tong questioned further as he sat on the wooden bench directing his friends to be seated on the stumps of wood, carved into seats, across the table. He listened as he began separating several plants, which he recently harvested from the garden near his home. Requests, such as this, have been made in the past. On this occasion, however, the petition was much more formal, more serious.

Wei Shou Tong was of medium build, emulating the strength of a sound physical build, as well as a certain calmness and assurance, unique to his stature as a grandmaster of Chinese martial arts and healer. He displayed an authority of nobility, yet the humility only acquired through years of disciplined labor, necessary in overcoming tremendous challenges. These were the challenges associated with fulfilling the requirements of becoming the Grandmaster of one of the most sought after kung fu systems in existence. Attaining the status of grandmaster is akin to recognition as professor emetrius in western culture. An aura of power and wisdom emerged through his calm mannerisms. The informality of visiting with old friends could not hide what was natural to his character and being. This was simply energy, emitted from within, through the shell of the physical structure, charisma in pure form.

"He is the young son of General Shyun...Kwong Long. He is very ill; and the family has been given no hope – only to prepare for his death," responded Mr. Chen somberly.

The morning air was humid, yet cooler than normal, for this time of year. Early spring was generally warmer in this subtropical island of Taiwan. A calm breeze reached across the yard of Master Wei's home, carrying the scent of spring. The songs of familiar colorful birds gently interrupted the overwhelming quietude of this abode. Time seemed to have escaped this place. Seconds became comfortable and well-appreciated minutes. As he glanced upward, noticing a Blue Magpie that had just landed on a branch overhanging the table that the men were seated around, the reputed great master of Preying Mantis Kung Fu and healer stood motioning to his friends, "Then we should not delay. I will see the boy."

The three men stood, then soon embarked upon the route set before them, to the Shyun household in Taipei. The spring sun began to warm the narrow dirt road, bordered with the thick vegetations of forest, which it separated. Attention to the sounds of their bicycle tires, churning up dirt pavement, and the rustling of palm branches from the breezes passing above the trees, gave way to the voices of these friends, occupied in conversation, speaking of old times and discussing recent political events.

This was a time of settling, following a period of great unrest. Taiwan, known as Formosa at the time, is the largest island outside the mainland of China. It was leased to Japan prior to World War II, during which time little was done to develop the island. After World War II, Taiwan was turned over to the Republic of China. Following the war, however, China remained in a state of unrest. Its people were in the midst of experiencing the turmoil of the communist revolution. During this political upheaval, the traditional ruling party, the Kuo Min Dang, continued as the legal government in China. However, following the loss of the civil war in 1949, the Kon Chan Dang, the Communist Party, took control of Mainland China. It was given the name "Peoples Republic of China."

Taiwan then became the formal home of the Kuo Min Dang, the Republic of China.

With the Communist Party in full control of mainland China, the tumultuous process of political and ideological purging had begun, in an effort to control dissention. Those opposed to the Kon Chan Dang were often sentenced to death, or sent to fight in the Korean War. It was during this time that Wei Shou Tang, renowned Third Generation Grand Master of Eight Step Praying Mantis, being employed by the Kuo Ming Dang, was wanted by the communist authorities for the killing of several communist soldiers during an incident. Wei Shou Tang, also known as Shou Tong, escaped to Korea.

Intending to preserve the heritage of China, the government of Taiwan sought after famous individuals, including many Kung Fu masters. During his stay in Korea, the Kuo Min Dang sought out Wei Shou Tang, because of his skill and reputation as a great martial artist and respected physician. He was finally contacted by operatives of the Kuo Min Dang, and brought to Taiwan during the time of the Korean War, and granted asylum.

Now re-established in Taiwan, Wei Shou Tang found the island to be mostly rural and undeveloped. Since mechanized means of transportation were somewhat limited, bicycles served to be practical and effective. This now allowed old friends to take leisurely advantage of the opportunity for conversation. The time passed quickly, as the men arrived at the home of mutual friends, resting briefly before going on to the home of Shyun Kwong Long.

The men were directed to the Shyun family home, where General Shyun warmly greeted them. "May I introduce Grandmaster Wei Shou Tong. He has agreed to see your youngest son," said Mr. Chen, the eldest of the men who approached.

"Please come in." beckoned General Shyun, as he led his guests into the house, which continued into an open courtyard. "My wife is preparing tea." The home was beautifully kept and decorated. Walls, some of which were the outer walls of rooms, contiguous to the house, surrounded the courtyard. Potted plants lined the perimeter of the courtyard, which gave the aroma of a recent watering.

"Thank you, General Shyun," stated Grandmaster Wei, as he and the other men were directed by the General to be seated around a large table, located near the exit of the house into the courtyard. "Tell me about your son, Kwong Long."

With great sadness he explained, "We have consulted many physicians, both traditional and western. They have given us no hope for his recovery. They have finally advised us to make preparation for his death."

"What is his main problem right now?" the healer questioned further.

"He cannot breath easily. It is difficult for him to walk because he gasps for air," explained General Shyun.

"Is he normally and active child?" Master Wei further questioned.

"Yes, very active before this illness began," replied his father.

"I would like to see your son now," requested Master Wei, hearing sounds of the young boy grunting for air from a distant room.

Wei Shou Tong was led to another room, where Kwong Long lay. He was breathing rapidly and with great difficulty. Wei Shou Tong approached him and found him to be very weak and unwilling to move, a condition inconsistent with the young child's personality, for he was normally very active, having compensated to the best of his abilities for this infirmity. Sitting by his side he reached for his right arm and extended it along the bed. With precise palpation, he felt the boy's pulse for several minutes focusing intently on the various aspects of rate, rhythm, intensity, and the ratio of beats to respirations. Kwong Long coughed several times trying to clear his lungs in an effort to breathe. As the almost five-year-old patient gasped for air, laboring at each breath, Master Wei questioned, "How long has he been like this?"

"The breathing has only been this difficult for the past week," replied General Shyun, as he thought grippingly of Kwong Long. His father spoke as he held to the memories of his son as an infant, first pulling himself to his feet and taking his first steps. He reflected on the pride and joy that permeated throughout the house, as he and his wife beckoned their son forward while they knelt to catch him, as his first step was about to be interrupted by a tumble. The hopes and dreams for the future were now so dismal. This man, who sat next to him, was their last hope.

"This started about eight months ago. He coughed but was not compromised. He continued to play with his friends. He would run and play games, chasing and being chased, with the other children. His coughing persisted for several days. We thought this unusual, and took him to see the doctor. He was given medicine, but the coughing continued. We took him to several other doctors, week after week, trying their treatments, but he never improved. He has become worse and worse. He stopped playing with his friends, and was short of breath, even when walking. It has come to this point, where today, he must sit upright, to maintain his breath. He was seen only a few days ago, and the doctor said that his lungs have filled with fluid, which is causing him to strain with each breath. He said no other treatments are available; everything has been tried....they have tried everything they know. My friends heard of your skills, and we are hopeful you can help our son."

With concern as to the ultimate outcome, Wei Shou Tong patted young Kwong Long's shoulder, as he suggested they sit for tea in the courtyard. Mrs. Shyun poured tea and returned to Kwong Long's bedside, as the men sat at the table. Master Wei looked carefully at Kwong Long's father, paused for a moment, unsure if he could help in this situation. He sipped from the teacup, and then placed it softly on the table, as he revealed his plan. "If you and your wife agree, I will take your son to my home. There, I will treat him. If he is healed, I will return with him in one year. If I am unable, I will arrange for his burial and you will not hear from me any further."

Very grateful for his kindness, General Shyun excused himself and sat with his wife, privately, for a lengthy period, discussing all that had been said by Wei Shou Tong. They carefully and helplessly considered the only option available. Willing to try anything at this point, it was agreed that their son should accompany the Grandmaster to his home.

Too young to understand the implications of this decision, Kwong Long's concerns centered around not having the ability to play with his friends. Although sheltered, as to the gravity of his illness, and despite the attempts of his family to curtain their feelings, he saw the sadness in his parents eyes as they told him he would leave with Master Wei for a time. He would live with Master Wei, at his countryside home for a time. They explained Master Wei would try to help him so he could once again be able to play with his friends and feel better.

It had been eight long months of progressive worsening of symptoms, yet now, the thought of leaving the security of his parent's attention and their love was terrifying. Until this point, his only concern was the inability to play with his friends, but now he was gripped by a fear - fear of leaving with this person he did not know; fear of the great unknowns that existed outside the walls of his home. Who was this man he would leave with? When would he return? How long would a year be? What would he do to him – would it hurt as some of the other treatments did?

The following morning a side cart was affixed to Master Wei's bicycle. Kwong Long was comfortably positioned in the cart, being placed over several blankets that cushioned the wooden seat. Soon they were on their way, tears streaming from Kwong Long's eyes, as he looked behind, toward his parents. Too weak to rebel, he cried out for his parents to take him back. Outwardly strong, standing firm, wishing their son well, his parents' hearts had melted within. Only bones and ligaments prevented them from collapsing to the ground with grief. Inexplicable morose had stolen their strength. They remained in this falsetto until Kwong Long was out of sight.

Clinging only to the hope of Master Wei's success, they were able to return to the confines of their house.

The blossoming of springtime in the countryside west of Taipei was of no solace to Kwong Long, as he wished only to be returned to his family. His first day at the home of Master Wei was met by one of several downpours. These were frequent during this time of year. It was the rainy season. The water would find its way under the walls of the simple dwelling, now home for Kwong Long, turning the patted dirt floor into a muddy pool. When the rains became so intense, wooden boards were placed over the dirt floor, allowing the interior to be as comfortable as possible. During this season, however, the sudden downpours and the rush of water from the hillside often occurred too quickly, not allowing sufficient time for the floor to be covered by the wooden planks.

Unlike the Shyun family's home, the house of Master Wei was, in comparison, very simple. It was typical of the dwellings found at the foot of the Cheng Ho Mountains. These were single story dwellings, consisting of wood plank walls and roof. The beds were constructed of similar planking, without mattresses to sleep upon. The wooden beds, simple in their construction, were raised above the floor with only enough space for storage beneath them. Hooks lined the walls that held a variety of utensils, clothing, such as jackets, plants and herbs, sorted and stored for drying. The beams overhead, supporting the roof, also served the purpose of hanging curtains, allowing for some degree of privacy. There was no running water or plumbing in this house. Water was available at the well, some walking distance away, approximately 5 minutes. A counter against the far wall, opposite the front door, allowed space for a large basin. It was freshly filled with water daily, to be used for cleaning. A separate pail was available, from which fresh water was drawn from the well for refreshment, preparing tea, and for cooking.

A fire pit, opposite the large table, located outside of the house along the west wall, was used for cooking food and boiling herbs, useful as remedies for various diseases. The table was fitted with a long bench on one side. Stools were positioned pragmatically along the opposite side, which proved to be the busiest location of Master Wei's home. Here, vegetables were prepared for cooking; herbs for medicines were chopped, cut, or crushed using a large mortal and pestle, which was stored on the counter within the home. This place served as the area where meals were eaten and friends gathered to visit. One could see into the home through a window, positioned above one end of this table. Some windows held glass panes, while others were fitted only with shutters. Beyond the fire pit was the woodpile, replenished frequently from the vast supply of fallen trees and small twigs found in the surrounding forest.

A path, leading from the road to the house, passed under a wooden archway with lanterns hanging from the two supporting posts on either side. Beyond the west side of the house were two additional paths: one, which led down a natural slope to an out-house; the other led up a slope, toward the mountain. Along this path, approximately a five-minute walk from the house was a natural well-spring, which served as the fresh water-source. Buckets of water were carried frequently from this well to the home. This activity was to become a common task for Kwong Long, as he would grow to find comfort and healing within the borders of this domicile. To the east flowed a stream, emerging from a large pool formed from the gentle waterfall rippling down the hillside forming the base of the mountain.

Master Wei was diligent about maintaining his gardens. Two gardens were most important. These were the vegetable and herbal gardens. Most of their sustenance would be harvested from the vegetable garden, on a daily basis. He had purchased a supply of flour from the city market. It was placed in a large storage bin inside the home. This flour was mixed with water to make buns.

A large variety of herbs were cultivated and harvested. Some were used fresh, while others were dried and stored. Most herbs were used for medicinal purposes. Medicines were prepared as teas, which served as a vehicle for administering their varied and multiple active ingredients. Others were packaged as poltices and applied topically. The remainder of the property was kept as a natural garden, where grasses interspersed the flora, indigenous to this area of Taiwan. The natural garden was comfortable and pleasing to the eye, offering a source of comfort and strength to the observer.

Upon his arrival, Kwong Long was very weak. The ten-mile trip from the city to this humble country homestead taxed the young boy significantly. His treatment was not delayed and began simply with a drink of water, freshly drawn from the well near his home. Soon, Master Wei prepared a meal that was considered easy to digest, comprised of fresh vegetables and cooked flour buns. This would become the foundation of the nutritional component of therapy for the remainder of his stay. Concerned by his young patient's weakness, meats of any type were not included in the prescribed diet.

No sooner than entering the gateway to Master Wei's home, Kwong Long yearned to return to his family. The boy's thoughts were not in concert with those of his physician in this regard. Looking up at the stranger, he could no longer contain himself and verbalized his desire to leave. Before his request was complete, Master Wei sat along the boy's side, extending his arm applying pressure to several points on his hands and along his arm. Pressure point massage, Tui Na, had begun. "Kwong Long, you cannot go home yet," he responded while continuing the massage. "There is much that must be done. You will stay here until you are free of your illness; until you are stronger; until you are able to play with your friends again." These words would become a familiar mantra because Kwong Long's focus would remain only to return to his home and family. Master Wei motioned to his young patient, directing him to recline slightly onto the straw mat. He then moved to the boy's opposite side, applying massage to pressure points on his foot and lower leg. His little patient's eyelids closed as his breathing became more relaxed. Soon he was asleep.

As the little patient slept Master Wei walked to area between the gardens and began his exercise routine. Three hours passed. Finishing the exercise, he heard Kwong Long stirring as he began to awaken from his sleep. Attending to his patient, he repeated the process of offering water, then prepared a small meal of vegetables and buns. When applying the Tui Na therapy, he started on the opposite side. Master Wei noted that Kwong Long experienced significant pain as he extended the massage to areas of his back. He would at times vigorously request that the massage be discontinued. Master Wei refused to allow his young patient to dictate therapy, and proceeded with the procedure despite the pain. On this occasion, exhausted by the massage, he allowed Kwong Long to rest once again. This cycle of therapy continued for several days, until the boy began to feel stronger.

Considering the progress that had been made over the past several days, Master Wei decided it was now time to move on to additional therapy. On this particular morning, as the sun began to rise, he called out to Kwong Long as he nudged his shoulder gently, "It is time to start exercise." After completing the usual routine with his patient sitting upright, legs dangling over the edge of the wooden bed, he instructed Kwong Long to extend his arms horizontally and move both hands in a circling motion. He directed Kwong Ling to circle the hands around and around several times, first in one direction, then the opposite direction. This was no easy task, because the young boy's weakened arms began to show signs of difficulty. His hands lowered with each turn of the wrist as he labored to maintain them horizontal to the ground. This simple routine was repeated two more times that day, followed by rest. With each prompting to begin, Master Wei responded to Kwong Long's requests to return home with the instructions, "You cannot go home yet. There is much that must be done. You will stay here until you are free of your illness; until you are stronger; until you are able to play with your friends again."

Several days passed once again, during which time Kwong Long became noticeably stronger. He was able to maintain his arms horizontally until the exercise was complete. He was less tired, although this minimal effort continued to be associated with shortness of breath. As had been his practice, Master Wei skillfully placed his fingers over the boy's wrist counting the number of heartbeats, relative to the number of breaths. A glimmer of hope emerged as a positive trend became apparent, over the last few examinations. Kwong Long rested frequently, but the proportion of time spent in sleep, during the rest periods, had decreased.

These continued to be difficult times, emotionally, since he continuously thought of home, his mother and father. His heart ached to be with them, to feel their love and compassion. Had they abandoned him, he wondered. But this could not be the case, because he never had cause to question their unconditional love for him. They had sent him away, to be cared for by this man, a stranger. Initially he feared this healer, but over these several weeks Master Wei had proven not to be danger to him. In his own way of understanding Kwong Long accepted that he had shown great care in helping him. With this thought he drifted off to sleep once again.

As Kwong Long rested, Master Wei walked to the far end of the garden picking several herbs along the way. He then entered the forest area, which was within hearing distance from the house, and carved bark from a tree. Moving to another area, near the edge of the tree line, he knelt, piercing the earth with his knife. He plucked a plant, along with the roots from the soil. On his return from the garden, he placed the herbal harvest onto the large table outside of the house, then looked in on Kwong Long. Still sleeping he quietly tore stems from two different dried herbs, which hung from string that was fastened to nails, placed in the rafters' overhead. Moving to the counter at the other end of the house, he removed several seeds from a jar. He carried a pail, half full with water, from the counter to the table, upon which the herbs were placed, and cleaned the soil from the freshly picked roots. Taking these ingredients, including the bark and herbs from the table, he placed them into a pot; added water, then cut slices from the root, allowing them to fall into the mixture. He then hung the filled pot over a small fire, which at this point was slowly settling into flaming embers, perfect for brewing herbal teas.

It was late afternoon when his little patient awoke. A refreshing breeze passed through the house, mitigating the heat of this late spring afternoon. "I have a tea for you to drink, Kwong Long," the healer indicated, as he drew the broth from the pot, which he placed on the counter earlier to cool. Master Wei sat along side his patient; brought the cup to his lips and stated, "Sip slowly." Within a fraction of a second, of taking the first sip, he tuned his head away, cringing at the awful bitter taste of the tea. "Take another sip," beckoned Master Wei as Kwong Long turned away again. "You must drink this medicine or you will not get better." Reluctantly, the little patient acquiesced and took the sip, grimacing in the most contorted fashion and making his disfavor exaggeratedly obvious. The third, fourth, fifth, and final gulp ended the ordeal. Kwong Long would be required to drink this brew three times every day, as part of the treatment regimen, which was planned for his healing.

Within a few days of adding the herbal preparation to his treatment, Kwong Long began to feel noticeably stronger. He had been under the care of Master Wei for approximately two months. At this point his strength had improved sufficiently, where it became difficult for the physician to contain his small patient. "Let me go home, I feel better....I don't want to be here any more!" demanded Kwong Long. While chants of rebellion and somewhat annoying, the demands were interpreted as a very positive signs of recovery. His young patient is doing much better, Shou Tong thought. While posing some difficulty, these were very encouraging actions on the part of Kwong Long. He had improved, but was still seriously ill. Had Master Wei not planned on keeping the boy for one year, the additional therapies, scheduled over the next several months, designed to sustain his healing, would likely never have been completed. Outwardly, much had been accomplished. To sustain the improvement for a lifetime, the treatment would be continued for the full year. Soon he would move onto more formidable therapies. A more significant improvement was necessary at this point.

"Shou Tong!" rang the familiar voice of Mr. Chen, as he and Mr. Fong approached the house. "How is our little friend?" questioned Mr. Chen. "I spent time visiting with the Shyun family. They have been very anxious to know of Kwong Long's progress."

"He is showing improvement…very positive signs," said Shou Tong, as he exited the front door, before responding to Kwong Long's repeated requests to return home. Shou Tong motioned to his two friends, indicating he would prefer them to walk near the gardens, far enough away from the house so as not to be heard. "The boy is much better but he must remain here with me, to complete the treatment. If his parents visit now, he will surely return home. All the gains, thus far attained, would then be in vain. As you can understand by his demands, he has improved sufficiently, that his strength has begun to return. Go again to the Shyun family, and tell them he is better. Yet, it will be in their son's interest to refrain from seeing him so soon. I will send word again."

"Thank you, thank you! I will visit them again tomorrow, since it is getting late in the day." Encouraged by the news and anticipating the Shyuns' joy, the men mounted their bicycles, and began their ride back to Taipei.

The next morning was met with stern resistance to the herbal tea. Kwong Long refused to drink the bitter preparation that he found intolerable, from the first day it was administered. But now, with his strength returning, he pierced his lips tight and turned his head away, causing Master Wei to spill a portion of the brew onto the floor. As if predicting this moment, the healer had cut a bamboo stick, having placed it the back pocket of his pants. He drew the stick, striking the wooden bed, near to where Kwong Long was reclining, and gently warned, "If you do not drink, you will be punished," motioning the manner in which he would strike the back of his small hand with the bamboo stick. Without hesitation, he looked at the cup of tea, reached out, grabbed it, then drink its contents.

Impressed by Kwong Long's good behavior, he walked over to his bed and pulled a large trunk from beneath it. Opening the trunk slowly, noticing Kwong Long peaking around the curtain that separated the areas, he pulled out a small toy.

"I have something for you!" hinting at the small object in his hands. This was a hinged puzzle of small, connected wooden pieces that could be shaped to resemble many different objects. This was something to occupy the young boy's mind, until he was strong enough to participate in more vigorous activities.

Later in the day, during the time normally devoted to massage, Master Wei reached for a box containing several acupuncture needles. As he withdrew the box from a trunk under his bed, Kwong Long's curiosity peaked once again. "Do you have a present for me?" he asked, as he thought back on his good behavior in drinking the tea earlier that morning. "No present," responded Master Wei. Kwong Long's curiosity turned to fear as he opened the box, exposing the needles. "This will not hurt, do not be afraid." Obviously, not believing the words of his healer, the boy pulled himself to the far-most corner of the bed, away from Master Wei. The Grandmaster took the needle and inserted it into his own hand. "See. No pain," said Master Wei, hoping to alleviate his fear. "This will help you more than the massage, now that your strength has returned."

Leaving the needle in his own hand, he gently held Kwong Long's hand and inserted the needle into a similar position on his patient's hand. He felt the boy relax. "See. No pain," said Master Wei with confidence. Soon after, several needles were inserted into Kwong Long's extremities. After a few minutes he instructed his little patient to begin some of the familiar exercises, which he had been doing for the past several days. When they were completed, he removed the needles.

With these added treatments Kwong Long was able to stand, then walk. After several days he was able to leave the house to follow Master Wei in the yard and garden. On this particular late morning, Master Wei knelt onto the ground and began weeding between the vegetables. Within a short time Kwong Long followed suit and knelt beside him. "Not that one!" Master Wei exclaimed, noting that Kwong Long had reached for a vegetable to pull from the soil. "Only pull ones that look like this!" he instructed as he pointed to a weed, which should be pulled. For the remainder of the morning they attended to this chore.

Within days Kwong Long was able to follow his physican around the yard, assisting with many of the simple chores, including gathering sticks from the forest edge and from the yard to maintain the fire.

"Come with me up this way," Kwong Long heard Master Wei calling from a distance ahead of him. "Now we will walk up the mountain slope to get some fresh water from the spring," said Master Wei. Excited by the prospect of seeing new territory, the boy hurried to the side of his healer. They walked side by side along the path's gentle incline on the periphery of the mountain slope. They quickly arrived at the source of a stream. Here, a spring of water bubbled from the between several rounded stones. Master Wei pulled two metal cups from his vest, handing one to Kwong Long. He placed the cup near the exit of the spring from the ground, and filled the cup. After inspecting the water he took a sip. The taste was refreshing. He then drank the remainder of the water. He motioned to his young patient to do the same, and soon they relaxed and talked about playing. When their rest finished they returned from the mountain slope.

Soon they were back at the house. "I have a present for you, Shang Tou, using the nickname he coined for Kwong Long!" announced Master Wei, as he led Kwong Long to the trunk, which was stored under his bed. Excitedly, Kwong Long hurried beside the Master to see what awaited him. Opening the trunk, and moving a few pieces of clothing aside, he saw a ball. He instantly knew this was meant for him. Master Wei smiled as Kwong Long jumped up and down. "Thank you, thank you" he shouted as Master Wei handed the ball to him.

"Go outside and play," he instructed. Without hesitation, Kwong Long was in the yard kicking and chasing after the ball. In a short time he became tired, held the ball and sat on a stool overlooking the area between the gardens as Master Wei approached. He watched in amazement as the Grandmaster began to exercise. Slowly, he circled his arms, then his waste and legs, stretching and turning. The speed of the exercise increased with time. He watched intensely as he saw his physician's body dropping low then shooting upward, striking with his hands and kicking in several different ways with his legs and feet. What was this pattern of motion he was privileged to witness? A grandmaster does not train in the presence of others. The exercise period seemed to last for only a short time, but soon after he finished, the time had arrived for the herbal treatment that was scheduled for each afternoon.

It was approximately 3 a.m. the following morning, when Master Wei awakened his little patient. Uninterested, he turned hoping to fall asleep again. With the healer's invitation to participate in his exercise routine, he became somewhat more willing to be awakened. He thought of how early it was, and how sleepy he felt. Yesterday, treatment was in the afternoon, and the day before at a different time. Kwong Long did not understand the timing of his treatments, and wished they could all be during the day. Despite his dislike of this apparant lack of a routine, Kwong Long grew to accept Master Wei's discipline. He accepted therapy more readily, and had become strong enough to participate in some of the basic exercises, the most important of which were breathing exercises. This acceptance allowed his healer to ease from the sternness, which he usually displayed, and resort to a more kind and relaxed attitude toward his patient. Before long the sun was on the horizon, with it's brilliance poking through the trees, about to heat the dampness from the ground they stood upon.

"Now breathe like this, Shang Tou," instructed Master Wei, as he demonstrated the technique of using the diaphragm to draw air into the lungs, rather than the chest muscles. In so doing, the belly expands outward on inspiration rather than the chest expanding. Kwong Long attempted to mimic his physician, arching his back with the abdomen protruding outward. "No, no, not that way. You must breathe in not just stick your belly out!" laughed Master Wei, as he repeated the instruction from the beginning steps. Soon Kwong Long was able to breathe in, expanding the abdomen; then breathe out, as he retracted the abdomen. Carefully, Master Wei watched, correcting the process, until a slow, unlabored, easy breathing pattern was repeated several times. Careful not to allow his patient to take too many breaths at first, he let the boy return to play. Within a few weeks Kwong Long would practice breathing, at precisely assigned times during the day, increasing the number of breaths as tolerated.

So noticeable was the progress, that Kwong Long started to participate in many of Master Wei's activities, including basic martial arts. He thought of how he disliked Master Wei months earlier, but now, Master Wei had become like a stepfather to him. "Stand like this. Hold your arms this way," instructed Master Wei, as he corrected the position of Kwong Long's feet. "Bend your front knee more!" As he relaxed from the stance and straightened his leg, Master Wei immediately used his foot to correct the stance. In most circumstances, young students were put to the test of arduous stance training, holding a position for several minutes, then hours. This was not the purpose for the time being. Shang Tou's strength must not be taxed too severely at this point, thought Master Wei. This was part of treatment, rather than martial arts discipline. Moving from one stance to another, Kwong Long's interest was captured. His mind wandered, imagining that some day, he would be like his physician, flying, dipping low, then jumping high; moving forward striking, etc.

The next day, after completing the morning meal, Master Wei entered the house to gather a number of herbs for the next treatment. He did not hear Kwong Long follow. Looking out the rear window of the house, he smiled as he watched the boy in the area between the gardens, where they had exercised the previous day, striking and kicking running one way then back, circling and striking. *Today my patient – next year my student*, Master Wei thought.

The following morning, aroused from a deep sleep, Kwong Long felt the strong hand of Master Wei gently shaking his shoulder. "It is time to get up, little one," he heard his healer, as he slowly opened his eyes to see dawn's sunshine breaking through the opened window. "I have another surprise for you today," said Master Wei, noting some caution in his patient's eyes. Kwong Long was somewhat hesitant, wondering what new therapy Master Wei had in store for him. "Today, you will return home!"

Tears began to flow from Kwong Long's eyes as he hugged onto his healer's arm. These were long awaited tears, stored up for months waiting for the moment he would see his parents again. He would not forget Master Wei, nor would his growing attachment to this man, who brought strength and vitality back into his body, cease. But, he wanted nothing more than to go home. His health had improved, day after day. Treatment had persisted to a point, expected to permanently maintain his healing.

"Hurry, get into the side cart and we will go to your parents' home," Master Wei demanded with a subtle smile. Within seconds, Kwong Long was out of the house standing in the front path. He then hopped into the side cart of the bicycle, anxiously waiting to begin the ride to Taipei. Master Wei mounted the bike and began the ride to the city. This was the first time Kwong Long was healthy enough to enjoy the ride in the bicycle side cart. While a leisurely pace was chosen, the cart bounced over ruts carved in the roadway by water that had previously streamed down the hillside over the patted dirt road. The side cart pounded against the edge of holes created from puddles of water that had accumulated. Master Wei's heart was full of joy as he listened to laughter, hearty at times, emanating from the side cart.

As they pulled up to the Shyun family home, General and Mrs. Shyun noticed the familiar features of Kwong Long, the vision of which, they kept in their minds continuously, every day, and in their dreams, nightly. Smiles and tears exposed their relief at the sight of their son, healthily jumping out of the cart, running into their arms. What seemed like an unending period of hugs and elation, gave way to a brief recess to meet Master Wei, as he walked toward the re-united family. "There is not a way in which we can thank you, Grandmaster! You have saved our son, and brought happiness back to our life!" exclaimed General Shyun, as he greeted Master Wei in the traditional manner.

Master Wei accepted the gratitude of Kwong Long's parents and left them to enjoy their reunion. His absence would not be prolonged, for Master Wei would soon accept Kwong Long as his student, training him daily for the next twenty years, as his Master had trained him. Ultimately, Shyun Kwong Long would become the next inheritor of the Eight Step Preying Mantis System of Kung Fu. But for now, Kwong Long would return to the life he enjoyed with his family and friends of his age.

The treatments, which Shyun Kwong Long received, were delivered over several months with the intention of sustaining the healing for a lifetime. In retrospect, with over fifty years having passed from the occurrence of his illness, Grandmaster Shyun's conviction, regarding the multiple phases of treatment (diet, breathing exercise, pressure point massage, herbal therapy, and acupuncture), is based not only on education and training in Chinese Medicine, but also on his personal experience as a patient, treated with this approach. Much can be learned from this experience. In particular, that diet, specific health related exercises, and breathing techniques (Chi Kung therapy) assist greatly in sustaining health, regardless if performed as a treatment, or as a means to improve and maintain health. The following chapters will detail much of the ancient conceptual framework, which has been highlighted in this chapter, as well as supporting information, generated in modern times.

Chapter 3

The Environment

Introduction

There are a number of modifiable environmental factors and personal behaviors that hold the potential to affect health and longevity. Some of the more obvious include behaviors known to be detrimental to health, such as cigarette smoking. Other less obvious behaviors include poor dietary habits that people find comfortable due to tradition or familiarity. It is well known, but often overlooked, that regularly eating foods high in fat and/or high in unnecessary calories (snack foods, soft drinks, desserts) is unhealthy. Healthier selections can be substituted, which include fruits, vegetables and water. However, these selections are often viewed as unappealing when compared to foods high in sugar and fat, from a taste perspective. Other less tangible factors which contribute to poor health including the inability to manage personal psychological issues, such as uncontrolled emotion, work related stress, or anxiety associated with the fast pace of life. These can lead to suppression of the body's immune function. Thus, avoiding various environmental and behavioral insults to the body can have a dramatic impact on health and longevity. Air pollution, water pollution, food additives, including flavoring agents and dyes, represent only a few examples. Many of these factors are a result of the life style that has evolved in modern society, and pose a considerable challenge to health, most notably, development of chronic diseases. Life styles, which allow for the influence of these types of environmental and behavioral factors either lead to or are highly associated with the development of the leading chronic diseases facing modern Western society. These include heart disease, depression, and immune system related diseases including allergy, cancer, and diabetes. Being chronic conditions, their onset is often insidious, and their natural history is one of a long duration. Unfortunately, appropriate attention to factors which lead to these diseases are often ignored, until significant and sudden health consequences emerge. Such consequences can include heart attacks, strokes, and complications of chronically elevated blood sugar, cancer, crippling arthritis, or incapacitating depression. At that point, efforts can only be directed at limiting further insults to the body, since the most significant opportunity for prevention has long passed.

Some consider the modern life style to have evolved to the point of being deleterious to health, in general. The advances in technology, along with its many benefits, have led to the leisure and comforts Western society has come to enjoy. However, these are not without costs. While many partake of the convenience and taste of fast foods, for example, the side effects from high cholesterol and unnecessary calories exemplify the current public health concerns, stemming from increasing obesity, cardiovascular disease, and diabetes in our population. The presence of toxic pesticides in the living environment, chemicals in cleaning products used on a daily basis, toxic substances that have infiltrated the food supply, including mercury found in various ocean fish, and other environmental pollutants, pose as serious of a health concern.

The foundations of many kung fu masters' understanding of health arose from the tenants of Chinese Medicine. From this knowledge base, is the understanding that about five to ten percent of poor health is due to environmental factors (air and water pollution, poor air quality in living spaces, for example) and approximately thirty to thirty-five percent of health problems are attributable to poor eating habits and diet; thirty percent to problems associated with the seven human emotions, and the remaining thirty percent to eating and sleeping inappropriately and at incorrect times of the day. Furthermore, when the four main requirements for human life are considered, including sunshine, air, water, and food, all appear to have been dramatically and negatively impacted by the modern technology and life styles. Therefore, most of the factors underlying poor health are theoretically modifiable. Therefore, such modification can be expected to significantly improve health and potential for longevity.

The principles of Chinese Medicine also dictate that, the source or root cause of a disease must be identified early in the process, prior to causing recognizable disease. Once identified and dealt with appropriately, good health should be preserved, for example, the offending factor has been removed. Given the four fundamental requirements for life and the major causes of ill health, a change in life-style holds considerable promise in promoting longevity. Specifically and simply, a person must make a change in those personal eating habits, living conditions, emotional patterns, exercise and sleeping habits associated with poor health. These include, a change from a poor diet and eating habits, including meal times, to healthy dietary habits; removal of environmental factors, which are known to lead to illness, for example, in as much as possible, live in an area or alter the living space environment to improve the air and drinking water quality, and limit exposure to direct sunlight; manage factors, which affect emotions negatively; and rest and exercise appropriately. Without such change and discipline, living one's life is akin to mopping up the water in the home each time it rains, rather than fixing the hole in the roof, through which the rain enters. While changes consistent with a healthy lifestyle are seemingly an obvious solution to acquiring good health and enhancing longevity, unfortunately, most prefer to adhere to the status quo. In other words, the short term positive rewards of eating fatty fast foods, drinking high calorie soda, adopting sedentary behaviors, allowing for uncontrolled emotions to dominate the thought process, succumbing to the temptation of great wealth to the point of overworking, and the like, appear to far outweigh the positive long term goals of pursuing good health and longevity, through adopting a sensible lifestyle of self discipline and moderation. Reflection on these matters and desire to change poor habits may only occur when an illness, such as heart disease is diagnosed. A change in the conditions that lead to such illnesses must occur several years prior to their development. Longevity and health require living within the proper conditions. A personal commitment to this end is the first and major step that must be taken to establish a basis for good health and potential for enhanced longevity. This chapter will be devoted to the conditions that Chinese martial art health experts believe pose the most significant potential for individuals who wish to improve their health and optimize the possibility for increased longevity.

Air

The subject of air pollution is not new. The effects of smog are well known to large segments of the population living in the United States, as are the effects of acid rain on our forests. Weather pattern changes and global warming, in general, are attributable, in large measure, to air pollution. Those living near areas with relatively higher concentrations of motor vehicle exhaust, for example, proximal to large freeways and other high-traffic areas have possibly experienced some of the associated health problems. This may be especially true during the period in which lead was included in gasoline.

Several states have passed laws prohibiting smoking in establishments, such as bars and restaurants, to minimize exposure to second hand cigarette smoke, a localized form of air pollution, known to be associated with lung cancer and cardiovascular diseases. Burning of incense is also not without problems, as this represents another form of localized air pollution.

The effects of air pollution also include removal of charged particles from the air. Charged particles, ions, are produced in nature whenever energy is transferred into the air (2-7). For instance, ions are generated from the lightning during thunderstorms, the friction from wind and rain, the splitting of water into droplets as water crashes over a waterfall or waves splash against the shore. The sun's ultraviolet light produces a layer of ions in the upper atmosphere, the ionosphere, which reflects radio waves back to the earth and is therefore useful in broadcasting. The sun's ejection of charged particles is responsible for the glowing colors of the aurora. Ions are charged, either positively or negatively. Ions near waterfalls, mountain forests, and the seashore tend to be negatively charged, while the atmosphere just prior to a thunderstorm, and areas which are paved with asphalt and concrete, such as areas within large cities, tend to be positively charged.

Airborne particles, such as dust, pollen, smoke and dirt attach to negative ions in the air. When negative ions are removed from the air in this manner, a regional shift occurs favoring the proportion of positively charged particles (7). Pollution from car exhaust, a reduced number of trees, lack of flowing streams, long distances from the seashore, and the presence of asphalt and concrete in city surroundings compared to the countryside, all favor the presence of a disproportionate amount of positively charged ions. Fluorescent lighting, electronic equipment, television and computer cathode screens, large amounts of plastic products, man-made fibers in carpets, upholstery and clothes, all also tend to reduce the amount of negatively charged ions, thus favoring positively charged ions in the living space atmosphere (8-10). Measurements of negative ions, for example, near a waterfall, register in the 50,000 ions per cubic centimeter (cc) range, while negative ions in the countryside approximate 1500 ions per cc (2,7). Those in a typical office area comprise only 50 ions per cc.

The significance of air, possessing a considerable reduction in negative ions, has been studied in several settings. For example, in one study of the farming industry, growth of barley, oats, lettuce and peas, in areas which were primarily positively charged, was dramatically stunted, compared to growth in air carrying twice the concentration of negative ions (7,11,12). In another study, people, who were grouped in rooms with disproportionately greater concentrations of positively charged ions, became irritable and fatigued (7,13). When these individuals were placed, for the same period of time, in rooms favoring negatively charged ions, brain wave studies demonstrated patterns consistent with relaxation and alertness. Biochemical studies show that positive ions correlate with higher concentrations of stress and body chemicals, including serotonin, adrenaline and noradrenaline, as well as allergy associated substances, such as histamine in the body (14-17). These studies indicate that twenty-five percent of people are strongly affected; fifty percent, considerably affected; and twenty-five percent, unaffected by these ion changes in the atmosphere. Administration of negative ion treatments has been shown to produce a positive effect in patients with respiratory diseases, such as asthma and hay fever, and help to control severe post-surgical pain and pain in patients due to severe burns (18-33).

Much of this information supports the notion held by Chinese martial art health experts that considerable time should be spent walking in a country setting, in wooded areas, near the ocean, waterfalls or running streams; and time should be minimized in cities with little green space. In so doing, health and longevity may be improved. Added advantage can be gained by walking barefooted, in a safe manner, on natural grass and the forest floor to maximize rejuvenation of the body's energy. Concrete floors should be avoided when exercising, while wood floors are preferred for exercise areas and in homes, in general, for these reasons.

Exercise areas, cooled by air conditioners, may also be problematic, due to high levels of positive ions being produced, as well as causing restriction in the flow of sweat secondary to cool room temperature, thus limiting the excretion of body toxins via this route. In addition, limiting time spent in areas where television sets remain continuously on, areas of poor air quality, and a preference for cotton rather than man made fabrics have a health benefit explained on the basis of ions in the atmosphere. Natural wood, cotton fabrics, soil, grass and trees tend to favor negatively charged ions, whereas synthetic fabrics tend to be positively charged. The above suggestions are made based on the concept of increasing negative electrons in the body, for health reasons. It is also appreciated that greater negative ion concentrations provide martial arts practitioners with increased alertness, more energy, and a feeling of overall better health. These individuals recommend, for general health reasons, concentrating time and effort in environments containing greater negatively charged ions, and minimizing exposure to substances and conditions associated with positively charged ions. Ion charges in the body should thereby, become balanced.

Children are considered to have a greater proportion of negatively charged ions, compared to adults. This allows for a relatively improved balancing of ions, following exposure to positively charged ions in the environment, as compared to adults. With increasing age, the ability to maintain this balance becomes lost, in favor of positive ions. A deficiency of negative electrons in the body is believed by martial art health experts to result in yin energy deficiency. Symptoms of yin deficiency include fatigue, dizziness, headache, constipation, dry mouth, itchy nose, decreased ability to concentrate, increased blood pressure and heart rate.

Water

Water is the foundation of life on earth. It occupies the majority of the earth's surface area and provides the atmosphere with moisture that recycles as precipitation. Water is the main component of plants and animals, including the human body, which is comprised of seventy to eighty percent water. Water enters the body through the air we breathe and the food and liquids we consume. Water can be absorbed through pores in the skin. Thus, the water in which we bathe, swim, and wash represents other sources of entry. Chlorine can be absorbed through pool water and chemicals in bath water can be absorbed, if the bathing period is long. Toxic substances can be absorbed through the skin when swimming in polluted lakes, rivers, and ocean areas. The potential for chemicals, infectious agents, including bacteria and parasites, and other pollutants to enter the human body through water is therefore, considerable and of concern.

Chemicals and other pollutants find their way into ground water from air pollution, waste disposal mechanisms, and directly from toxins produced through any number of industrial processes. They manage to contaminate streams, ponds, rivers, oceans and the plants and animals, exposed to the polluted water. Toxic substances can be recycled as water evaporates, then returns as precipitation. When plants and animals die, the residues work their way back into the ground water supply, once again. Martial art health experts accept that, at the very least, consuming water containing unsafe levels of chemical pollutants can impair the immune system; slow new cell formation in the body's cell turnover process; and force organs, including the kidneys and liver, to over-exert in clearing the body of toxins. Together, these can initiate the process of chronic disease.

As a result of Western society's understanding of this problem, tap water undergoes a purification process prior to entering the home, which is intended to limit microbial contamination and reduce the amount of toxic substances to levels considered to be safe. Several sources of bottled water can be purchased, which are marketed based on purity. Water can be boiled, or undergo a distillation process, to destroy microbes and remove chemicals. Well water must undergo sufficient purification to be considered safe for use.

Many of the current purification mechanisms, however, may be inadequate for individuals, attempting to optimize health and longevity. For example, boiling removes soluble oxygen from the water. While water from springs and streams contains soluble oxygen, there is no guarantee of its purity. Distillation leaves water slightly acidic, and if consumed regularly, forces the kidneys to expend extra effort in maintaining a normal acid-base balance in the body. Concern has been raised over the adequacy of the purification processes used to remove chemicals and infectious agents from tap water, prior to entering the home, as well as the standards set for minimal amounts of toxins. Due to these perceived deficiencies, additional attempts to purify the water supply can be made. For example, filters are available, which can be placed in the home to provide a more vigorous level of water purification, prior to consumption.

According to the National Wildlife Federation, irrespective of the care people take in avoiding pollutants, the vast majority of individuals contain at least trace amounts of industrial chemicals and pesticides in their bodies (34,35). Some of the most notable of these toxic agents include DDT, PCBs, PBB, dioxin, furans, lead and mercury. They enter the body through the food supply, water, and air. Unfortunately, the higher an animal is on the food chain, the more likely higher amounts of these toxins are in the body. The reason for this partly lies in the ability of these agents to stay within the body for long periods of time. With each successive step in the food chain, accumulation occurs. In addition, each time a person consumes food or water containing toxic substances, such as these, further accumulation occurs, since they are difficult to be cleared from the system. These accumulated toxins are particularly problematic for the fetuses of pregnant women, which are in the key stages of development, as well as for children, who are influenced significantly by hormone-like toxins.

It is estimated that twelve percent of the lifetime amount of toxic substances taken into the body occurs during the first year of life (34). These substances affect learning; are associated with hyperactivity in children; lower sperm count in men; reduce immune system function; and are linked to cancer. In particular, hormone-like toxins are linked to breast cancer in women, and testicular and prostate cancer in men. Other pesticides are linked to leukemia and neurological disorders in children. Serious genetic damage may also be occurring, which can be passed on to offspring.

It is increasingly being recognized that both the acute and chronic effects of exposure may be harmful. Sudden exposure to high levels of these toxins causes significant harm to wildlife and humans. Exposure, to what has previously been accepted as safe levels, may be as harmful when occurring over the long term. Toxicological studies generally determine harmful levels of these substances when exposure occurs over a short period of time. An increasing amount of evidence suggests that pollutants can affect vital biological systems, at amounts well below those thought to be carcinogenic or cause hormone problems, when the long term is considered (36-38). These effects are termed "subtle" or "sub-clinical". In addition, amounts considered safe for the adult may cause considerable harm in the young child or fetus. The effects to the young can include birth defects, immune suppression, and gender confusion. The florid short-term signs of toxicity observed in wildlife, might also serve as a marker for the subtle effects, occurring in humans.

Two of the most popular pesticides used in the US are classified as organophosphates and carbamates (35). Pesticides in both of these groups function to poison the nervous system of insects. These have the same effect on the human nervous systems. They interfere with the acetylcholinesterase enzyme in the brain, leading to disruption of signals in the nervous system. Short term exposure to high concentrations have been long known to cause many symptoms including agitation, insomnia, muscle weakness, respiratory distress, nervousness, irritability, forgetfulness, confusion, and depression. An increasing amount of evidence in animals and humans indicates that low-level exposure, over long periods of time, to organophosphates may affect neurological function and development (34-38). A strong probability, therefore, exists that children, exposed to low levels over a long period of time, may experience respiratory problems such as asthma, lower cognitive abilities, behavior problems, and other subtle neurological problems (39-41). Studies also point to links between chronic exposure to these pesticides and brain tumors and leukemia in children. These types of cancer have increased dramatically since the 1970's (42-44). Other studies have shown a relationship between exposure of parents to these pesticides and birth defects in their children (45,46).

Studies have demonstrated that over eighty percent of adults tested, show levels of pesticides in their system (47). Because of the differences between adults and children, in the manner in which they absorb and excrete these substances, it is expected that toxin levels in children may be much higher, and therefore, place them at greater risk of negative health consequences. Children are exposed to pesticides from many sources, including non-organically grown fruits and vegetables, pesticide use in homes and schools. Over ninety percent of American homes are sites of pesticide use, and pesticides are commonly used in schools (48-52).

Given the various routes pollutants can enter the human body, several alterations can be made to minimize exposure. These include a review of the chemicals used in the home and surrounding yard area for cleaning and pest control. Those, which pose even a potential health problem, can be avoided. Alternative, yet effective natural products for cleaning and pest control should be considered. Additionally, attention should be given to reduce bathing time to a practical length to minimize absorption through the skin. Showering can be substituted for bathing to minimize exposure. Consideration should also be given to altering water recreation preferences; minimizing exposure to chlorine in swimming pools; and avoiding polluted waters of lakes, rivers, and ocean areas. Since it is often recommended that adults drink approximately 2500 to

3000 ml of fluids per day, consideration should be given to installation of a reputable water filtration system in the home, at least for the portion of the water supply used for drinking and cooking. Alternatively, a reputable brand of bottled water could be used for consumption. Natural juices derived from totally organically grown fruits or vegetables, without additives, can be used to replace some of the daily fluid requirement, if these products are available.

Sunlight

Sunlight, solar radiation, is one of the most basic foundations for life on this planet. It maintains global temperatures in a range compatible with life. Sunlight is necessary in energy formation among plants, and without sunlight all life on this planet would cease to exist. Sunlight is necessary for plants to produce oxygen, an essential step in maintaining sufficient oxygen content in the atmosphere. Sunlight is also required for vitamin D to be produced in the body. Vitamin D is required for calcium absorption in the gastrointestinal tract.

Despite the necessity for sunlight, over-exposure to sunlight can lead to several health consequences in humans (53-54). Excessive exposure is associated with increased risk for developing various skin cancers, cataracts and other eye diseases, accelerated aging of the skin, and decreased immune function.

Sunlight is composed of a spectrum of electromagnetic waves, including ultraviolet radiation (UV), which is invisible to the eye; visible light, which allows us to see; and infrared radiation, which serves as the main source of heat and is the most important to health. Much of the harmful UV light is filtered by a layer of colorless gas, ozone, located in an upper layer of the atmosphere, the stratosphere. Ozone can also be found at ground level, but is harmful to living organisms at this level (55). Ground level ozone is produced when sunlight acts on motor vehicle exhaust. It is found in smog. In contrast to the problems presented by its presence at ground level, concern has been raised since the 1970's, with regard to depletion of ozone in the stratosphere. Holes in the ozone layer over the Arctic and Antarctic regions, as well as thinning of the ozone layer over the mid-latitudes, allows higher levels of UV radiation to reach the earth's surface. A number of effects have been observed from excessive UV radiation including health problems; damage to water ecosystems where a reduction in the most basic food source in the oceans, phytoplankton, can occur; reduced crop yields including barley, canola, soybean, and oats; and forest survival.

Of the direct health related problems, skin cancer is the major concern. Skin cancer has reached epidemic proportions in the United States (53,54). Caucasians have a higher risk of skin cancer because of a decreased amount of pigment in the skin. It is estimated that twenty percent of Americans will develop some form of skin cancer in their lifetime. The most serious form of skin cancer, melanoma, is one of the fastest growing types in the United States. Cases have doubled in the past two decades. Non-melanoma skin cancers are less deadly, and have high cure rates, if detected and treated early. These include basal cell carcinoma, the most common type of skin cancer; and squamous cell carcinoma, which spreads to other parts of the body, unlike basal cell carcinoma. Other types skin problems, caused by excessive exposure to UV light, include actinic keratosis and premature aging of the skin. Actinic keratosis is comprised of pre-malignant skin lesions that are a risk factor for development of squamous cell carcinoma. Premature aging of the skin occurs years after the majority of a person's over-exposure to the sun has occurred. Ultraviolet radiation also increases the chance of developing cataracts, which are responsible for sight problems in millions of Americans. Other eye problems caused by UV light include tissue growth that can impair vision, pterygium; skin cancer around the eyes; and degeneration of the macula, the part of the retina where visual perception is most acute. The immune system of the skin can also be affected, leading to increased infection.

The sun also provides infrared radiation, which acts to warm objects directly, termed radiant heat, even though the air temperature may be relatively cooler (55). At normal exposures, infrared radiation provides warmth and relaxation. Air pollution can inhibit infrared rays from reaching the earth's surface, to some degree. Large objects, such as tall buildings and mountains, prevent much of the infrared rays from reaching the shaded areas. Over-exposure to the sun's infrared light can cause heat stroke, particularly among the very old and very young.

Other aspects of sunlight have been appreciated among Chi Kung practitioners and many Chinese martial arts masters. Chi, the energy within the body, is in the same wave range, infrared range, as infrared radiation, when emitted externally. This energy can be transferred to objects including, food, when prepared by an individual. In contrast, food prepared mechanically, such as that required in preparation of large quantities, does not benefit from this energy transfer. In part, this may explain the preference for home cooked versus prepared foods. In addition, appropriate exposure to the sun is thought by martial art health experts to reduce the incidence of arthritis and skin disorders. It is also believed, that exposure to the sun is responsible for maturation, noting that people who live in areas of limited sunshine, as seen in the arctic regions, mature more slowly than those living in areas with normal amounts of sunlight. For reasons of risk versus benefit, exposure to direct sunlight should be limited to early morning and early evening. For example, limited periods of time may be spent in direct sunlight between 6 a.m. to 9 a.m. and 4 p.m. to 6 p.m., in a effort to reduce the harmful effects of solar radiation.

Food

An old Chinese saying is translated, "Whatever you eat is what you will look like." The truth of this saying has endured centuries and will likely continue to endure, reflecting the influence diet exerts on modern man, as well. The environment has such considerable impact upon the food supply that it must be addressed in this chapter, as well as the next. Topics including proper nutrition, food preparation, mealtime, and use of foods to alleviate specific symptoms of disease, involve the topic of food, but from a different perspective; these topics will be given a separate chapter. The information in this chapter will be restricted to foods and dietary behaviors that should be avoided. The next chapter will address foods and dietary behaviors that are understood to lead to health and longevity, based upon the experience of those martial artists, who have appropriately practiced this discipline over the centuries.

With the changes occurring in modern society that reinforce the fast pace of life, high protein, high calorie, and many fast foods that are high in fat content, are at an increased demand (56). While fats, carbohydrates, and protein are needed for proper cellular metabolism and cell growth, excessive amounts of these dietary components can ultimately lead to a decrease in the performance of several organ systems. As excessive energy is spent for digestion and storage of unnecessary calories, sedentary behaviors emerge, lung expansion decreases, and an overall reduction in vitality ensues. While these manifest as several outward signs of sluggishness, due to overeating or eating excessively fattening foods, other subtle, more deleterious long-term consequences mount in probability. These are not as easily witnessed, and can include decreased ability and resilience of the endocrine, cardiovascular and immune systems, and an over-taxing of the kidneys.

Children, unfortunately, are rapidly becoming a segment of the population that are as easily and possibly more affected than are adults by "fast-foods". Most do not like "healthy" foods, such as vegetables, and easily succumb to the temptation of eating foods high in fat content. Foods with increasing popularity among children are high in oil content, which is a major source of fat in the diet. Obesity in children is currently a major public health concern in the United States. Vegetables have high amounts of fiber, which assists in producing the appropriate frequency of stool expulsion from the body. Fiber, thereby, helps to remove many unwanted, unhealthy, and/or toxic substances from the body. Foods high in fat content, such as hamburgers, hotdogs, and fried chicken, lack fiber. Soft drinks are high in sugar content, or conversely, include sugar substitutes that may be of greater health concern. Canned foods contain preservatives. These commonly consumed foods are high in calories and fat. Depending on the remaining contents in these common diets, an imbalance of fiber content may also exist. Regular consumption of these foods can establish a foundation for ill health at a young age. Eating unhealthy foods, and eating unhealthily, is not only problems during childhood, but lead to future problems as the body ages.

Overeating

Data reported commonly through the news media, and within the scientific literature, indicate without question that, obesity has rapidly become one of the major heath concerns in the United States, both among adults, and more importantly among the young. While the short-term consequences of obesity in the young are unsightly and problematic, in terms of lack of physical activity, the long-term effects of overeating are far more disturbing, as the spectrum of diseases and negative effect on lifespan are considered. Epidemiologic research indicates that susceptibility to a number of degenerative diseases increases concurrently with an increasing standard of living, seen with industrialization (57,58). When the array of environmental and dietary factors is considered in this research, it appears that, caloric intake alone, accounts for much of the risk.

While increased caloric consumption is associated with negative health consequences and decreased life span, caloric restriction is conversely associated with decreased degenerative disease and increased longevity. Recent gerontologic research has generated sufficient data to support the notion of an anti-aging effect of caloric restriction (59-62). For example, less heart disease and an increased number of individuals living to 100 years of age appears to be associated with reduced caloric intake, in certain populations of South Africa. Caloric restriction also appears to maintain a youthful state in physiologic processes, and a delay or slow down of the progression of age, associated these processes (63). It is hypothesized that, reduced caloric intake results in a decrease in oxidative stress from free radicals, thus reducing cell damage (64,65).

A considerable amount of information has been generated in animals, to elucidate the effect of dietary intake on lifespan, and other health related concerns. Age related changes in certain areas of the brain have been reduced, as a result of dietary restriction in mice (66). Specifically, the decline in sensory-motor coordination was retarded, and improved performance was observed, with dietary restriction. These findings also indicate that, the benefit of dietary restriction on brain function and longevity is likely due to reduced oxidative stress, the effect of free radicals. Studies in rodents have clearly demonstrated the relationship between increased caloric intake and increased body weight; greater incidence of tumor occurrence; higher susceptibility to chemical carcinogens; and a shorter life span (57). While it is recognized that other factors influence longevity and carcinogenesis, attention is being given to the extent to which caloric intake changes the ability of the body to cope with stresses, both internal and external to the body, such as chemical, physical, and biological carcinogens. Research in this area has shown that physiologic changes occur in response to decreased caloric intake, such as a decreased body temperature and increased water consumption (57,67). With a reduced caloric intake, metabolism, expressed as metabolic output per gram of lean body mass, does not change, and reproductive capacity decreases. With regard to reproductive capacity, it is thought that less offspring are required to maintain continuation of the species, when life expectancy is increased. This observation is explained, in that energy intake can upgrade or downgrade functions related to free-radical stress response (66). With lowered caloric intake the metabolism of sex-specific hormones changes. Cell damage is reduced, as a result of a decrease in free-radical formation. Moreover, the ability for DNA repair is also preserved or enhanced, regardless of the cause of DNA damage, including exposure to carcinogens (57,58). Additionally, the fidelity of DNA replication increases, and oncogene expression is stabilized, thus decreasing the potential for development of cancers. Other animal studies suggest that, a shift occurs from longevity and endurance, seen with calorie-restricted diets, to body growth and reproductive fruitfulness with higher calorie intake (58,59). Reproductive fruitfulness represents a marker for poor survival probability. In other words, increased production of offspring becomes necessary to sustain the survival of the species, as longevity is reduced.

In summary, these findings indicate that processes are upgraded that improves response to a wide range of environmental stressors, when caloric intake is decreased. This allows for better survival and a downgrade of reproductive activity. Ultimately, calorie restriction results in an increased reproductive and total life span, reduced stature and reproductive activity, increased metabolic efficiency, decreased mutation-causing response with an increased death rate of mutated cells, decreased inflammatory response, increased DNA repair enzymes, and modified cell mediated immunity. Overall these changes improve the body's defense against environmental stress, such as radiation and chemical carcinogens.

Additional research in animals (rodents) has produced a clearer picture of the mechanism of the negative effect of overeating on health and longevity, as well as the beneficial effects of caloric restriction (67). Similar studies are currently underway in larger primates, with preliminary data paralleling the data derived from rodents (64). Final data on longevity will not be available until 2020, due to the longer natural life span of primates, relative to rodents. On the basis of the consistency in results, application of this information to humans is very likely.

Given the added benefit of consistency of time tested nutritional practices of Chinese martial arts health experts over centuries, along with conceptually similar caloric restricted diets administered to experimental animals, showing the greatest longevity and health, it can be assumed these practices should be given serious consideration, in developing personal nutritional behaviors. Since other research indicates that much of these benefits appear to be lost if caloric restriction is initiated in advanced age (68,69), starting such changes in early adulthood appears to be more beneficial. The rule of thumb is, among Chinese martial art health experts, healthy dietary habits should begin as soon as possible, and not delay beyond starting at approximately 35 years of age. It is commonly understood that alteration of dietary behavior, beyond 50 years of age, will produce little, if any, benefit. Research also indicates that the benefits of decreased caloric intake only apply if the nutrient quality is maintained (57). Therefore, the nutritional quality of a proper diet must be preserved, in the caloric restricted setting, for the benefits on health and longevity to be realized.

Cholesterol

While a holistic approach to health and longevity is extremely important to achieving the desired outcomes, including a sensible approach to other dietary aspects, this section will focus on the effects of excessive fats and cholesterol. Cholesterol and triglyceride are two types of fats, which are important for the body in producing energy, making hormones, and helping to build cells (70). Normal, and even minimally low amounts of fat, is needed in adults for these beneficial functions. The liver normally manufactures sufficient cholesterol and other fats, as needed by the body. Another source of cholesterol is dietary. Excessive dietary fat is problematic (71). Higher than required amounts of these fats, present in the body over a long period of time, poses significant health problems, most notably, to the cardiovascular system.

Despite caloric restriction, the type of food consumed must be given appropriate consideration and attention. While diets high in protein have gained popularity, in the setting of caloric restriction, they remain unbalanced with regard to the proportions of other important food groups, such as fruits, vegetables and carbohydrates. As will be pointed out in the next chapter, a balancing of food groups in the diet has benefits equally as important as limiting weight gain and lowering cholesterol. For example, Chinese martial art health experts have appreciated the effect any type of meat including beef, pork, chicken, wild game such as rabbit or venison, can have on the acid-base balance of the body. Meats are considered acidic and can make the body acidic. The body pH must maintain a proper pH balance, similar to yin and yang balance. As people age, the body normally becomes more acidic. Alcohol and soda pop are also considered acidic. This, along with all the other nutrition problems associated with high caloric and high fat foods, will predispose to illness following 20 to 30 years of exposure. Acidic foods, in general, cause the kidneys to overwork in an attempt to maintain a balance in pH. Over taxing of the kidneys is traditionally considered a root cause of many illnesses. People with acidic bodies tire easily with exercise, and become short of breath easily. Meat also contains added hormones, as part of farming practices used in the modern meat industry, allowable in the United States.

In general, abnormally high amounts of cholesterol and triglycerides can occur in the body because of hereditary reasons, as a result of other diseases, and because of diets, which are high in fat content (72). Liver disease; a type of kidney disease, nephrotic syndrome; thyroid disease, hypothyroidism; and diabetes mellitus are a few of the diseases associated with high cholesterol. Of the reasons for high cholesterol, consumption of food high in fat content, obesity, lack of physical activity, and stress over long periods of time, are major contributors. More and more persons living in America and other Western cultures have cholesterol levels that are well above normal limits, required by the body. When more cholesterol, than the body needs, circulates through the blood, over long periods of time, a build up can occur on the walls of arteries. This process leads to the formation of thick, sticky deposits, called plaques. Plaques can form anywhere in the body. Over time, they can grow in size, clog and cause reduced flexibility in the vessels, resulting in a decreased flow of blood to the affected area. This condition is referred to as atherosclerosis. If this occurs in vessels leading to the brain, a stroke may occur. Similarly, if this occurs in vessels feeding the heart, a heart attack can occur. Other organs and tissues can similarly be affected, such as the kidney, intestine, and muscles (leg muscles, for example). Fats can deposit in the skin, xanthomas; tendons; spleen; and liver, causing "fatty" liver.

A number of well-known risk factors exist specifically for high cholesterol. These include obesity, and eating diets that are high in saturated fat and trans fatty acids. Trans fatty acids are found in processed foods, fried foods, and hydrogenated foods. Other risk factors include, low fiber diets, low physical activity levels, stress, smoking cigarettes, living in an industrialized country, and having untreated under-active thyroid disease, diabetes, or polycystic ovary syndrome.

Several forms of cholesterol exist in the body. The high-density form, HDL, can actually assist in ridding the body of the "bad" types of cholesterol. Exercise can raise levels of HDL. Malnutrition, obesity, low levels of physical activity, and cigarette smoking are among the factors that reduce HDL. High triglyceride levels can be caused by similar factors including, hereditary reasons, high calorie diets comprised of sugar and refined carbohydrates, obesity, diabetes mellitus, alcohol use, kidney failure, stress, and hepatitis.

Several changes can be made to diet and lifestyle to help reduce cholesterol, triglyceride, and trans-fatty acid in the body (72). The diet can be altered to include consumption of foods low in saturated fats. Diets low in red meats, dairy products, and egg yolks are examples. The diet may be supplemented with other foods, such as whole grains, fruits, and vegetables, including their seeds. Plant sterols, which are found in vegetables, fruits, and seeds, appear to interfere with cholesterol absorption. These foods are rich in vitamins, such as folic acid, pantothenic acid (Vitamin B5), vitamin E and minerals. Minerals such as 1500 mg to 2000 mg per day of calcium, and chromium found in brewers yeast, have been shown to reduce cholesterol in the blood. Fiber, included in the diet, helps reduce cholesterol more than simply consuming low fat foods. Essential fatty acids, found in fish and walnuts, including omega 3 and omega 6 reduce cholesterol. Soy protein contains isoflavones, which are believed to also reduce cholesterol. L-carnitine may be helpful in reducing cholesterol and triglycerides, as well as increasing HDL. Alpha-linolenic acid, found in walnuts and used as a substitute for thirty-five percent of monounsaturated fats, in low-fat diets, can also reduce cholesterol. This substance also acts as a sponge, cleaning up free radicals, thus, providing an anti-aging effect. If oil is to be used, olive oil appears to be the least harmful. Heating olive oil, however, may preclude this advantage. Weight reduction, stress reduction, increased physical activity, and smoking cessation are other important changes that can impact on reducing cholesterol and triglyceride levels.

Meats

Modern farms rely on high-efficiency systems, forcing animals, raised for slaughter, to be housed in close-quarters with their food delivery and waste removal relying on minimal human effort. This is in contrast to the historical method of allowing animals to roam and graze. In the high-efficiency process, a number of alterations to naturally raising have been conceived (73). For example, waste paper, old phone books and newspapers have been used in creating a source of roughage. With these waste products, the animals consume materials such as polychlorinated biphenyls and other petroleum based printing chemicals, which remain stored in the animal's fatty tissue, only to be consumed by humans. Some of these materials are known carcinogens. Overcrowding of the animals and poor nutrition has led to the use of antibiotics and hormones, to improve weight gain and prevent infectious diseases. Antibiotics impact bacterial resistance patterns. Concern has been raised over the potential of hormones to cause hormone imbalances in humans that consume them, leading to early onset of puberty in females, and possibly certain types of cancer, years later (74). Several countries, including those of the European Union, have adopted a conservative approach, banning the use of these steroid hormones, until evidence exists proving them to be safe, in the long term. In addition to these hormones, food additives including stabilizers, preservatives, dyes, flavoring agents, artificial sweeteners, and emulsifiers are included in many processed foods. Many of these are proven to be harmless, however, the long-term effects of low-level exposure, contained in some foods, may have not been considered. The stress, resulting from the methods used in raising and slaughtering these animals, causes release of several hormones, which remain in meats when consumed (75).

Concern has surfaced, regarding changes in rules that reclassify the safety of animal carcasses containing cancers, tumors and open sores, as "safe for human consumption" (76). It is thought that cancer, glandular swelling or lymphomas, sores, and infectious arthritis, among other diseases in animals, pose no health danger. In the case of tumors, some reports note that the lesions are cut out and the unaffected carcasses are passed on to the market. Despite a "safe for human consumption" designation, many find the prospect of potentially consuming this type of disease-exposed meat to be more than repulsive.

Meats have come under fire as a vehicle of transmission of a number of substances, which are harmful to health (77-80). As pointed out above, toxic chemicals can be found in animals, from which our meat supply is derived. Of similar concern, is the potential for transmission of infectious agents in the meat supply. Statistics available from April, 2002, according to the Centers for Disease Control, indicate that during a 5 year period from 1996 through 2001, approximately 76 million cases of food-borne illnesses per year leading to

325,000 hospitalizations and 5,000 deaths occurred (81). These products included meat, poultry, and other foods. While the meat supply is considered safer than ever before, these statistics are concerning. Several notable illnesses have gained much attention, including transmission of E. coli 0157:H7 in beef, which releases a toxin, causing a sometimes-fatal kidney problem combined with hemolytic anemia, hemolytic uremic syndrome (82). Other risks to humans are still unknown, for example, consumption of meats contaminated with the infectious agent believed to be responsible for mad cow disease (83). Not only has the beef market been affected, but also consumption of game animals, such as deer, may hold a similar risk. In addition, improper meat storage, including storage following consumer purchase, can allow bacteria to grow (84). This requires that appropriate care be given, to insure sanitary conditions throughout the entire spectrum of the industry, from the time of raising animals to home storage and food preparation. Processed meats also contain preservatives, adding to the potential for long-term concern.

Fish and Other Seafood

Certain types of seafood, in particular, shellfish, contain high amounts of cholesterol. Storage of fish, once caught, can pose problems with regard to freshness. Many believe ocean fish must be eaten fresh, without having been stored, to be healthy. After fish are caught, they must be stored into cold rooms while at sea. Depending on the storage time and the adequacy of storage conditions, the meat may no longer be fresh. Catch may undergo refreezing to avoid deterioration; however freezing may lead to damage of the fish meat. Fish may also be caught from polluted water. The consumer is seldom aware of the nature of water in which fish are caught, whether it was polluted or not.

Some pollutants, problematic for fish and the humans that consume them, are ubiquitous, such as mercury (85). Mercury occurs naturally in the environment. A more toxic form of mercury, methyl mercury, is produced by bacterial transformation of mercury that is dissolved in water. Methyl mercury is rapidly absorbed from the gastrointestinal tract and promptly enters the brain of adults, children and the fetus of pregnant women. It is then slowly converted back to mercury. Other organs can also be affected, including those of the cardiovascular, immune, and reproductive systems. Chronic exposure of low doses of methyl mercury, from maternal consumption of fish during the pre-natal period, has been associated with poor performance on neurobehavioral tests of children, in particular, those focused on attention, fine motor function, language, visual-spatial abilities, and verbal memory (86). Animal studies also confirm the detrimental effects on the developing nervous system. Once mercury is absorbed, the body slowly releases it. Studies have show that half of the concentration is released from the body every 44 to 56 days (87). Accumulation, over time, can occur if mercury is consumed more frequently than this, for example, on a weekly or daily basis. The effects are most harmful in the fetuses of pregnant women.

Fish absorb methyl mercury, especially predatory fish, such as swordfish and shark. The U.S. Food and Drug Administration believes consumption of fish is safe, if eaten infrequently as part of a balanced diet, for example, no more than once per week (85). It is advised that women of childbearing age, who may become pregnant, limit consumption of shark and swordfish to no more than once per month. The same concern has emerged for tuna fish. The FDA believes consumption restrictions are not necessary for the top 10 seafood species, since levels of mercury are generally less than 0.2 parts per million, a level believed to be safe for normal weekly consumption of 2.2 pounds. Not everyone agrees with this advice (88).

Considerable controversy exists with regard to the amount of mercury exposure due to silver amalgam, used by dentists to repair dental caries for years (88). Several groups believe a link exists between low-level exposure to mercury vapors, emanating from these dental fillings, and the development of neurological diseases, such as Alzheimer's disease. Some European countries have banned amalgam use as a result of these concerns, now that alternative materials exist to replace amalgam. Similar concerns exist for systemic exposure to other metals, such as aluminum. New standards in the pharmaceutical industry will reduce or eliminate aluminum from intravenous nutrition products, based on concerns over heavy metal poisoning due to this element (89).

Other problems are evolving with regard to consuming fish, primarily, farm-raised salmon (90). Salmon is the primary farm-raised fish, with other fish likely to be included in the near future. The concern centers on the presence of PCB's, a type of dioxin), which has been related to birth defects, and thought to be a carcinogen. Higher concentrations of PCBs were found in the farm-raised fish compared to wild, caught fish. Apparently, farm-raised fish are not regulated by the Environmental Protection Agency, since they are grown commercially on farms. Rather, the Food and Drug Administration (FDA) regulates them. The FDA standards are quoted to be 500 times less protective than those of the EPA.

Milk and Eggs

Another potential source of pollution observed since 1993 is dairy products, derived from cows that have been injected with recombinant bovine growth hormone (rBGH). This hormone is given to cows in the US to increase milk production, however, its use is banned in several countries, including Canada and the European Union. While little scientific data exists, it is believed that consumption of milk and other dairy products, including cream, cheese, yogurt, buttermilk, cream cheese, ice cream, iced milk, and baked goods using products derived from cows given rBGH, may be linked to breast, colon, and prostate diseases (91). This belief may be responsible for its ban in many modernized countries throughout the world. Cows given this hormone also have health consequences, including cystic ovaries, uterine disorders, digestive problems, enlarged hocks, knee lesions, and mastitis (92). Recombinant bovine growth hormone causes release of a chemical, insulin-like growth factor (IGF-1). IGF-1 is found in high levels in milk derived from cows, treated with rBGH. While natural to the body, excessive levels of this substance has been associated with breast cancer, prostate cancer, colon cancer, acromegaly, hypertension, diabetes, and enlarged breasts in men.

Egg yolks are high in cholesterol and egg white is high in the protein, albumin, making it difficult for some to digest. The egg also receives hormones, given to the chicken, to increase the frequency of egg production.

Taste Enhancers

A number of products are currently available, and frequently used, to enhance the taste of foods and beverages. These include table salt (sodium chloride), MSG (monosodium glutamate), and sweeteners, including sugar and aspartame. The inclusion of these substances in home-prepared meals can be controlled, to some degree. On the other hand, meals consisting primarily of processed foods and foods prepared outside of the home, for example, restaurant foods, frozen foods, canned foods, fast foods, do not allow discretion over the amount of these substances placed in them. To decrease the amount of taste enhancers, a reduction in the amount of these foods is required. In many cases, those who consume prepared and processed foods, consume far greater amounts of taste enhancers than desired.

Salt (Sodium Chloride)

Excessive dietary salt has long been looked upon as a dietary factor associated with poor health and decreased longevity. While the acute effects of occasional exposure to excessive dietary salt are not considered problematic, long-term exposure is believed to be a health issue, especially for those with cardiovascular and kidney disease. Modern medicine appears to support this belief. The contributory role of dietary salt to high blood pressure is well established for certain patient groups (93,94). Salt has also been explored as a factor responsible for promoting gastric cancer. Laboratory evidence indicates that no direct relationship exists between dietary salt and gastric cancer. However, evidence in laboratory animals indicates a potential role for dietary salt in gastric cancer caused by other carcinogens found in highly spicy foods (95).

Published animal, clinical, and epidemiological reports were examined to determine if a role for excessive salt intake is a risk factor for development of osteoporosis (96). The findings of this research suggest that, while salt is implicated as a weak contributor, only a minority of people experience increased sodium and calcium loss in the urine, due to increased salt intake. The effect is overwhelmed by other factors such as estrogen level. Factors, which appear to provide favorable affects on bone health, include increased intake of potassium, magnesium, zinc, vitamin C, and alkaline-producing fruit and vegetables. On the other hand, another study showed that a reduction in urinary sodium excretion by one-half produced the same effect on reducing bone loss as increasing dietary calcium in a study of 124 postmenopausal women (97).

Possibly due to prehistoric man having adapted to low amounts of sodium in the diet, the harmful effects of high sodium diets are not unexpected. Diets high in sodium can raise blood pressure in people and animals, susceptible to the effects of sodium chloride (98). It also appears, that high potassium diets reduce the rise in blood pressure caused by high salt diets. Low to normal potassium in diets promotes retention of sodium chloride by the kidneys. Along with ingestion of high amounts of sodium chloride, the rise in blood pressure is produced. People with high-normal blood pressure are at higher risk of stroke, heart attack, or heart failure according to the Framingham Heart Study (99). According to the American Journal of Cardiology, reducing salt intake in the diet is more effective at lowering blood pressure in people with mild hypertension than exercise (100). All groups of salt sensitive patients, regardless of race, age, sex, and weight differences, experience increases in blood pressure with increase salt intake and visa versa (101). In genetic models of hypertension, increased sodium intake is associated with changes in the structure and function of arteries. This deleterious effect appears to be separate from the effects of increased blood pressure (102). In total, this information points to the potential for considerable health consequences to the cardiovascular system as a result of increased salt intake.

MSG (Monosodium Glutamate)

MSG enhances the flavor and aroma of foods. Food companies rely on its ability to increase the acceptability of commercial food products. It also can suppress undesirable flavors and eliminates the metallic taste associates with some canned food products. Consumption of MSG in the USA has increased from approximately one million pounds, in 1950, to over 300 million pounds, today. Several names appear on USA food labels that contain MSG or glutamate, including glutamate textured protein, monosodium glutamate hydrolyzed protein, monopotassium glutamate, glutamic acid yeast extract. Some bouillons, broths, and stock flavorings contain MSG (103,104).

MSG works by exciting nerve cells, causing a discharge of electrical impulses. The danger of MSG lies with its ability to over-stimulate cells possessing glutamate receptors, leading to cell damage or even cell death. Several illnesses are thought to be associated with exposure to MSG during infancy or during the prenatal period. This association is based on the pharmacology of endogenous glutamate. The pharmacologic effects include side effects, such as learning disabilities, emotional problems, and endocrinologic abnormalities (103). Childhood exposure is suspected of playing a role in abnormal brain and cognitive development. Cumulative exposure in adulthood is suspected by some to be associated with headaches, including migraines (104). Its role in worsening seizure disorders, strokes, dementia, Alzheimer's disease, allergy, Parkinson's disease, fibromyalgia, obesity, and ALS has been explored, however, its contribution to these illnesses is extremely controversial (105-113). The scientific evidence supporting a link between these diseases and MSG remains lacking.

Known reactions to MSG, such as excessive thirst, inability to concentrate, and headaches are thought to be dose related, in that some people react to small amounts, while others react to larger amounts (103,114). The effects can occur immediately upon exposure, and up to 48 hours later. It is not known whether the amount of MSG consumed in the diet is sufficient to cause health problems, even if a cause-effect relationship was to be established. Also, a number of other food-derived chemicals may protect against the ill-effects of MSG, including omega-3 fatty acids, which are found in flax seeds and fish oils.

From a theoretical basis, and anecdotal reports of ill effects following exposure, consumption of large amounts of MSG should be avoided. Repeated and cumulative exposure from consuming prepared, canned, and commercial foods, sauces, soy sauce, gravies, flavorings, extracts, and concentrates, can be substantial. For those who have chosen to alter their diets, to comply with a more natural approach to nutrition, elimination of MSG from the diet could be considered a healthy choice.

Aspartame

Aspartame consists of three different chemicals. These include, aspartic acid, phenylalanine, and methanol (115-117). Along with glutamate, aspartame is classified as an excitotoxin, in that, excessive levels in the brain exceed the normal neurotransmitter function, and destroy the nerve cell (104). Under normal circumstances the barrier, between the blood and brain, does not allow various toxic chemicals to enter the brain. However, if high amounts are in the blood, over long periods of time, a small percentage may still cross this protective barrier. The blood-brain barrier is not as efficient in the very young, allowing a higher percentage of undesirable substances to cross into the brain from the blood. For this reason, consumption of these excitotoxins is not encouraged for children.

Over time, aspartate can destroy brain cells (115). However, clinical symptoms may not be evident for years into this chronic process. Long term exposure to aspartame is believed by some to be associated with several chronic illnesses, including multiple sclerosis, ALS, memory loss, hormonal problems, hearing loss, seizure disorders, Alzheimer's disease, Parkinson's disease, hypoglycemia, dementia, brain lesions, and neuroendocrine disorders (115,118). Acute reactions to aspartame include, headaches and migranes, nausea, abdominal pains, fatigue, sleep problems, vision problems, anxiety attacks, depression, and chest tightness due to asthma (119-121).

Some individuals, even those whose body processes phenylalanine properly, have excessive levels of this substance, due to chronic aspartame ingestion (122). High levels of phenylalanine in the brain can reduce the amount of an important neurotransmitter, seratonin. Reduced levels of seratonin are associated with emotional problems, including depression. Excessively high levels of this chemical are thought by some to cause seizures and other serious psychological disorders, such as schizophrenia.

Diketopiperazine (DKP) is a by-product of aspartame, possibly formed during prolonged storage, and has been implicated in the development of brain tumors (115). It is interesting to note the increase in various disorders, with possible links to aspartame and MSG, during similar periods over which consumption of these products has increased. These include brain tumors, for which the incidence has increased sixty-seven percent, between 1973 and 1990, in persons over 65 years of age (123-125)). An increase of 10% has occurred in all age groups. Other diseases, which have increased substantially over similar periods, include diabetes mellitus and mood disorders such as depression.

Sugar

White sugar is refined sucrose. It is produced by processing the juice of sugar cane or sugar beet, removing all fiber, protein, and minerals. Approximate consumption of sugar, in the average American diet, is a shocking two pounds per week (126). Considering all sweeteners, the average American consumes one hundred forty-seven pounds per year. This is not surprising, when the number of food containing sugar, corn sugar, and high-fructose corn syrup, are included. These foods are breads, breakfast cereal, ketchup, mayonnaise, peanut butter, spaghetti sauce, soft drinks, and the many commercially prepared fast food meals. Mixed juices, water with some real juice, contain a large amount of sugar.

Refined sugar is quickly absorbed from the gastrointestinal tract into the blood stream. When this occurs, glucose levels rise sharply, causing insulin to be released from the pancreas in normal individuals. Insulin seeks to control the level of glucose in the blood. But, in response to the rapid absorption of sugar, the effect of insulin outlasts the sudden effect of sugar. This ultimately causes the amount of glucose in the blood to fall, leading to hypoglycemia, blood sugar that is too low. Hypoglycemia stimulates hunger, in an attempt to increase blood glucose to normal levels. If blood glucose falls too low, other effects occur. The adrenal glands are stimulated causing the conversion of glycogen into glucose. Cortisone is also released from the adrenal glands, which can inhibit the immune function. High insulin levels, in response to high sugar consumption, can inhibit release of growth hormone, which in turn reduces the immune function.

If, in response to hypoglycemia, a person consumes more sugar, the body undergoes a see-saw effect, between too much glucose and not enough glucose (127). Symptoms of dizziness, weakness, fatigue, depression, aggression, insomnia, and even loss of consciousness can occur, as a result. Over time, diets high in sugar can result in cardiovascular, liver, and kidney complications due to the excess build up of cholesterol. This is an effect of the body being unable to use the fat and cholesterol produced from sugar. Fats can be deposited in several organs, including the heart, liver, arteries, and kidneys. When this occurs, fatty degeneration may result. The effects of which, include coronary artery disease of the heart, arthrosclerosis, fatty liver and kidneys.

Sugar is lacking in the vitamins and minerals required for its own metabolism in the body, specifically, the B vitamins, chromium, magnesium, and zinc (126). Without replacing these, and other vitamins and minerals, body stores of vitamins C and D, phosphorous, iron, selenium, vanadium, tin, boron, bismuth can be decreased in the bones, teeth, and tissues. Some of these minerals and vitamins are needed for the proper disposition of fats in the body. When depleted, cholesterol levels can rise, fatty tissue can increase, metabolic rate can decrease, and the way to ill health started.

Caffeine

Although caffeine is a natural substance, and found in over sixty different plants, several negative effects should be highlighted. These include nervousness, jitters, and insomnia in some people (128). In other words, the nervous system is over-worked and an unnecessary expenditure of energy occurs. According to martial art health experts, unnecessary energy expenditures can be detrimental, from a health perspective, since less energy is available for necessary body functions. Caffeine also increases acid production, worsening symptoms of gastro-esophageal reflux (heartburn). Irritability and headaches can occur in people who abruptly stop consuming caffeine after long periods of use. Caffeine may also have an effect on blood pressure.

Coffee has been linked to arthritis (129). According to study reports of approximately 19,000 people, who were monitored for the presence of "rheumatoid factor" in the blood, a marker for arthritis, the amount of coffee consumed per day was strongly associated with rheumatoid factor. Those who drank more than 4 cups of coffee per day were twice as likely to test positive for this factor; and those who drank 11 or more cups per day were 15 times as likely to have this factor, compared to those who do not drink coffee. In a larger study, the link between coffee and arthritis was not demonstrated (130).

Alcohol

Among the many negative consequences of alcohol consumption, cirrhosis of the liver is a major health concern. Liver disease, due to alcohol consumption, can develop after more than 10 years of heavy consumption (131). The amount of alcohol that can injure the liver varies greatly among individuals. In women, as few as 2 to 3 drinks per day, and in men, as few as 3 to 4 drinks per day, has been linked to cirrhosis. The injury may be due to the effect of alcohol on blocking the normal metabolism of proteins, fats, and carbohydrates. Liver damage can affect other organs, including the stomach, intestines, kidneys, and the immune system.

Methods of Cooking

Popular methods of cooking include the use of traditional stove and oven heat, barbecuing, and microwave ovens. Concern has been raised over barbecuing and micro waving because of the potential for producing carcinogens in the cooking process. Concern, specifically for microwaves, includes the effects of radiation leaks.

Barbecuing

While a popular cooking method, especially during the summer season, barbecuing is not without risks, and should preferably be avoided by those who choose to improve health and longevity. Meats contain creatine. When heated to high temperatures during barbecuing, creatine combines with amino acids, the building blocks of protein, forming heterocyclic aromatic amines (HAAs). HAAs are suspected cancer-causing agents (132). Other cancer-causing compounds, polycyclic aromatic hydrocarbons (PAHs), develop from the smoke produced when fats drip from cooking meat onto hot coals. As the smoke rises, a portion of these compounds can attach to the surface of the food being cooked on the grill. Cured meats, including hotdogs and sausages, contain nitrites. When cooked at high temperatures, such as those often produced when barbecuing, the formation of nitrosamines occurs. Nitrosamines are another group of cancer-causing compounds.

While eating substantial amounts of red meat, such as beef, pork, and veal may increase the risk of various types of cancer, including colorectal, pancreatic, breast, prostate and renal cancer, according to the National Cancer Institute, grilling or frying meat is believed to double that risk (133).

Microwave Ovens

Microwaves are a form of electromagnetic energy that travels at the speed of light. Within a microwave oven, a magnetron creates microwaves that, in turn, interact with food molecules to change their polarity millions of times per second. As a result of this rapid changing of polarity, especially with water molecules, the friction causes the food to heat up. In addition, substantial damage occurs to the surrounding food molecules. Microwaves, created in this fashion, are a result of alternating current. This is different from the natural microwaves, created by the sun, that do not cause frictional heat in molecules (134).

It has been noted that some of the first cautions arose from Eastern Europe, regarding use of microwaves, and centered on baby formula. Micro waving baby formulas creates synthetic isomers that are not biologically active. Changes in certain proteins also occur. For example, the protein unit, L-proline, is converted into its d-isomer, which is known to be toxic to both nerves and kidney cells. In addition, portions of the formula may become superheated, causing burn injury in the infant. As a result, recommendations against micro waving baby formula emerged (134).

It was also noted that several years later, it was discovered that, blood samples, taken from individuals who consumed food prepared in a microwave oven, showed different results, when compared to blood samples, taken from individuals consuming traditionally prepared foods (134). Specifically, a decrease in hemoglobin and cholesterol values was observed and a change in the ratio of good to bad cholesterol. Lymphocytes were also lower in patients consuming microwave prepared foods. Much earlier, Russian investigators identified carcinogens, including d-Nitrosodienthanolamines in virtually all foods exposed to microwave radiation. In addition, a sixty to ninety percent decrease in nutritional value of these foods was noted to occur. Decrease bio-availability of several vitamins, including those of the B group, vitamins C and E, and essential minerals, are affected. Russian authorities noted that microwaving cereal grains and milk led to conversion of some amino acids into carcinogens. Formation of carcinogenic substances was also observed when frozen fruits were thawed using microwaves. Specifically, glucosides and galactosides were converted into carcinogens. Similarly, plant alkaloids in raw, cooked or frozen vegetables were converted into carcinogens. Free radical formation was observed when plants were microwaved, especially root vegetables.

A report indicates, according to a survey of microwave repair service personnel, approximately fifty-six percent of microwave ovens, two years or older, leaked levels of radiation ten percent higher than the safety limits, set by the FDA (134). Findings of Russian experiments with microwaves detail substantial health consequences of exposure to microwave emissions, including a breakdown of the "life-energy field"; degeneration of cellular voltage, such as internal cellular membrane potentials; breakdown of electrical nerve impulses; long term loss of vital energy; magnetic "deposits" throughout the nervous system and lymphatic system; hormone changes in both males and females; and brainwave disturbances of alpha, theta, and delta patterns, associated with negative psychological effects (134).

Summary

In this chapter, environmental factors, including their potential impact on health and longevity were considered. Some represent the traditional view of Chinese martial arts health experts, while others add to its evolving knowledge base. Many of these factors represent technological advances, providing society with certain advantages. However, the improvements realized may not be without costs. For example, the pesticides used in agriculture, protect plants. But these chemicals may predispose to health problems. While irrefutable scientific evidence for such problems may not be available, the popularity of organically grown foods attests to the public's attitude toward this issue. Similarly, fresh foods are being given more preference, compared to canned and frozen foods, in an attempt to avoid preservatives.

The rationale for choosing to avoid exposure to various environmental and dietary factors varies considerably. Some consider consuming more organically grown vegetables and fruits to simply be a good idea, thus avoiding chemicals, maintain a good balance in pH, and promote a healthy immune system. Others consider oxygen's role in cell metabolism, arguing that, fresh foods contain more oxygen. With more oxygen, cells are likely to function better, thus promoting appropriate cell repair, cell turnover, a healthy immune system, and assist in clearing waste products, a potential source of illness. Regardless of the rationale, centuries of good health outcomes, attributable to what is considered healthy eating and limited exposure to detrimental environmental factors, supports the concept. In some cases, considerable scientific evidence is emerging, supporting many of these concepts. For example, it has long been recognized that the body undergoes starvation with consumption of too little food, but several chronic illnesses are being linked, through scientific examination, with over-eating. In the final analysis, whether scientifically proven, or by some personally developed rationalization, avoiding potential problems offers a conservative approach that many people choose to adopt. In so doing, no personal harm is created, and often much good, in terms of health and longevity.

The environmental challenges to health were presented in this chapter, as interpreted by Chinese martial art health experts. The following chapter will focus on nutrition as a means to maintain health, fitness and promote longevity. The information in the next chapter is based on adopting positive dietary behaviors, rather than avoiding potential harmful foods and environmental factors. For example, diets consisting of whole grains, rather than bleached rice or wheat, are recommended. Inclusion of some fruit seeds in the diet offers the added benefit of consuming the life energy, stored within them. Food temperature is discussed, in that consumption of ice-cold foods reduces body energy and slows circulation. Allowing beverages to warm to room temperature, over a two-hour period before drinking, for example, is beneficial in this regard. The timing of meals and snacking is also important from the perspective of preserving organ energy. The liver can be overworked during its rejuvenation period, from 1 a.m. to 3 a.m., if food consumption occurs prior to going to sleep at night. When this occurs, the liver does not receive the full benefit of the rest period. Over the long term, the prerequisites for illness can, thereby, be established. Eating foods out of season requires storage of fruits and vegetables that have not ripened on the vine. When brought to market, additives, such as sugar, may need to be added. In short, foods, eaten out of season, may lack important nutrients and contain additives, which should be avoided. To achieve a goal of improved health and longevity the body condition must be changed. This requires, in part, a change to a healthy diet.

Diet is only one of several factors that need to be addressed. Other chapters will discuss exercise, rest, emotion, and breathing, specifically. How we deal with these factors will have a tremendous impact on the potential for improved health and longevity. For those who view longevity as reaching the average life span, much of the information and perspectives outlined in these chapters may be viewed as having little value. However, if the goal is to improve longevity, beyond that which is considered average, a conservative approach, incorporating reasonable life-style changes, designed to avoid exposure to foods or environmental circumstances that may interfere with extending one's life span may be welcomed.

Chapter 4

Diet, Health, and Longevity

Introduction

Diet, emotion, physical activity, and rest are interrelated with respect to their influence on health and longevity. The major dietary challenges to health in modern society include high fat foods and foods high in sugar, which lead to heart disease, obesity, represent a risk factor for several cancers, and at the very least, complicate the control of diabetes. The fast pace of modern life often can lead to several destructive habits, apart from eating foods high in fat and refined sugar. The fast pace of modern life also induces considerable stress with an array of emotional implications. Uncontrolled and intense negative emotion can predispose to both psychological as well as physical illnesses. Emotional stress can impede the resilience of the immune system in fighting disease and be a major cause of insomnia. These can influence appetite and motivation for participation in physical activities. The lack of physical activity is also associated with poor health. In contrast, proper exercise enhances muscular-skeletal strength through movement and cardio-pulmonary health through the flow of blood, air, and body fluids. Those with good emotional balance are often healthier and happier. It has been long recognized that a good diet, proper sleep, physical activity/exercise, and the control of destructive emotions represent four main cornerstones of good health. Positive health habits, such as eating a good diet, build and maintain a body, which retains a minimum of harmful substances that interfere with good health, such as high cholesterol. A healthy diet also assists in maintaining a strong immune system. However, addressing one cornerstone, such as diet, while ignoring the others, may not result in the outcomes desired with regard to lasting health and longevity. The simple lesson learned over the centuries, in particular, among Chinese martial art health experts, is the value of a holistic approach. In other words, a building cannot be expected to stand when only three of the four corner-posts, holding up a house, are strong. The house will eventually collapse. Addressing the four main cornerstones of good health has proven to result in success, while focusing on one or the other may not lead to the healthy and long life expected. In this light, attention must also be given to exercise, emotional control, and the proper amount of rest and sleep. According to the National Sleep Foundation greater than fifty percent of the adults in the United States suffered from insomnia in 2002 (135). While insomnia is caused by many reasons the most common causes were identified as depression, anxiety, and tension. The four cornerstones of good health may be viewed separately, but are inter-related and their impact on health, inseparable. Not only does emotion affect rest and sleep, but diet and the desire to exercise as well.

Modern Western medicine is beginning to accumulate scientific evidence substantiating this holistic approach. For example, in controlling high blood pressure, more promising results were demonstrated when a combined approach was used (Established Plus DASH group), compared to other interventions that were more focused (93-95,98,101,102,136-142). Specifically, lifestyle changes, including weight reduction, if overweight; diet control, inclusive of reducing salt and other forms of sodium intake with an emphasis on consuming foods high in fruits, vegetables and low in dairy fat products; increased physical activity; limiting the consumption of alcohol; and smoking cessation were associated with the greatest control of blood pressure. A higher degree of weight loss occurred in those, who were initially overweight at the start of the study, and participated in the combined approach.

When overweight, weight reduction is well recognized as a critical key to health and longevity. Obesity and being overweight increases the risk of problems from hypertension, high and disproportioned levels of lipids in the blood, type 2 diabetes, coronary heart disease, stroke, gall bladder disease, osteoarthritis, sleep apnea, respiratory problems, cancers including endometrial, breast, prostate, and colon cancers, and increases in all-cause deaths (57-69,143-149). Studies published indicate daily diets, high in fruits and vegetables, as well as physical activity, were separately associated with a reduction in the risk of stroke, risk of death from stroke, and death from stroke (150,151,152).

In the context of a holistic approach to health, sunshine, air, water, and food are important considerations. In the previous chapter, several environmental issues were discussed, which address these four considerations. A change of behavior was emphasized, with the intent of avoiding consumption of foods that are considered deleterious to health, and minimizing exposure to polluted water, air, and excessive sunshine. It was stressed that, behaviors such as these must change, since they underlie the foundation of many illnesses. In this chapter, dietary practices, which are considered good for health, will be focused upon. The body must, however, be allowed to exist within proper internal and external conditions for good health and longevity to prevail. Proper diet is basic to establishing good health. The positive impact of a healthy diet can, however, be negated by exposure to an unhealthy environment, such as excessive exposure to the sun, a major cause of skin cancer.

Behavioral change requires discipline. Proper attention, emphasis, and effort are necessary in making diet, in particular, a priority. Exercising this type of discipline is directed toward long-term, rather than short-term goals, including the prevention of chronic illness and promotion of longevity. One can lose sight of these long-term goals in the midst of the trials and tribulations of controlling diet, over the short-term. Moreover, restaurant and prepared foods can be of poor health promoting quality, yet their ease of use and availability are appealing in the rush of today's society. Practices such as eating more raw vegetables and fruits, grown organically, to accomplish long-term health goals including enhancing the immune system and maintain a proper acid-base balance within the body, require extra discipline. This type of discipline often requires eating raw vegetables and drinking bottled water, while friends and colleagues consume pizza, chicken wings, beer, and diet soda. The temptation to succumb to this type of poor eating can at times be strong, however, avoiding the end results of bad dietary habits, ranging from fatigue to heart disease and obesity, are well worth the effort.

In this chapter, general recommendations, based upon the practices of Chinese martial arts masters, will be offered. These will include the type of foods consumed, methods of preparing such foods, and most importantly, the appropriate meal times. The basis for these dietary habits stems from centuries of trial and error experience. Modern wisdom, and, in some cases, scientific information is consistent with, and supportive of, these dietary practices. Topics, including the effect of foods on acid-base balance; acid-base balance and electrolytes; the relationship between foods, free radicals and antioxidants; the health benefits of fresh fruits and vegetables; the importance of fiber in foods; and the value of nuts, seeds, and sprouted seeds will be presented. Foods have also been used in the treatment of disease within the Chinese martial arts and Chinese medicine, in general. A basic discussion of this topic will also be presented. Since this latter subject is linked to emotion, according to the Five Element Theory, the effects of emotion on organ function will also be given brief attention in this chapter.

The Effect of Foods on Acid-Base Balance

To appreciate the relationship between food types and their acid-base characteristics, a brief review of acid-base concepts and biochemistry is necessary. The degree of acid or base potential is measured by convention, as pH. The term pH is a mathematical reflection of the hydrogen ion concentration in solution; the potential of a solution to produce Hydrogen ions, i.e. pH. While pH ranges from 0 to 14 in nature, the range within biological systems generally lies between 3 and 9. When the pH is below 7, the solution is considered acidic; when above 7, the solution is considered basic or alkaline. The potential of any substance when in solution, to be slightly acidic or basic versus highly acidic or basic, is dependent upon the degree to which the positive and negative components of that substance can distance themselves from one another, ionize. For example, water is made up of positively charged hydrogen ions, H+, and negatively charged hydroxyl ions, OH-. These ions hold fairly close to one another, and are very weakly separated or ionized. Water is considered neutral in pH, holding a value of approximately 7. In other words, 1 positively charged hydrogen ion exists for every 10,000,000 water molecules (1 in ten to the power of 7). If relatively more hydrogen ions exist in solution, the solution is considered acidic. For example, if 1 hydrogen ion exists for every 1000 water molecules (1 in ten to the power of 3), the solution is considered acidic, with a pH of 3. On the other hand, if relatively less hydrogen ions exist in solution, the solution is considered basic, alkaline. For example, if 1 hydrogen ion exists for every 1,000,000,000 water molecules (1 in ten to the power of 9), the solution is considered basic, with a pH of 9. When substances are added to water, they are able to affect the degree of association between the hydrogen (H+) and hydroxyl

(OH-) components, to either a greater or lesser degree, making the solution either more acidic or basic, when compared to the neutral point, pH of 7 (153).

Within the human body, which is mostly composed of water, the normal pH of blood is 7.4, and can range between 7.36 and 7.46. The human body is, therefore, slightly basic in nature. The body strives, at great lengths, to maintain this normal range in blood pH. If the body becomes too acidic (less than a blood pH of 7.36) or too basic (greater than a blood pH of 7.46), dramatic consequence exists to health and ability to sustain life. A change above or below this narrow and normal range can result in changes in the ability of most organ systems to function, including the lungs, heart, kidneys, brain, and the immune system, depending upon the degree of change from normal.

The body has a remarkable ability to adjust itself and maintain a normal pH. This ability is part of the process of self-preservation. For example, when exercising, the body becomes more acidic, due to metabolic by-products produced in muscles. To maintain the acid-base balance, the rate of breathing increases to rid the body of the extra carbon dioxide produced, which contributes to the acidity. When this occurs, the lungs "help" rid the body of the excess acidity created, and maintain balance. Increased breathing also provides more oxygen, which is required by the body to keep up with the increased metabolic demand, due to the exercise. Without the increase in breathing rate, carbon dioxide would build up, causing further acidosis. In addition, anaerobic metabolism would occur, as a result of insufficient oxygen, causing lactic acidosis. If the body is not able to fully compensate, by breathing away carbon dioxide and taking in more oxygen, the kidneys will retain bicarbonate to help neutralize the excess acidity. If exercise continues and the body is not able to compensate through this added mechanism, the body will eventually become too acidotic. When these acid-neutralizing mechanisms can no longer compensate, the body would be forced to stop exercising. Assuming the person is healthy, the body will feel weak; the muscles would become tight, cramped and possibly painful. The person will feel fatigue. All of these effects will force the body to stop exercising, in order to deal with the extreme condition placed upon it by the physical exertion, beyond the body's capabilities to compensate.

This example of the effect of exercise on acid-base balance, highlights the effects of an abrupt, or acute, insult on the body, and the mechanisms the body uses to normalize the acid-base balance of blood, measured as pH. Many other circumstances exist that can cause the body to acutely become overly acidic or basic, resulting in an internal mechanism to correct the blood pH toward the normal range. On the other hand, long-term, chronic, low-level insults on acid-base balance can also occur. Eating proportionally excessive meats or meat products, over a long period of time, is an example of a long-term insult to the body's acid-base balance. Eating in this manner causes the body to become slightly acidic. The body may compensate for the slight acidity by craving certain foods that make the body more basic. An increased workload to various organs also occurs, since it is necessary to clear and balance acidity. The immediate result, seen on a daily basis, is a normal blood pH. Similar to the body's reaction to acute insults, the body may also react to chronic insult, but gradually over a long period of time. In the acute scenario, this is achieved by causing fatigue, forcing a person to stop exercising. In the chronic scenario, overworked organs ultimately become weakened, and eventually perform less efficiently and effectively, leading to illness. The quality of life becomes affected and the potential for longevity reduced.

The body has several mechanisms to normalize pH in the body. These include retention of bicarbonate by the kidneys in response to acidity, and release of bicarbonate in response to alkalosis. Phosphates and ammonia can also bind to acids in the body, which are then excreted by the kidney. Various amino acids, protein building blocks, can bind to and neutralize acids within cells. Other ions, such as calcium, sodium, and potassium interact with acids to help clear them via the kidney. Hormones, including anti-diuretic hormone (ADH) and aldosterone, regulate the amount of sodium, potassium and water in the body. These hormones assist the kidney indirectly in maintaining acid-base balance. As the body adjusts for acid-base imbalances, the regulating ions are either retained or lost. Similarly water is retained or lost. The consumption of foods and fluids must compensate for this process, as balance is sought, with regard to acids and bases within the body. Thus, in addition to the kidneys, which regulate acid-base balance metabolically; and the lungs, which regulate acid-base balance through respiration; the organs that regulate absorption of nutrients and water must also be considered. These include the stomach, small and large intestine, liver, and pancreas.

Most diets cause the body to become acidic, thus forcing several organs of the body to overwork in maintaining a normal blood pH. The most important of these organs include the kidneys, lungs, stomach, small and large intestines, liver, and pancreas. Grains, meats, and dairy products are acid producing (154). Diets, excessive in these foods, force the body to overwork. Over the short term, the stress to the body can easily be managed. However, after years of continuous consumption of these foods, the organs responsible for maintaining a normal pH can become weakened. Several recommendations are offered with regard to dietary changes based on age, organ pathology, exercise, and emotion. These recommendations consider the type of foods, time of day foods are consumed, flavor of foods, and preparation of foods. An example of these recommendations is based upon the concept that vegetables and fruits are base producing. For example, some have suggested that, a normal diet for healthy individuals should include 80% base forming foods and 20% acid forming foods (153,154).

A distinction should be made between foods, which are acid producing, foods that are naturally acidic, and the acidity naturally resulting from body metabolism (153-155). The acid, which the body normally produces as a result of body metabolism, is easily and naturally dealt with, through respiration. Acid produced, for example, by physical activity causes an increase in respiration. Increased respiration, in response to physical activity, is a natural mechanism to compensate for the slight acidity metabolically produced. This type of acidity does not require the body to resort to extraordinary metabolic mechanisms to neutralize an acid pH. Fruits and certain vegetables, that are naturally acidic, may contain greater acidity than acid producing foods. The body, however, can manage the acidity from fruits and vegetables in the same manner as it manages acidity produced by body metabolism. The acidity, resulting from acid producing foods, on the other hand, must also be neutralized differently, either chemically or metabolically. This is required to provide for the additional mechanisms of elimination, through the bowels or kidneys. Minerals stored in the body can be used to neutralize the acid produced by acid forming foods (153,154). Under normal circumstances the minerals are replaced through consumption of fruits, vegetables, and other foods. If these minerals are not replaced in the diet, other minerals, such as calcium, are substituted. These substitute minerals have other primary functions. When used as substitutes to neutralize acid, their primary functions suffer. Consumption of acid-producing foods in advanced age can increase the drain of calcium from the body, and thereby increase the chance of osteoporosis (153,154). Continual exposure to acid-producing foods also forces organs, such as the kidneys, to overwork for long periods of time to maintain a normal pH. This is similar to driving a car 120 miles per hour for weeks on end. The organs, as is the case with an engine, will no longer be able to function at that heightened level for any extended period of time.

Acid forming foods include meats, fish, fats, grains, dairy products, including cheese and butter, most nuts and seeds, beans and peas, table sugar, and proteins (153,154). Base forming foods include most fruits and vegetables, soybean, tofu, kidney beans, almonds, and corn. Several fruits and vegetables are naturally acidic including lemons, oranges, grapefruits, pineapples, and tomatoes, but are base producing when consumed. Both acid and base forming foods are essential to the body and, therefore, good for health. In general, maintaining a normal balance between acid and base forming foods allows for maintenance of a normal body pH without overly taxing organs, such as the kidneys. Maintaining a normal pH facilitates the proper functioning of enzymes, distribution of electrolytes, cellular metabolism, and organs.

Eating the correct foods, at the wrong time during the day, is thought to be more detrimental to health than eating the wrong foods, at the right time of the day, by Chinese martial art health experts familiar with these issues. The proportion of these two basic types of foods, the time consumed during the day, and overall amount must be considered for optimal health. It must be kept in mind that, negative emotional states and lack of proper exercise can override the benefits of a proper diet. These additional subjects will be covered separately in subsequent chapters.

Acid-Base Balance and Electrolytes

The most important electrolytes and ions in the body include sodium, chloride, calcium, potassium, and bicarbonate. Chloride, for example, helps maintain a balance of fluid inside and outside of cells, proper blood volume, blood pressure, and pH of the blood and other body fluids. Most of the chloride is absorbed in the intestine during ingestion of food and added table salt, sodium chloride. The kidneys excrete excess chloride. The level of chloride in the blood usually rises and falls in concert with sodium levels in the blood. Therefore, the hormone that regulates the amount of sodium in the blood, aldosterone, indirectly regulates the amount of chloride. The level of chloride in the blood is also related to the amount of bicarbonate in the blood. When bicarbonate increases in the blood, chloride decreases, and visa versa. As is the case with chloride, the body naturally regulates the amount of all electrolytes and ions in the system. For example, with a net loss of sodium and chloride from sweating, the body will crave salt to replenish these electrolytes.

Aside from breathing and heart function, the most important activity, the body performs, is maintaining a balanced pH, acid-base balance. Electrolytes share an integrated relationship with acids and bases in the body. When the body becomes too acidic, the body naturally compensates by retaining basic salts. Under normal conditions the body has enough salts and is capable of performing the necessary adjustments. Under sudden and extreme conditions, the body may not be able to compensate. For example, an acute ingestion of a toxic amount of potassium can result in death due to toxicity to the heart. Fortunately, this is a relatively uncommon situation, since vomiting usually occurs following oral ingestion, precluding the occurrence of toxic potassium blood levels. On the other hand, the body can succumb to the effects of chronic low-grade acidity. Net acid-producing diets, for example, can produce a low-grade acidosis in healthy persons. The degree of acidosis increases with age, presumably because of a progressive deficiency of organ function and base reserve, necessary to compensate with increasing age. As the body becomes slightly acidic, organs, such as the kidneys compensate by retaining base substances, and the lungs, by exhaling carbon dioxide. The body also may tap into base electrolyte and salt reserves, when necessary. Using these reserves, however, depletes the base electrolytes from maintaining their normal and natural function. This can result, for example, in heartburn and stomach upset as base reserves, intended to balance the high acidity in the stomach, are drained to balance pH elsewhere. Calcium loss from the bone may also occur, as base salts are drained from bone to balance pH.

A proper diet, in this regard, should not impose the chronic metabolic stress of low-grade acidity on the body. Reducing acid producing foods, increasing base producing foods, such as fruits and vegetables, in part, provide the body with a natural mechanism to avoid chronic low-grade acidosis, while also providing the body with the necessary electrolytes and nutrients the body needs to function optimally.

Free Radicals, Foods, and Exercise

Free radicals are unstable molecules that damage cells. Free radicals can be viewed as bullets, used by the body to defend itself against invasion. These unstable molecules can result from the body undergoing an inflammatory response. For example, a simple cut in the skin can cause local inflammation. As the body detects the invasion of foreign entities, such as bacteria, the skin becomes red, slightly swollen, and painful. These signs are in response to chemical messengers in the body, cytokines, which coordinate the natural inflammatory process, associated with protecting the body. Ultimately, immune cells and free radicals destroy the invading entities. The body heals, and inflammation resolves. In this example, free radicals play a vital role in survival. However, when free radical function extends beyond the natural and normal response, healthy cells can be harmed, leading to disease. Longevity, in turn, can be affected. Free radicals are also believed to underlie the aging process, in general, and contribute to the causes of many different age-related illnesses (156-162). These illnesses include inflammatory diseases such as arthritis, heart disease, and neurological diseases, such as Alzheimer's disease.

Free radicals have a normal role in protecting the body, as well as a harmful effect, when excessive (159). Within the spectrum of their normal function, free radicals play a vital role in several biochemical processes of the body. Oxidative free radicals, for example, help metabolize sugars, kill bacteria, and maintain flexible blood vessels. On the other hand, induction of free radical formation from stimuli in the external environment can lead to damage of normal cells and normal cellular processes (160). Mutagenic substances and cancer-causing chemicals in prepared meats, for instance, can contain or stimulate production of harmful free radicals in the body (161,162). The body normally counters excessive free radicals via antioxidants. In health, a balance is achieved in this regard. However, the body has limitations in providing sufficient antioxidants to deal with free radicals induced by an unending onslaught of external stimuli, such as poor dietary products, consumed over a long period of time. Thus, some dietary modification is required to reduce induction of these free radicals. To maintain a proper balance between free radicals and antioxidants, consumption of foods that are bad for the body (see previous chapter) should be avoided, and more fruits and vegetables, which contain antioxidants, should be eaten (150,163). This provides a natural method for reaching balance. To derive the maximal benefit from fruits and vegetables, these foods should be organically grown, fresh, and naturally ripened. The necessary flavanoids, vitamins, phyto-estrogens, and other beneficial substances will be maximally available under these conditions. This is not to say that consumption of excess antioxidants, in the form of antioxidant supplements, is more beneficial. Supplemental antioxidant consumption can tip the balance to the other extreme, reducing the normal healthy function of the body's natural free radicals, which provide normal protection against bacteria and cancer cells, for instance (163).

Medical research is quickly uncovering a unifying concept that underlies the mystery surrounding many diseases, inflammation (164). It appears that inflammation can present acutely, as well as chronically. Acutely, inflammation flares up, in response to external intrusion, such as infection. Chronically, low-level inflammation can occur, causing a slow-burn effect that can promote the development of several illnesses, including heart disease, high blood pressure, diabetes, and neurological diseases, such as Alzheimer's disease. In the body, fat cells can act as producers of inflammatory substances, resulting in this slow-burn effect (165). Several interventions can reduce this type of inflammatory process, including exercise; reducing saturated fat in the diet; increase consumption of fruits and vegetables that provide the body with a rich, yet appropriate, supply of antioxidants; and good oral care to reduce chronic inflammation of the gums. While not proven as a cause of heart disease, a strong predictive association for heart disease exists for oral diseases such as pericoronitis, infection around the third molar; tooth decay to the point where root remnants only remain; gingivitis, inflammation of the gums; and cavities (166-171).

Animal research suggests that vegetables may prevent or help treat the inflammatory disease, systemic lupus erythematosis (lupus), and other diseases linked to inflammation, such as heart disease (172). People with heart disease may also benefit from the antioxidant effects of fruits and vegetables. In addition to reducing inflammation, it has been appreciated for a number of years that, vegetables, such as broccoli, cabbage, and cauliflower, may be protective against several types of cancer (150,151,173-180). Beverages derived from vegetables including dark beer, red wine, or purple grape juice, contain flavanoids that offer a mechanism to fight the free radicals that occur, when the body metabolizes various foods (181-183). Flaxseed, a component of diets in Asia for thousands of years, contains a high concentration of omega-3 fatty acids, which likely lower cholesterol, stabilize blood sugar, and lower the risk of several types of caner, including breast, prostate, and colon cancers (184). Omega-3 fatty acids also reduce inflammation associated with many diseases, including arthritis, Parkinson's disease, and asthma. The fiber, phytoestrogens, and antioxidants found in flaxseed, may also contribute to these beneficial effects.

Other research indicates that antioxidants, such as vitamin E, can neutralize free radicals, but when combined with exercise, the effect is more pronounced (150,152,177,185). Exercise boosts antioxidant formation, which combats free radicals. Exercise provides the added benefit of reducing obesity, high blood pressure, and diabetes, which contribute to free radical cell damage. Free radical formation, as a result of exercise, is also thought to stimulate the body's production of natural antioxidant enzymes. Since the body tends to produce more free radicals, and fewer antioxidants to counter them, after approximately 40 to 45 years of age, consumption of foods containing natural antioxidants, including fruits and vegetables, as well as moderate exercise, become more important to health and longevity at this age.

This is not to say that, establishing a foundation of these behaviors, starting earlier in life, is not as important (186,187).

Health Benefits of Fresh Fruits and Vegetable

Epidemiologic studies support the link between diets, high in fresh fruits and vegetables, and the low risk of many chronic diseases. Several factors can be pointed to, which may provide these health benefits, including the types of nutrients, vitamins, minerals, and fiber content present in fresh fruit and vegetables. Studies of remote Andean inhabitants have identified their traditional diets, as possible contributors to the extraordinary longevity and low incidence of diseases such as cancer, heart disease, and inflammatory illnesses, including arthritis, experienced among this population. The conclusions drawn among researchers indicate, diets rich in whole grains, fresh fruits and vegetables, in addition to being low in fat and animal proteins, appear to be associated with their longevity and low incidence of these chronic diseases (151).

Many disease-preventing, protective compounds have been identified in fruits and vegetables. These are referred to as phytochemicals and many may possess several potential means of promoting health, including adjustment of enzymes that detoxify foreign harmful substances coming in contact with the body; stimulation of the immune system; reduction of platelet stickiness, thus preventing blood clots; adjustment of cholesterol production and hormone metabolism; reduction of blood pressure, and antioxidant or anti-inflammatory action (173-185,188,198). Many of these mechanisms overlap one another, some with stronger supportive evidence than others. For example, evidence supporting the value of whole grain breakfast cereal indicates a reduced the risk of heart attack by twenty-three percent, and lower the risk of death from any cause by twenty-seven percent (199). While the advantage of whole grain cereal is unclear, researchers point to the effect of whole grains on lowering cholesterol and blood pressure, improving the processing of insulin and glucose, and beneficial content of micronutrients, antioxidants, minerals, and fiber. Recent information supports the value of eating broccoli tips. Eating this part of the vegetable is associated with protecting the heart against cardiac disease (190).

C-reactive protein (CRP) has long been known as a marker of inflammation in the body. Moreover, sustained high levels of CRP are associated with an increased risk of stroke, early signs of type 2 diabetes, heart disease, and sudden cardiac death. This protein appears to play an active role in forming blood clots, causing heart attacks and stroke (200). While CRP plays an important role in the body's normal biochemistry, the existence of high levels in the body for long periods of time appears to lead to serious health consequences. CRP levels can be lowered through the same means as lowering cholesterol, including weight loss, consuming fewer calories per day, and adopting a very low fat diet (201). Low fat diets generally include proportionally greater fruits and vegetables.

As antioxidants, phytohemicals are thought to restore a natural balance between free radical formation and antioxidant defense. As pointed out above, an imbalance, in this regard, is thought to play a role in cardiovascular disease, cancer, cataract formation, the overall process of aging, inflammatory and neurological diseases. Fresh fruits and vegetables are good sources of trace minerals that can interfere with, and disable, free radicals, before they react with cells. Other substances in fruits and vegetables, which act as antioxidants, include vitamins C and E and beta-carotene. More potent antioxidants, found in these food types, are the flavanoid group of compounds (163,173,175,177,178, 181-183,190,194,198,202). Adjustment, in terms of upgrading the ability of detoxifying enzymes to protect against mutagenic substances, is a key factor in the body's ability to protect itself against environmental toxins entering the body through respired polluted air, absorption from the skin, or by way of the food and water consumed. The enzyme systems in the liver and gastrointestinal tract, responsible for metabolizing these harmful substances, can be enhanced by a number of phytochemicals, including flavonoids, isothiocyanates, and allyl sulfides. The nutrients in foods and other phytochemicals, including vitamins, also have the potential to improve immune system function. The immune system is a complex interplay between immune cells, immune system chemical messengers, antibodies, and immune system products that kill invading pathogens and cancer cells.

Platelet aggregation, or clumping, contributes to a wide range of diseases, including cardiovascular disease. The mechanism of platelet aggregation in the disease process may involve inflammation. Numerous compounds, found in fruits and vegetables, are capable of reducing the adherence of platelets to one another, thereby reducing clumping and clot formation (151,152). Compounds found in garlic are some of the most widely studied for their anti-platelet activity.

In addition to inflammation, plaque formation, due to elevated serum cholesterol and triglyceride concentrations, represents a significant contributor to cardiovascular diseases, including coronary artery disease and atherosclerotic disease in non-cardiac blood vessels. Vegetables and fruit have demonstrated the ability to lower cholesterol by reducing cholesterol absorption in the gastro-intestinal tract, as well as modify the biochemical process leading to high cholesterol. Saponins, for example, are believed to bind cholesterol and prevent absorption into the blood, as well as reduce inflammation (183). Saponins are found in red wine and are believed to originate from the skin of grapes. Saponins can also be found in olive oil and soybeans.

The phytochemicals found in green foods, soy products, and grains, as a group, are known as terpenes. These compounds function as antioxidants, with the carotenoid subgroup being studies the most. The carotenoids are found in yellow, orange, and red pigmented vegetables and fruits, including tomatoes, parsley, organs, grapefruit, and spinach (202). Of the more than six hundred carotenoids, beta carotene is the most familiar. Only about ten percent of this group of carotenoids possesses vitamin A activity. Beta carotene is the most active in this regard. These carotenes may offer protection against specific types of cancer, including lung, colorectal, breast, uterine and prostate cancers. The protective effect may be greatest when these carotenes are consumed together. They also increase immune response and protect the skin against UV radiation. Another class of terpenes, found in citrus fruits, the limonoids, may be more specific to protecting lung tissue.

Phytosterols are found in most plants, but concentrate in green and yellow vegetable seeds, such as those of pumpkins, yams, soy, rice and various herbs. These phytosterols compete with cholesterol within the intestines for absorption into the body. This competition reduces the absorption of cholesterol and facilitates the excretion of cholesterol from the body, via the stools. Phytosterols may also reduce inflammation and the development of colon, breast, and prostate cancer.

Phenols are a group of compounds offering blue, blue-red and violet colors to berries, grapes and eggplant. This group of compounds protect against oxidative damage, blocking specific enzymes involved with inflammation. They also interfere with platelet aggregation by interfering with prostaglandin formation, a group of substances involved with inflammation.

The flavanoids include flavones, flavanones, and flavanols. Comprising over fifteen hundred compounds, this broad group possesses a wide range of actions against inflammation, free radical activity, toxins, platelet clumping, and inhibition of specific enzymes. For example, flavanoids may block angiotensin-converting enzyme, ACE, and thereby reduce blood pressure in people with hypertension (202). They can block cyclo-oxygenase, thus reducing the production of prostaglandin, and thereby decrease platelet clumping and inflammation. The flavanoids may also block formation of estrogen, due to blocking the enzyme, estrogen synthetase, and thereby interfere with estrogen-dependent tumor growth.

Isoflavones are similar to flavanoids, and possess properties that are responsible for hindering tumor growth, specifically of the breast, uterus and prostate. It has been noted that people who consume diets rich in isoflavones, found in soy foods, rarely develop these cancers (202).

Glucosinolates, found in cruciferous vegetables can activate enzymes, and detoxify substances in the liver. These substances also activate enzymes that regulate white blood cell and cytokine activity. By products of these compounds are thought to be associated with the blocking of enzymes related to tumor growth (202).

Similarly, Allyl Sulfides, found in garlic, leeks, shallots and onions, might have a protective action against mutagenic substances, and therefore cancer. They may also enhance immune function and provide protection to the cardiovascular system.

Indoles are found in high concentrations in fruits and vegetables high in vitamin C content. Together, with vitamin C, indoles may bind to carcinogens in the intestines (202). When bound, carcinogens are prevented from being absorbed by the intestine. Bound carcinogens may also be prevented from leading to local disease in the gastro-intestinal tract.

A number of other plant compounds act as potent antioxidants, including isoprenoids, coenzyme Q (ubiquinone), and lipoic acid. Further understanding of the role of lipoic acid, as a free radical scavenger, may prove to be an important step in understanding how fruit and vegetable antioxidants slow the aging process, and offer the potential for enhanced longevity.

Plant and Fruit Enzymes

Naturally occurring (endogenous) enzymes in plants, including fruits and vegetables, are responsible for their growth, and may remain active after harvested and stored. They maintain the metabolism of the fruits and vegetables, but also have harmful effects on their color, flavor, odor, and texture. As a result, attempts are made, prior to and during the storage process, to eliminate or neutralize the activity of these enzymes, which are responsible for the harmful effects on aesthetic properties. Several naturally occurring enzymes, found in fruits and vegetables, assist the body in the digesting protein and fats, derived from other food types. These beneficial enzymes include amylase and lipase, and are among others that assist with the digestion of fruits and vegetables themselves, such as pectin methylesterase (203,204).

Several other natural substances, found in fresh fruits and vegetables, can also affect color, flavor, odor, texture, and nutritional value, once harvested and stored. These act in a manner similar to the effect of endogenous enzymes. In an effort to retain a desirable appearance and texture, various processes and chemicals are introduced to harvested fruits and vegetables, in their storage and marketing, to destroy or neutralize these enzymes and products. Unfortunately, fruits and vegetables harvested prematurely, stored for long periods, or altered enzymatically, may not have had an opportunity to develop or retain the optimal quality and quantity of the health-promoting compounds. Therefore, eating fresh fruits and vegetables is optimal for consumption. Fresh and mature products provide the natural compounds associated with good health and longevity. Without modern harvesting and storage methods, on the other hand, these fruits and vegetables may not be available for wide consumption. Therefore, as general rule, every effort should be made to consume seasonal fresh fruits and vegetables, grown in your geographic area.

Cooking can destroy many important compounds found in raw fruits and vegetables. Therefore, raw fruits and vegetables should be consumed for optimal benefit. The seeds and skin of these foods contain high concentrations of many important compounds. If grown organically, the seeds and skin should also be consumed, whenever recommended, palatable, and feasible.

Fiber Content of Foods

Whole grain carbohydrates, fruits and vegetables with skin, such as peas, beans, cabbage, cauliflower, apple, cherries, pears, peaches, and plumbs, are rich in fiber (205). Fiber occurs naturally in two forms, insoluble and soluble (206,207). Insoluble fiber is cellulose, which cannot be absorbed by the intestines, and remains in the bowel to form stool. Insoluble fiber or roughage promotes normal bowel function in healthy individuals. Soluble fiber absorbs water, slows the rate of digestion, and absorbs fats and sugar. Appropriate fluids with the adequate bulk provided by carbohydrates, contributes to normal bowel function. In addition to promoting normal bowel function, dietary fiber assists in lowering cholesterol levels in the body, by reducing the rate and extent of fat absorption. Reducing cholesterol assists in preventing atherosclerosis, which causes high blood pressure and heart disease. Dietary fiber is not contained in animal products, such as milk and meats. It must be kept in mind that other behavioral and dietary factors may have a greater impact on lowering cholesterol, including reducing the total amount of fat in the diet; avoiding foods and cooking oils, that are high in cholesterol and saturated fat; participating in regular physical activity; and losing weight if overweight.

While low in fat content, insoluble dietary fiber also provides a sensation of fullness without the calories. Fiber, thus, assists in reducing the total calories consumed per day, weight reduction, and weight maintenance efforts. If an increase in dietary fiber is associated with a reduction of sugar intake, the management of diabetes, specific to dietary control, may also be improved.

Through fostering normal bowel function, dietary fiber helps treat chronic constipation. This may reduce the risk of colon cancer and other bowel diseases, such as irritable bowel syndrome, diverticulitis, and hemorrhoids. Consumption of fruits and vegetables has a greater association with lowering the risk of colorectal cancer than fiber from other sources, such as cereal fiber (208-210). Other behavioral factors, which contribute to constipation, such as the lack of physical activity or exercise, insufficient fluid intake, use of constipating medications, and diseases affecting bowel contents or bowel function, should also be addressed in this regard. The advice of a medical professional should always be sought if chronic constipation exists.

Recommendations, offered by U.S. government agencies and the National Cancer Institute, suggest adults should consume an average daily intake of twenty to thirty grams of dietary fiber with an upper limit of thirty-five grams (205). Adequate fluid intake should accompany fiber intake. Since the average intake of fiber by adults in the United States is approximately twelve to seventeen grams per day, a change in diet, providing an increase to twenty to thirty grams per day, should be accomplished slowly. A gradual increase is advised in an effort to avoid the side effects of a sudden change in dietary fiber to this higher level. These effects can include an upset digestive system, gas, and abdominal pain. Fiber supplements should be avoided, unless recommended by a medical professional.

The Value of Nuts and Seeds

Nuts and seeds, in particular sprouted seeds, offer a potent source of nutrients. The belief that these foods possess the highest reproductive energy of the plant is consistent with the Chi Kung concept of essence. Essence is considered to be responsible for growth and reproduction in humans, according to Chinese medical theory. Thus, Chinese martial arts health experts believe consuming these foods represents a source of concentrated energy. In fact, seeds contain all of the important nutrients required for human growth (210). Seeds are very good sources of protein, unsaturated fatty acids, many vitamins including the B-complex series and vitamin E, and high in mineral content. They also offer a source of fiber in the diet.

Nuts possess similar nutrients. Nuts are rich in linoleic acid, a free radical scavenger thought to retard the aging process. However, nuts are high in fat content where forty to sixty percent of the nutritional value is composed of fat.

Spouted seeds provide additional nutritional value compared to unsprouted seeds. The sprouting process increases nutritional value several fold (210,211). For example, the riboflavin content of sprouted barley seed is more than six hundred percent greater than dry barley seed. Similarly, the niacin content is over one hundred seventy percent greater. Vitamin C content is increased over two hundred fifty percent in sprouted lentil seeds compared to dry seeds.

Due to theoretical reasons, as well as observational evidence regarding nutritional value, many recommend adding seeds, spouted seeds, and nuts to the diet. Some controversy exists regarding this recommendation because of the fat content of nuts. Nuts are, therefore, not routinely recommended in this Chinese martial art system.

Oxygen Content of Water

Considerable marketing effort is evident for products advocating the notion that oxygen, when supplied to the body through water, super-oxygenated water, provides some additional benefit over the normal process of breathing oxygen (212-214). Evidence supporting improved athletic performance, as a result of using these products, is used to promote various health claims. The main objection, in the author's opinions, to the concept of using the gastro-intestinal tract to enhance the delivery of oxygen, lies with the fact that oxygen cannot be delivered, via water, in sufficient amounts to add any real benefit to the body, over respired oxygen. Respiration, via the lungs, is a very efficient and natural mechanism to oxygenate the blood and body tissues. If additional oxygen is necessary in healthy individuals, the body will increase the depth and rate of respiration, automatically. From a clinical standpoint, breathing exercises and physical activities, which promote increased respiration, are far more effective than attempting to increase oxygenation of the blood via a nutrient-absorptive membrane, such as the intestine.

Two processes are used to increase oxygen in water: a synthetic process, which forces oxygen into water; and a natural method, involving the addition of alkaline salts to water. Mineral enriched water may actually provide some health benefit because of the base-forming potential, rather than the increased oxygen content.

With respect to promoting appropriate oxygen content in the blood, enhancing the natural process of oxygenation, breathing, through appropriate and well established methods, Chi Kung exercises and exercise, in general, appears to be a more reliable, realistic, and far less expensive means to accomplish this end.

General Concepts and Practices

The general dietary concepts and practices presented in this section stem from Chinese Medical theory, and therefore a brief review is presented. From the Chinese Medicine perspective, as people age, the digestive system increasingly becomes challenged, and weakens without proper care. This is particularly true for those over fifty years of age. The degradive scenario often involves excessive amounts of foods being consumed, accompanied by less frequent bowel movements. Here, both the stomach and spleen, which also includes many functions of the pancreas, according to Chinese Medicine, become compromised. According to this organ function model, the stomach is the first recipient of consumed nutrients and liquids. Nutrients and fluids are absorbed and sent to the spleen for distribution. Food then passes from the stomach to the small intestine, where a second phase of nutrient and fluid absorption occurs. Throughout these steps, interaction exists between the digestive organs, stomach and small intestine, and the spleen. This model also recognizes the role of the liver, at least in terms of promoting the digestion and distribution of nutrients, fluids, and energy. Once processed through the small intestine, a final step occurs within the large intestine, until contents are finally passed as stool. This model is somewhat consistent with the western view, at least in terms of the downward flow of intestinal contents and absorption of nutrients. The biochemical processes, involved in digestion, absorption, and processing of nutritional components, result from the combined action of several organs, including the stomach, small and large intestines, liver, and pancreas.

Weakness in the stomach and spleen can be attributed, in part, to an over-consumption of meats and fish, and an insufficient consumption of fruits and vegetables, which contain the fiber. Fiber assists with the downward flow of intestinal contents. With the type of chi deficiency occurring with advanced age or illness, little strength is available for normal peristalsis and evacuation of stools. Fiber allows for easier passage of contents though the intestine, and evacuation of stool from the bowel. The stomach and small intestine are able to pass contents along more easily and smoothly.

Constipation can affect health in several other respects, as well. The feeling of being full and uncomfortable reinforces diminished physical activity. Lack of physical activity allows constipation to persist. In turn, retention of stools does not allow for the normal passage of waste. This prevents the removal of many toxins from the body within the stools. When constipated, the body undergoes prolonged exposure to these toxins. The dietary practices described below should produce at least two bowel movements per day, or optimally, three per day. The body is considered to be in good condition when bowel movements follow the three main meals per day.

Grain and other high fiber fruits and vegetables quickly pass from the stomach. In terms of Chinese Medical theory, "heat" is not produced in the stomach. This is desirable, since foods, such as meats, which require residence in the stomach for a greater length of time, produce "heat." In addition, with sufficient fiber, a feeling of fullness ensues and fewer calories are consumed; cholesterol is reduced; and bowel function is improved. Fruits and vegetables do not contain fat, additionally providing a mechanism to lower overall cholesterol levels.

These foods contain a considerable amount of vitamins, minerals, and other nutrients, in addition to fiber.

A lack of appetite should not serve as a reason to avoid meals. Stomach insufficiency is associated with a lack of appetite. The practice of consuming the prescribed amount of calories and liquid, according to the practices described below, even when the desire to eat is lacking, is advantageous. With proper nutrition, the consumption of the appropriate nutrients assists in resolving stomach insufficiency. In this regard, foods are used in the self-treatment of various symptoms and attention must be given to food flavors. Foods used in the treatment of symptoms will be covered in a separate section.

Grains and Vegetables

Grains and the seeds of many fruits and vegetables are thought to contain life energy, and therefore, generally good for health. For this reason, vegetables, which contain seeds, are preferred. These include peas, beans, lentils, tomatoes, cucumbers, and squash. Spinach, broccoli, and other leafy vegetables offer considerable roughage in the diet, in addition to vitamins and minerals. Broccoli and other flowering vegetables may offer some protection against heart disease and various cancers of the intestinal tract, for example colorectal cancer. In general, vegetables are considered neutral with respect to their ability to warm or cool the body, according to Chinese Medical concepts.

In addition to the above foods, the traditional diet of martial arts masters within the Eight Step Preying Mantis System includes a reliance on grains, such as wheat and pearl barley, green beans, yellow beans, red beans, mung beans, which cool the body, cabbage, onions, carrots, potatoes, and corn. Sweet potatoes are also included, but eaten only in the morning. The others can be eaten at any time of the day. Vegetable roots, for example, potatoes, are high in carbohydrate, offering a good source of caloric energy. Other roots, such as carrots, are high in fiber. Seaweed is high in minerals, including calcium. The fruit of several vegetables, high in vitamin C content, contain a greater proportion of water and natural sugars. Mushrooms are high in protein and B complex vitamins. All of these foods are considered beneficial for the health of the stomach and spleen.

Preparation of grains or beans requires washing before cooking. Sufficient water must be added for cooking. The cooking time is approximately three to four hours. Breads, made from whole grains and prepared in a low-fat method, are also considered beneficial. The vegetables are best consumed raw. Consuming sprouted seeds, for example, green bean seed sprouts, are also considered beneficial, due to their enhanced nutrient content. Care is taken in their purchase, choosing organically grown products.

Fruits

In general, fruits chosen for consumption, should be locally grown, in season, contain seeds, and allowed to mature naturally on the plant. If organically grown, the skin of the fruit should be eaten. In addition, consuming the seeds of the fruit, when possible, is considered advantageous to health. Fruits should not be cooked, since heat destroys many of the nutrients. Fruits are considered naturally cooling to the body.

Around the world, latitude dictates climate, which in turn dictates the type of fruit natural to the area, and those which are able to be cultivated in a given region. For example, northern China is located at the same latitude as New York State. Given the existence of similar natural resources, similar fruits could be grown in both areas. Since the body becomes adapted to a given climate, the body also becomes adapted to the fruits grown in that climate. The body is, therefore, optimally benefited from locally grown fruit, rather than fruit imported from climates of dramatically different latitudes. For example, people from New York State would be expected to receive greater benefit from fruits natural to, and grown in, New York State, versus fruits grown in tropical climates. This is believed to be the case, since both the individual and the fruit are adapted to the particular climate. If one were to move to a tropical climate, consuming tropical fruit would be more beneficial to the body, once adapted to that climate.

Consuming fruit that is harvested in season is also considered most beneficial to the body. Fruit, harvested in season, is matured naturally. Fruit that is harvested prior to ripening naturally and stored eventually ripens. However, the fruit may become nutritionally deficient, and therefore, be more acid producing to the body. The color of ripened fruit also is a consideration among many Chinese martial arts masters of this system. The color of naturally ripened fruit corresponds to a particular season in many cases. In general, during the spring season, a greater proportion of green colored fruits are chosen for consumption; during summer, more red colored fruit; during Indian Summer, more yellow fruit; during autumn, more white fruit; and during winter, more deeply colored fruit.

Seeds contain the ability and energy for reproduction, as well as a source of roughage. For optimal benefit, fruits containing seeds are chosen. In addition to the pulp, consumption of the skin and seeds offers nutritional advantages. The skin is thought to be base forming, once consumed, and therefore, beneficial to the body. If the skin is too thick, for example, the skin of a banana, the fruit can be placed in a blender. However, the skin is most often discarded and only the pulp eaten. The skin of fruits should be consumed, whenever palatable and possible, if organically grown. This is particularly important with regard to apples. The skin retains pesticides and should be avoided, if not organically grown. Apple skin is high in antioxidant compounds. Some would consume orange, lemon, or lemon skins if ground in a blender. Similarly, common sense should prevail with regard to consuming the seeds of fruits. Consuming grape seeds would be considered acceptable, while consuming avocado seeds would not.

Consumption of any fruit should occur within a two-hour period to avoid oxidation and discoloration. Consumption of freshly juiced fruit should occur within thirty minutes, to optimally preserve nutritional value.

Preparation

Because of their high fat content, oils and butter should be avoided in preparing food. Oil is difficult to digest and raises cholesterol. As mentioned in other sections, high cholesterol can lead to cardiovascular disease. For example, atherosclerosis can result from sustained high levels of cholesterol, causing the diameter of the vessels to be decreased and less flexible. This will restrict or decrease blood flow, leading to infarction in any tissue, most notably, the heart (myocardial infarction) or the brain (stroke). Other major organs can be affected as well, such as the liver and kidneys. If vessels become weakened, as a result of atherosclerotic disease, a rupture of the vessel wall can occur, leading to internal bleeding. If in a vital area, such as the brain, a stroke can result.

Methods of food preparation, including barbecuing and use of microwaves, hold their own specific problems, and are discussed in detail in the previous chapter. Similarly, because of the problems associated with pesticides, food additives and other preservatives, organically prepared foods are preferred. Avoiding processed foods that contain these substances may also be advantageous.

In general, when preparing food, boiling, steaming, or using water in place of oil when frying, avoids the difficulties associated with fat. When boiling, attempt to use a maximal temperature of fifty degrees centigrade. With higher temperatures, an increased destruction of nutrients and enzymes can occur. Consumption of raw fruits and vegetables offers the greatest benefit (215). As a general rule, restrict the cooking of vegetables to fifty percent, attempting to retain as much of the nutritional value as possible.

Consuming Meals

Breakfast

The optimal time to consume the breakfast meal is between 6 a.m. and 7:30 a.m. Exceptions are not made for those who work the night shift. Working during the night is considered unhealthy, since the liver, in particular, does not receive the proper rest and regeneration, during the period of predominant chi flow to that organ, 1 a.m. to 3 a.m. In general, the optimal time to sleep, based on the cycle of chi flow through the organ channels, is from 9 p.m. to 4 a.m. or 5 a.m.

The content of the breakfast meal should include two different types of fruit, two different types of vegetables, and a source of carbohydrate, such as a potato or whole grain bread, wheat bread, for example. Breakfast should constitute approximately one-half of the total daily caloric intake. With chronic disease, extra carbohydrate should be consumed, for example, one potato. An added source of vegetable enzyme should also be included to assist digestion. The fruits and vegetables should be seasonal and locally grown, if possible; they should optimally be consumed raw. The potato can be steamed or eaten raw. A sweet potato can be substituted at the breakfast meal. Breads should be prepared from whole grains, and eaten without being toasted.

Foods should be chewed well to assist in digestion. Raw vegetables should be chewed approximately thirty times per mouthful. Chewing also assists in salivary production, which helps the digestive process.

A sufficient amount of water should be consumed during the breakfast period. A healthy adult should consume approximately three liters of water, throughout the waking hours, not less than two and one-half liter and not more than four liters. It is preferable to avoid drinking the majority of liquids prior to the evening hours, preventing waking up during sleep due to the need to empty the bladder.

Lunch

The optimal time to consume the lunch meal is between 12 Noon and 1 p.m.

The content of the lunch meal should consist of the same type of foods as the breakfast meal, however the quantity should be half as much. For example, the meal can consist of one fruit, one vegetable, and carbohydrate, such as potato or bread.

Sufficient water should be consumed according to the above suggestions.

Dinner

The optimal time to consume the dinner meal is between 5 p.m. and 7 p.m.

The content of the dinner meal should consist of similar foods, as consumed for the lunch and breakfast meal. The quantity should consist of one fourth to one third of the total daily food intake. The dinner meal can be tailored to offer considerable variation, in an effort to avoid the boredom of eating the same foods, day after day, meal after meal. For example, cooked beans can be substituted frequently; a small amount of meat or fish can be included a few times per month. Seek out recipes, which remain within these guidelines, yet offer interesting alternatives.

Sufficient water should be consumed according to the above suggestions.

Between Meal Snacks

If hungry between meals or during the evening hours following dinner, fruits can provide an excellent, healthy substitute to traditional high fat, high carbohydrate, and high sugar snacks.

Influence of Age on the Proportion of Dietary Components Consumed

Healthy individuals, less than thirty-five years of age, are capable of tolerating the effects of various types of foods, including animal protein and fat. Assuming the caloric intake of any meal is not excessive and nutritional components are balanced, with no more than thirty percent of calories derived from fat, considerable variability and choice of foods can be considered appropriate. The individual should also display an active lifestyle.

Certainly, exceptions to choosing such a broad variety of foods exist, including a familial predisposition to high blood cholesterol. In this case dietary changes are often recommended, which include a reduction in the consumption of fats. In addition, an examination of the actual percentage of fat in the average meal, found in the United States, may reveal a much higher percentage of fat, than is recommended. If this is the case, a reduction of fats to the recommended proportion of total calories is recommended. These recommendations pertain to adults. Neonate and infants, on the other hand, require fats in the diet for normal growth and development of the nervous system. Fat free diets are, therefore, not recommended for infants and neonates. Specific dietary recommendations are available for toddlers, children, and teens, and can be obtained from the pediatrician's office.

Between thirty-five and fifty years of age, a change in the proportion of dietary components provides health advantages. During this period, the effects of long term exposure to acid producing foods, free radicals, and body changes, require the added health benefits of vegetable and fruit nutrients, fiber, and enzymes. Dietary adjustments to incorporate these should be considered. A greater proportion of whole grain products, fruits and vegetables, accompanying a reduction in the proportion of meats, fish, and dairy products in the diet, offer a reasonable alternative to the traditional "American" diet. These dietary changes help minimize energy expenditure and workload of the internal organs, which work diligently to maintain proper balance in pH, free radical-antioxidant activity, and detoxification of harmful substances entering the body from the environment. The less energy the body must expend, as it exerts in performing these functions, the more energy is available for normal repair and replacement of cells and tissues, mental acuity, physical activity level to improve circulation, better overall health, and longevity.

Over fifty years of age, an almost complete elimination of meats, fish, and fat from the diet becomes critical, with respect to promoting health and longevity. Beyond this age, the body must conserve on energy, and expend as little as possible on balancing the effects of diets, high in these components. The advantages of fruits and vegetables, taking the place of animal proteins and fats, become extremely important to health and longevity for the reasons cited above. It should be kept in mind that, diet must not be the only consideration in this regard. Proper exercise, control of emotion, and breathing exercises assist in promoting circulation, reducing unnecessary energy expenditure, and improve oxygenation for overall better health, immune system function, removing environmental toxins, and cell repair and replacement.

The immune system, in general, appears to be a key contributor to longevity. It is well known that, the immune system weakens with advancing age, making the elderly more susceptible to disease. It is also well known that several factors allow the immune system to weaken over time, and include, environmental toxins, sedentary lifestyles, diets poor in nutrients that promote a healthy immune system, and stress. In addition to proper diet, exercise, minimizing exposure to environmental toxins, stress reduction is an important component in preserving a healthy immune system. Stress often leads to excessive and destructive emotions, such as anger and depression. Control of such emotions, through a variety of means, including exercise, prayer, mediation, or seeking the help of a therapist, may assist in avoiding the consequences of these powerful feelings. Excessive emotion will be addressed separately, both in this chapter and subsequent chapters. Diets, high in anti-oxidants, can protect the rapidly dividing cells of the immune system from free radical damage. The oxidative stress associated with free radicals appears to play a role in degeneration of neurological function with age. Diets, rich in B-complex vitamins, found in many whole grains, fruits and vegetables, and omega-3 fatty acids, found in wild salmon and flaxseed, also help to improve brain function, including memory, an important asset with advancing age.

Dietary Treatment of Disease

Several centuries ago, the relationship between consuming various foods and alleviating symptoms of illnesses were identified. For example, consuming basic or cooling foods was noted to assist with stomach acidity or heat in the stomach. Here, a balance could be achieved, as the cooling effect of a particular food was used to balance the heat produced within an organ. The Yin and Yang Theory applies in this context, where heat, excess yang, results from of a deficiency of coolness, yin. To bring the body or organ back into balance, yin, coolness, must be supplemented. Therefore a cooling, yin, food would be indicated. In contrast, if the body demonstrates the symptoms of excess cold, as a result of yang deficiency, yang (spicy) foods would be indicated. Foods are assigned to possess yin or yang characteristics, based upon flavor and/or outcomes from consuming these foods, in the setting of various diseases over centuries of experience. These outcomes indicate their yin versus yang character.

The relationships between organs and foods, in particular, food flavors, are also engrained within the Five Element Theory. In this theory, not only are the yin and yang characteristics considered, but also are many, non-obvious organ relationships. These relationships dictate whether foods should be avoided, under various conditions of illness, or food flavors should be added in the presence of other symptoms. In short, the Five Element Theory relates among many other factors, organs to flavors, emotions, and symptoms. This theory is dependent upon identifying whether symptoms indicate deficiency or excess. Identifying these characteristics becomes important when considering the method used to return balance to the system. With deficiency, the Mother-Son relationship between the organs, within the Five Element Theory, is primarily applied. With excess, the Control relationship between the organs, according to the Five Element Theory, is primarily applied. Adjusting flavors is intended to bring balance, using the Mother-Son relationships, if symptoms indicate deficiency, or Control relationships, if symptoms indicate excess. A more complete presentation of the Ying and Yang Theory and Five Element Theory can be found in *Abimoxi Fundamentals, The Way of Martial Arts Healing* (216).

According to the Five Element Theory, emotions are associated with organs. This association indicates that, excess or uncontrolled emotion can affect the organs, and organ dysfunction can also result in excess emotion. For example, anger is associated with the liver. Excessive and long-standing anger can result in liver problems. In contrast, liver problems, such as liver "heat," may result in anger. Similarly, long-standing exhilaration, as may be the case when winning a lottery, is thought to damage the heart; worry, the spleen; fear or panic, the kidneys; and sadness, the lungs. Rapid changes from one emotion to another are also considered unhealthy. According to this theory, the organ affected by emotion can resist normal control by another organ, further exacerbating the emotion. This is due to excess in the recipient organ. In other words, the recipient organ is resistant to normal control due to excess. To re-establish control, eating foods with specific flavors can assist the appropriate controlling organ. In the case of excess in the liver causing anger, balance can be achieved by consuming spicy foods, such that the normal control of the lung over the liver is re-established. Emotion, itself, can also be used to balance uncontrolled emotion according to this theory. For example, anger can be balanced by sadness; excessive happiness, uncontrolled exhilaration and excitement, can be balanced by fear; worry can be balanced by anger; fear can be balanced by pensiveness; sadness can be balanced by happiness.

Organs and Associated Flavors	Organs and Associated Emotions
Liver – Sour	*Liver - Anger*
Heart – Bitter	*Heart - Happiness*
Spleen – Sweet	*Spleen – Pensiveness/Worry*
Lung – Spicy	*Lung - Sadness*
Kidney – Salty	*Kidney – Fear/Panic*

The fast pace and stressful nature of today's workplace, family, and social interaction, can significantly impact emotional health. Stress and negative emotions are known to lead to poor sleep, decreased physical activity, substance abuse, and overeating; all of which negatively impact health and longevity (135). The information provided above may be considered complementary to accepted Western treatment methods for emotional, psychological, or physical ailments. It must be remembered that, stress reduction, prayer, and meditation are also complementary to accepted Western treatment modalities. Professional assistance from a licensed health professional must always be sought for any illness, including emotional problems. Complementary approaches should not be confused with alternative approaches. Proponents of alternative approaches sometimes ignore approved Western medical practices, provided by licensed health professionals.

Avoidance of specific flavored foods is thought to prevent exacerbation or worsening of problems in various organs. Certain flavors gravitate to specific organs, thus, giving strength to that organ. Sour gravitates to the liver; bitter gravitates to the heart; sweet gravitates to the spleen; spicy gravitates to the lungs; and salt gravitates to the kidneys. Avoidance of certain flavors is based on the Control relationship within the Five Element Theory, in an effort to prevent over-control of an organ suffering from deficiency. For example, because the lungs, which are given strength by spicy foods, normally controls the liver, spicy foods should be avoided in cases of liver problems to prevent over-control; salty foods should be avoided in cases of heart problems; sour foods should be avoided in cases of spleen problems; bitter foods should be avoided in cases of lung problems; sweet foods should be avoided in cases of kidney problems.

Various foods could be consumed preferentially, to assist organs with illness related to deficiency. This concept is based on the Mother-Son relationship within the Five Element Theory. For example, sour foods assist the heart; bitter vegetables and fruit assist the spleen; sweet foods assist the lungs; spicy foods assist the kidneys; and salty foods assist the liver.

In the case of deficiency illnesses of various organs, avoidance of certain flavored foods and consumption of other flavored foods can be combined. For example, in the case of a liver deficiency illness, spicy foods should be avoided to prevent over-control of the liver by the lungs, and salty foods should be consumed to assist the liver by the kidneys. In the case of heart deficiency illness, salty foods should be avoided to prevent over-control of the heart by the kidneys, and sour foods should be consumed to assist the heart by the liver. In the case of spleen deficiency illness, sour foods should be avoided to prevent over-control of the spleen by the liver, and bitter foods should be consumed to assist the spleen by the heart. In the case of lung deficiency illness, bitter foods should be avoided to prevent over-control of the lungs by the heart, and sweet foods should be consumed to assist the lungs by the spleen. In the case of kidney deficiency illness, sweet foods should be avoided to prevent over-control of the kidney by the spleen, and spicy foods should be consumed to assist the kidneys by the lungs.

In cases where disease is due to excess, the Control relationship also applies. With excess the tendency is over-control against the recipient organ. This is in contrast to deficiency, where over-control is due to an underlying deficiency of the recipient organ. In the case of excess causing over-control, the recipient organ must be fortified. Sour foods are required to fortify the liver against excessive control by the lungs, which correspond to spicy. Bitter foods are required to fortify the heart against excessive control by the kidneys, which correspond to salty. Sweet foods are required to fortify the spleen against excessive control by the liver, which corresponds to sour. Spicy foods are required to fortify the lungs against excessive control by the heart, which corresponds to bitter. Salty foods are required to fortify the kidneys against excessive control by the spleen, which corresponds to sweet.

A licensed doctor of Chinese medicine is able to diagnosis organ deficiency or excess, based on symptoms and other diagnostic means. The diagnostic process is not obvious and may not correlate with organ dysfunction, as defined by Western medicine. Therefore, self-treatment is not suggested. The above information is offered for educational purposes only. With this in mind, various foods have been categorized according to taste. For example, bitter foods include apricot seeds, asparagus, wild cucumber, celery, cherry seeds, coffee, grapefruit peel, hops, kohlrabi, lettuce, radish leaf, dandelion root, rhubarb, bitter melon, spinach, and chard. Spicy foods include black pepper, castor bean, cinnamon bark, clove, garlic, ginger, mustard leaf, marjoram, nutmeg, peppermint, radish, red pepper, spearmint, anise, white pepper, chili, and cayenne pepper. Salty foods include abalone, barley, chive seeds, clams, crab, duck, ham, kelp, oyster, pork, salt, and seaweed. Sour foods include apricot, crab apple, grapefruit, green grapes, lemons, pickles, olives, pineapple, plums small red or adzuki beans, star fruit, tomato, and vinegar. Sweet foods include abalone, apple, banana, barley, bean curd, beef, beets, brown sugar, cabbage, carrots, cherry, chestnuts, chicken, eggs, coconut, corn, mushrooms, dates, cucumber, oranges, eggplant, figs, duck, grapes, honey, kidney beans, longan, longevity fruit, malt, mango, milk, mung beans, muskmelon, papaya, peaches, persimmon, plums, potatoes, pumpkin, pears, raspberry, red beans, rice, saffron, soybean, squash, strawberry, string beans, sugar cane, sunflower seeds, sweet potatoes, tangerines, oranges, watermelon, water chestnuts, walnuts, and wheat.

Chapter 5

Breathing

Introduction

Deep regulated breathing represents a sophisticated practice, handed down generation-to-generation among martial arts masters for centuries. This type of breathing practice is most commonly referred to as Chi Kung (217). Breathing, in its less sophisticated practice, is a fundamental body function; yet with proper development has considerable impact upon health, fitness, and longevity. It is this impact that makes breathing worth discussing at length, in terms of Chi Kung practice.

At the most basic level a person has life, when breathing is ongoing; when breathing ceases, life ceases. While this observation is quite simplistic, several aspects of breathing, which one may consider to be at a similar basic level, are not as obvious. These breathing-related factors integrate with health, fitness, and longevity. For example, when breathing is normal, and appears effortless, a person is generally considered in good health. When healthy, the breathing mechanism responds to demands of the mind and body. For instance, when sitting and relaxed, breathing is slow and effortless, occurring with minimal lung expansion. On the other hand, when physical or even psychological demands require the body to have an increased amount of oxygen, lung expansion increases along with respiratory rate. In contrast, if the lungs do not compensate for such increased demands, breathing may appear shallow, and the person will appear to be out of breath. With these signs, it is generally accepted that, illness or disease is present. The illness or disease may, or may not, directly involve the lungs. The disease may involve the heart, be due to severe infection in the blood, or possibly a hormone problem, such as diabetes.

A very important observation, regarding those who exercise regularly and effectively, is that breathing is controlled and relaxed, allowing for a prolonged and effective exercise period. Individuals, who are naive to demanding exercise routines, often do not consider the need to control breathing in this manner. Lack of regulated breathing frequently leads to periods of gasping for air, in an effort to make up for this type of deficiency in exercise technique.

Thus, breathing, being considered a reflection of a person's health status, provides insight into an individual's strength and vitality (218). For example, it can be apparent, whether a person is physically capable or weak. Strength and vitality are also apparent. For instance, it can be observed, whether a person is mentally vibrant, or lacks the ability for even minimal motivation. The lungs and pulmonary function represent a window into these characteristics. A person with vitality is able to speak with appropriate volume and strength, projecting words, in such a manner that, others can adequately hear and be somewhat motivated by the conversation. It could be said that, a great amount of chi, energy, is present. With inadequate chi, the voice would appear weak and depressed. This description also reflects the basic aspects of breathing, which are not quite so obvious. The status of internal organs, in this scenario, the kidneys, would likely be weak. Other physical weaknesses and inabilities are associated with disease, such as difficulty in speaking and/or walking, due to a blockage of blood flow to the brain, following a stroke. Similarly, a blockage in the flow of chi may result in weakness and inability. It is understood, within the larger scope of breathing practices, Chi Kung, that jing, the original essence of energy within the body, undergoes a transformation into chi. If a blockage in this process occurs, organ function may be affected. For example, lung chi and kidney chi are connected, under normal circumstances. With illness, this connection is blocked. Similarly, heart chi and kidney chi are connected. Insomnia results, if the connection is blocked. A person can easily sleep when the connection is maintained. Deep breathing exercises are able to free blockages in chi flow, allowing normal function to return. These are only a few examples of the effect of breathing on health. The subject of breathing, therefore, extends well beyond that which is commonly appreciated at a basic level.

Breathing also impacts longevity. A lifetime of proper breathing is an important component of preparing for advanced age. Often, the various contributory components, responsible for an outcome, are viewed independently. In reality, these components are integrated, and as a whole, result in a specific outcomes. This is also the case with breathing. The ability, willingness, and knowledge to properly deal with the various other factors that overstress the body can be accomplished through appropriate nutrition; proper rest; good attitude; and attention to spiritual issues (219). These, in addition to breathing, are an integral part of preparation for longevity. For example, life should be simple and quiet; the diet should include consuming less meat and more vegetables and fruit. Under optimal circumstances, life expectancy should minimally reach one hundred twenty years. However, the lack of attention to these details becomes evident, once people reach approximately fifty years of age. At this age, considerable change occurs in the body. To mention a few obvious changes, strength can be lost in the legs, the graying of the hair begins, and wrinkles occur. Blue veins may become noticeable under the surface of the skin as the skin loses thickness. It is understood, among individuals who practice breathing exercises to increase and circulate chi in the body that, the root cause of age related changes involves a decrease in chi. A decrease in chi can affect blood forming elements, and the circulation of blood to various tissues. Chi is understood to carry or foster blood supply to various tissues and organs. The body begins to degenerate as chi decreases. At this point, the body can no longer compensate for the effects of overstress, without intervention. Correction of this process involves increasing blood elements by stimulating the bone marrow, through breathing exercises and nutrition. An easily recognized sign, indicating the body is in poor health, is the lack of saliva production, when practicing deep breathing exercises.

Proper care of the body can be viewed in a manner similar to that of regularly changing the engine oil of an automobile every three thousand miles. If adhered to, vehicle engines will general show good performance, with little need for mechanical repair. Such engines will outlast those, which have not been attended to in this fashion, by thousands of miles. Ideally, if attention is given to proper care of the mind, body, and soul, prior to fifty years of age, the breakdown of the body, and many of the health problems that emerge, may be significantly delayed, allowing for considerable longevity. Much of this proper care begins with, and continues to involve, deep breathing exercises.

In addition to the practice of deep breathing exercises, after fifty years of age, a person should be rid of bad habits, such as smoking and drinking alcoholic beverages. These habits exacerbate weaknesses in the body. Ideally, these bad habits would have been dealt with well before this time. However, fifty years of age is the point, after which, little can be done to reverse the resultant internal damage. As discussed in the previous chapter, after this age meats in the diet should be avoided, since the body cannot afford to expend the energy, necessary in processing this type of food. Between the ages of thirty-five and fifty years, one should eat less meat; while before thirty-five years of age, eating meat will have little negative impact on the body.

Proper rest is another important aspect of health and longevity. Taking appropriate rests after fifty years of age becomes necessary. A person should be sensitive to the body's need for rest. When the body requires rest, rest should be taken at that point. Rest is of much less benefit, if delayed to a different time that fits another schedule. When the body requires the rest, every reasonable effort should be made to comply. In many cases, illnesses are manifest after fifty years of age, because the reserves of the physical body become diminished, through lack of attention to these matters.

Several ancillary issues are related to proper breathing. Air quality is important to consider when practicing deep breathing exercises. Air, within a tightly sealed home, contains many particles, such as dust, and may be lower in oxygen content compared to exterior air. Exterior air can also be of poor quality, especially if near areas of pollution. In either case, poor air quality can affect health negatively, over time. Deep inhalation, of this type of air, is like allowing the lungs to function as a vacuum cleaner. On the other hand, breathing fresh air deeply is like getting a transfusion of blood, since the air is clean and rich in oxygen.

Background and History

With these observations and concepts, much can be gained, through the practice of deep breathing and understanding its influence on exercise potential, health, and longevity. The benefits of deep breathing have only recently drawn attention and interest in Western culture. Beginning several thousand years ago in Asia, particularly among Doaist practitioners of China, and continuing, generation after generation, even to the present day, the empirical, trial and error, study of breathing and practice of Chi Kung has evolved into a sophisticated art (217). This art has been referred to by several names including Tu Na (breathing), Dao Yin (directing the chi), Shing Chi (moving the chi), Fu Chi (feeding the chi), Shao Shi (adjusting the breathing), Jing Kung (quiet work out), Tsan Sho (Buddhist exercise), Zr Guan (stop thinking), Lien Dan (produce the ball), Shuen Kung (misery work out), Shing Kung (sexual work out), Sho Lien (creative exercise), Juao Tsan (sitting meditation), Ne Yang Kung (internal nurturing exercise), and Yang Shan Kung (nurturing or long life exercise). Chi kung practice, inclusive of deep breathing methods, is also considered the oldest and original method of self-healing in China. It's origins in Chinese history share a heritage akin to acupuncture, Tui Na (massage of pressure points), and herbal medicine. As the several synonyms listed above indicate, Chi Kung has many applications, in addition to the healing arts. The applications are interrelated and include, but are not limited to, health and longevity, self-healing, medical healing, martial arts, and spiritual pursuits.

From a historical perspective, the application of deep breathing, both inhalation and exhalation, as a mechanism to reduce pain, promoted the general development of Chi Kung breathing exercises. Later, in the development of Chi Kung practice, the use of the small circle breathing exercise was applied to help reduce the type of arthritis pain experienced just prior to changes in weather. The small circle exercise involves the coordination of breathing with the mind, directing energy, chi, within the body. This exercise is similar, in concept, to the direction of cardiopulmonary blood circulation; where blood, from the heart, passes through the vascular bed of the lungs to pick up oxygen, required for body metabolism, i.e. energy, then travels back to heat, via the pulmonary artery. This circulation is in contrast to the larger systemic circulation, where the flow of blood from the heart travels to all other areas of the body, then back again to the heart. It was thought that, as circulation slowed, pain would ensue or become worse. The resultant pain could be alleviated by the small circle exercise, through adjusting the blood circulation and energy flow. Many parallels to this concept can be identified in modern medicine, developed in Western societies. For example, attempts to increase blood flow, through injured areas of the body, by using heating pads and warm soaks, have been shown to hasten the healing process, and reduce pain. Several other causes of pain are due to reduced blood flow. These include the crisis pain of sickle-cell disease, the pain of Reynaud's disease, and similar pain seen in advanced stages of diabetes mellitus.   All result from decreased blood flow to various areas of the body, such as the hands and feet. Attempts at improving blood flow have produced reduction in pain. For example, through the use of various medications in treating Reynaud's disease, red blood cells are enabled to penetrate through narrowed vessels, thus improving oxygen delivery.

Theories within Chinese Medicine

Other factors in the external, natural environment were noted to influence the internal environment of the human body, and therefore health. These included the observation that, breathing the cleaner and fresher air, found at higher elevations was associated with better health. Additionally, temperature differences, depending upon seasons of the year, especially dramatic shifts in temperature, as well as differences in humidity and dampness, appeared to affect health. These simple observations supported the belief that, the human body represents a microcosm of the external natural environment or universe. The vast array of combined knowledge in this area, ultimately, evolved into the Five-Element Theory. This theory suggests, for example, that, movement of air, wind, in the external natural environment, has a correlate within the internal environment of the human body, chi flow. Just as air cannot be seen, neither can chi. However, the effects of air, when in motion, wind, can be observed, through the effects of its energy. Wind passing through trees causes branches to move. Wind passing over a calm lake produces ripples and waves in the water. As with the wind in the natural environment, the movement of chi, within the internal environment, produces observable effects, through its energy. Just as the wind can be harnessed in the sail of a boat, causing the vessel to move rapidly over the water, the movement of chi can increase many abilities of the human body, through harnessing its energy. It was observed that, chi, when flowing appropriately within the human body, can increase strength, improve health, and heal disease. These effects were of sufficient reproducibility that, the methods involved in exercising and directing chi have been passed on, generation to generation, for thousands of years. These methods represent a branch of Chinese medicine, and a very necessary, and important component of the martial arts.

Internal Viewing

Concentrating on breathing in and out deeply is considered the method of practicing chi. When a person is quiet and relaxed, from this type of breathing, the practitioner can sense chi travelling within the body. As such, in the early days of development, Chi Kung exercises with this intent, were referred to as internal viewing methods. Internal viewing ability allowed for sensing the function of the internal organs, within the living body. The sensing of living internal organs allowed for the mapping of channels, pathways of energy flow, throughout the body, which link the organ systems. Special points, small terminals that store chi along the channels, were identified. Their manipulation through massage, Tui Na, or stimulation with needles, Acupuncture, provided an external means of promoting chi flow. These external modes of intervention produced a similar response, in terms of health and treatment of disease, as the internal Chi Kung self-healing methods. As with Chi Kung, these methods were discovered through experience, and improved upon, generation by generation.

The process of internal viewing allows for the examination of the living host. This is in contrast to study of anatomy, using cadavers. In this sense, viewing of cadavers is an external viewing method. The advantages to the use of cadavers include, objective examination reproduced by multiple individuals, thus, substantiating the understanding of human anatomy. The benefits to internal viewing are not as obvious. Only when a person is alive does motion exist, such as chi flow. To study this flow, including the various pathways, the living host must be studied. Through the process of internal viewing, the twelve original channels, meridians, eight special channels, and the numerous acupuncture points, were elucidated. It was identified that, the twelve original channels connect the entire body, with each channel being connected to one another. It was also discovered that, each channel is associated with a particular organ, as well as a period of maximum chi flow. In addition, eight special channels were identified that normalize chi within the twelve original channels. This is accomplished through the release or absorption of chi from the special channels, if insufficient chi or chi overabundance exists within the original channels. Confirmation of the discoveries, resulting from internal viewing methods, lies with reproducible observations among a vast number of individuals, within and between generations. In addition, external means of manipulation of acupuncture points resulted in reproducible outcomes, which also substantiated the findings of the internal viewing methods.

With respect to self-healing, the process of internal viewing can be used to identify areas of illness. Once identified, chi can be directed, by the mind, to the area where illness is present, providing the mechanism for healing. Specifically, through the practice of Chi Kung, the mind is trained and breathing is adjusted, to direct chi and open blockages along chi pathways, the channels. A balance between yin and yang, for health maintenance purposes, the adjustment of blood, and an increase in original, pure, chi from jing, the raw source of energy within the body, can also be accomplished through this process.

Immortal Chi Kung and Health

As mentioned above, directing chi for healing was also found to have application to health maintenance, which, in turn, affects longevity. For these purposes, the small circle and big circle pathways were practiced, specifically. These pathways and practices are discussed in more detail in the book entitled, *The Principles and Practice of Sitting Chi Kung*. Later, it was discovered, that, the soul could be nurtured. Through this method, the process of reincarnation was identified. The development of specific practice methods for religious purposes was referred to as Immortal Chi Kung. In this context, it is understood by those who practice Chi Kung, that, people are born with an original life essence, which is converted into chi. This pre-birth essence is referred to as jing. The presence of considerable essence is akin to having a bank account with a large amount of money deposited, such that, one can live off the interest, not requiring withdrawals on the principal. A person with sufficient jing is like a tree that has enough water to grow and flourish. The leaves will always remain green with healthy roots, trunk, bark, and branches. The result of the tree possessing this natural supply of water is a beautiful outward appearance. Shen is the term, referring to the outward extension of jing, which has been converted into chi in sufficient amounts. Approximately midway between the umbilicus and the pelvic bone, within the abdomen is housed an area, referred to as the dan tien or "ocean of chi". Behind the dan tien lie the kidneys, which retain jing. With respect to health, those who have healthy and strong kidneys maintain jing, in sufficient amounts to produce enough chi to ward off illnesses, due to external causes.

Through Chi Kung exercises, a great amount of chi is generated, which can be transformed back into jing. This is similar to having received the type of education and training necessary to attain a well paying job, such that a considerable portion of earnings can be placed in the savings account, rather than spent on necessities. The more one practices, the more is saved, and transformed back into jing. In this sense, practicing chi means to increase one's own abilities. In other words, Chi Kung practitioners train the dan tien, such that chi can be produced in large quantities, which then can be transformed back into jing. Thus, several possible transformations are possible: jing to chi; chi to jing; chi to shen. Chi Kung, therefore, is used as the Jing-Chi-Shen conversion process. This type of Immortal Jing-Chi-Shen practice is considered the treasure of the human body. The mind is used to direct chi for storage, where it can easily be accessed if needed.

The mind is able to direct chi, just like it directs the body to move, via the nervous system. The mind is a powerful tool, in that, whatever a person understands and is able to use, positive results emerge. For example, the chi, which is transformed from jing, original life essence, original chi, is spirit. When the mind is used to produce chi, the outcome is similar to connecting electricity to a new home, thus having ready access to a power source for every imaginable appliance. If a person has enough chi, it can be transfered back into jing, thus, increasing jing in the body. Shen, the extension of chi outward, requires some of the energy; but adequate amounts will remain, which are available to be transferred back to jing. The best time to nurture chi in this manner is during periods when the body is quiet, such as during meditation, so that the least amount of energy is expended in the process. If a person can conserve on energy expenditure, then more chi can be transferred back to jing, and thus, be available, for instance, to increase life expectancy. Wu ji (quiet mind) and characters, a discussion of which is beyond the scope of this book, allow chi to be transformed back into jing. This is part of the Immortal Chi Kung practice. When the mind is empty, quiet, the brain becomes very relaxed. This relaxed state is understood to be very good for rebuilding energy. From the outside, the body looks quiet, but chi is moving inside. Similarly, when the brain is quiet, chi is moving efficiently. A quiet mind is needed for chi to move easier through the brain. To generate energy, a person must start with breathing, which helps to quiet the mind, along with inducing other beneficial effects.

When a person has sufficient jing, the soul can be nursed or nourished. When this occurs, a person is then able to go back into the immortal realm and develop "sixth-sense" abilities. With Wu Ji, also called Ru Ding (empty mind), the soul is able to go out from body. The progression of development to this point is first, through practice for health, then longevity, then nurturing of the soul. As the soul is nurtured, the future can be appreciated. The soul is then equipped to go out of the body, the immortal stage. In this stage a person is not sleeping, but very relaxed, using only minimal energy. This is similar to hibernation. At that time, a person can feel their consciousness travel around, within the body; and it is possible to adjust and correct problems within the body. Teachers of this practice recommend, if the soul goes out from the body, the distance should be limited. This practice should only be accomplished two to three times per year. Practice should be done over three to six days duration. Each time this is practiced, the person should not eat food; only drink fluids.

With respect to longevity, those who have sufficient jing stay young longer. Youth is the outward extension of jing, shen, which has been converted into chi in sufficient amounts. When people look older than their age, it is because there is not sufficient jing. Of note is the effect of sexual life on jing. For men, sexual activity depletes jing; whereas, for women, sexual activity is associated with an increase in jing. For the Chi Kung practitioner, attention is given to the sex life, with regard to conserving jing and protecting the kidneys, to maintain good health and longevity.

Deep Breathing Methods

With time, over several generations, nine different kinds of breathing methods were identified. These include: breathing in and out through the mouth, breathing in and out through the nose, breathing in through the nose and out through the mouth, breathing in through the mouth and out through the nose, breathing in only and breathing out only (lung capacity must be considered for each), breathing in and out with holding of the breath, not breathing in or out, and umbilical breathing in and out. Chi Kung practitioners indicate that, when using umbilical breathing, the person does not feel like he or she is breathing. The breath is light, relaxed, and not forceful. When breathing very light, even a feather, placed in front of the nose or mouth, will not move.

Concepts

External and Internal Breathing

From the information provided above, it can be appreciated that two general categories of breathing exist: external breathing, using the lungs; and internal breathing, using chi. With internal breathing, chi predominates, and is responsible for the "breathing" process. It is, therefore, often stated among Chi Kung practitioners that, chi is like the blood of the soul. The mouth and nose are external structures, through which air passes in and out of the lungs. External breathing impacts internal breathing, since the internal organs are massaged. Chi Kung, therefore, uses external breathing to promote internal breathing. Internal breathing increases the ability to adjust the chi and the blood within the human body, as the mind directs chi. This is a very important aspect of Chi Kung practice. The mind must be empty, quiet, and relaxed for this to occur, since only the mind, in this state, can be used to direct the chi in the body. When the mind directs chi, through the various channels, internal breathing is occurring. This is the reason chi is thought of as the blood of the soul. It is like oxygen plus nutrients in the blood of the physical body. The quiet and relaxed mind is capable of directing chi, just as the brain directs blood flow. For example, when a person lies or becomes embarrassed, the face turns red. This occurs as a result of the nervous system causing dilation of blood vessels in that particular area. Just as the nervous system is capable of shunting blood to the surface of the skin of the face to produce "flushing," the mind can direct chi to specific areas.

The Mind

When practicing Chi Kung, the mind is the main factor. It represents the driver, the general, and the director of the process. The mind must, therefore, be cared for properly. Chi can clear the mind, as it is directed through the inside the top of the skull, the Bai Hui point. Passing of chi through the Bai Hui improves health, in general, because the brain controls the entire body, including all of the organs via the nervous system and release of hormones. The small circle exercise circulates chi through the Zen and Du channels, the Conception and Governing channels. This circle extends from the tailbone up to the top of the head, then down, past the dan tien, back to the tailbone. The small circle is important, since it affects the Bai Hui point, clearing the mind of any blockages. This is analogous to movement of legs and hands, which requires direction from the mind. A breakdown of the process is obvious, for instance, when considering individuals who have suffered a stroke. In many cases, the stroke is due to a blood clot, serving as a blockage of blood flow within the brain. As a result, direction for movement or speech from the brain is hindered. If treatment is instituted to break down the blood clot, soon after the blockage is identified, further clotting can be prevented, and the blockage can possibly be opened.

Oxygen is needed for the body, especially the brain. With chronic, mild oxygen insufficiency, signs of illness will occur, such as a poor memory, slow reaction time, dizziness, and drowsiness. When the body senses a deficiency in oxygen, particularly sudden oxygen insufficiency, yawning occurs. Yawning occurs frequently as people age. Yawning promotes deep breathing, which, in turn, increases gas exchange in the lungs, leading to increased oxygen in the blood. The person then feels refreshed. Deep breathing, as an intervention for this problem, helps by using the entire capacity of the lungs.

More available oxygen, therefore, enhances the functioning of the brain and the mind. Enhancement of mental abilities, including creativity, is another example supporting the idea that, deep breathing is good for the body.

A person can live days without water and food, but only a few minutes without oxygen. Correspondingly, the benefits of sufficient oxygen to the brain and other organs are vastly more important to the body, than the well recognized benefits of a proper diet. But, this is not to discount the importance of diet. These are inter-related. The human being is like a machine. Proper nutrition and the digestive process provide the fuel. Oxygen is necessary to turn the fuel into energy. In a sense, oxygen mixes with nutritional components in the metabolic process. Both are required to produce energy. Age can affect this process. Enzymes, needed for digestion, are reduced with increased age. Deep breathing exercises can reverse this problem. Through deep breathing and internal breathing, the organs are massaged and stimulated, which, in turn, helps release of hormones. Some of these hormones stimulate digestive enzymes. In addition, when people use deep breathing exercises daily, the internal organs will be supplied with sufficient oxygen to promote proper functioning of the digestive system, and help ward of illness by stimulating the immune system. The best time to exercise in this manner is 11 p.m. to 1 a.m., since maximal oxygen is available, allowing for healing and health maintenance.

External breathing, only using the lungs, has certain limitations. Deep breathing, on the other hand, leads to internal breathing, and generation of chi, which, in turn, can provide for health maintenance and self-healing, when necessary. It must be remembered that, the mind is the director of this process. The mind directs chi, and in this scenario, by concentrating on areas of blockage. The blockage is then opened, as chi is directed through those areas. Proper functioning of the mind is dependent upon it having received appropriate oxygen over time. Deep breathing is essential in this regard.

Influence of Emotions

Several emotions and thought patterns affect the mind, such as stress, anxiety, nervousness, and panic. Through the hormonal response to these emotions, an increase blood pressure can occur, which, in turn, can lead to other diseases chronic diseases (220-223). For example, the digestive system can be affected. When affected, a person may no longer feel hungry, lose weight, and develop ulcers. Several chronic diseases have been linked to the effects of long-term stress, including cardiovascular, gastrointestinal, and more serious psychological disorders, such as depression. This is exemplified by an old Chinese saying, which advises people not to get mad or panic, because the liver will be injured. The liver is a gastrointestinal system organ.

Stress combined with emotions, such as anger, can also exacerbate the consequence of atherosclerotic vascular disease (224), due to years of diets high in fat content. When stressed, blood pressure is increased. Anger promotes a higher cardiac output. It is understood by those who practice Chinese medicine that, the combination of plaque in arteries, increased blood flow, and high blood pressure together can lead to strokes. The root of the problem is stress and anxiety. This is analogous to clogged pipes in an old house that experience sudden changes in water pressure. With sudden bursts in pressure, some of the clogged material can be dislodged, cutting off water flow downstream. Individuals under thirty-five years of age can often tolerate stress and anxiety. However, after many years of high blood pressure and other uncontrolled emotional issues, the body can no longer compensate. More serious consequences with disastrous outcomes, such as heart attacks and strokes, may be the end result.

People in their thirty's and forty's can frequently be under considerable pressure, due to circumstances surrounding marital stress or difficulties at work. These circumstances can lead to depression, which may result in sexual disorders, and fatigue. This type of fatigue, the feeling of being tired all the time, indicates that the body's energy is very low. The root of these problems lies within the mind. The lack of certain hormones, as seen after menopause, can also lead to increased difficulty in tolerating stress. The use of deep breathing, through the dan tien, while meditating and practicing the small circle exercise, can induce calmness. A calming of the mind reduces stress, anxiety, and increases energy to the brain (220,223).

Underlying all of these psychological issues is the lack of chi. The practice of Chi Kung addresses the root of the problem, however, the response is not immediate. Patience is required for sufficient time to attain the desired results. Western medicine addresses the symptoms with relatively rapid results. However, the root of the problem, insufficient chi, is not necessarily addressed. In some cases, energy expenditure continues, while masking the symptoms with medication. Ultimately, this may, in turn, lead to a worsening of the underlying cause, lack of sufficient chi.

The Spirit and Health

Several psychological disorders, lung, and digestive system diseases can be addressed through the practice of Immortal Chi Kung, since the mind is the center for practice and the brain must be energized. Disorders and illnesses including a lack of appetite, coughing, diarrhea, constipation, incontinence of urine, cramps, ulcers, and insomnia can be addressed. However, a qualified practitioner must be involved in this type of therapy. A quiet mind is naturally therapeutic for anxiety (225). Problems including outbursts of temper, nightmares, panic, hyperactivity, fatigue, fearfulness, and insomnia may also be addressed. Chi Kung practitioners refer to this process as cooling, or calming, down the nervous system. As stated above, deep breathing initiates the process by assisting in quieting the mind.

There are many different methods intended to improve health and foster longevity, but only a limited number of effective methods are available. Many people practice, making their best effort in one of several methods, only to find disappointment. Health and longevity may not be impacted in a positive manner, mainly because of mistakes in practice. Correct practice must be complete in a holistic sense. That is, Chi Kung methods, intended to adjust the body for health and longevity, must recognize the Jing-Chi-Shen transformations. Jing is the original internal essence, raw material. Chi is the internal energy, product of the raw material being acted upon. Shen is the energy transferred outside of the body, the finished product, delivered externally. Jing, Chi, and Shen work together, as one. Chi is produced from the jing. Increased jing will lead to increased chi. As chi increases, some will surface to the outside of the body, Shen. If jing is decreased then chi is decreased. Therefore, jing is understood to directly influence chi. When Chi Kung is practiced, an adjustment occurs, allowing chi to be transformed back into the raw material, jing. This becomes beneficial, since the increase in raw material avoids the need to use the original jing. The three factors together, Jing, Chi, Shen, lead to health and longevity. In contrast, when jing becomes depleted, then life cannot continue. In other words, the raw material to produce life energy is no longer available, and death ensues. To affect longevity, jing must be made, and original jing must be conserved. This concept is similar to investing one's inheritance, then living off the proceeds, such that, the principle inheritance is maintained. The inheritance survives longer.

Sixth sense abilities develop when Jing, Chi, and Shen are combined, such as the ability to visualize the soul, and other supernatural characteristics, available pre-birth. With this type of practice, training the soul, attention is given to the spiritual, and the Chi Kung method is referred to as the Immortal Way.

General Aspects of Deep Breathing

Deep breathing is an essential component of the fundamental aspects of practice, and affects health in a beneficial manner. Usually after middle age, the body's organs will begin to degenerate. Symptoms of old age arise. For example, shortness of breath, even with minimal exercise, and deterioration in memory can be observed, primarily after, but even before fifty years of age. When this occurs, the organs responsible for restoring and delivering oxygen, the lungs, blood elements, and heart, and the nervous system, start to degenerate. Deep breathing delays the degenerative process.

Breathing reflects a person's health status. Observing breathing can define whether a person is healthy or ill, strong or weak, powerful or low in energy. The lungs and heart can be either strong or weak. In general, with good health, they are strong; with ill health, they are weak. Chronic illnesses, common to the elderly, are problematic for those individuals who get little to no exercise. For example, people, who are confined to long hours of sedentary work and assume a similar sedentary lifestyle during leisure time, become weak. Because of this type of weakness, breathing exercises are particularly important for health and human life. The reverse breathing exercise in Chi Kung practice can increase nutrients to the organs, thus improve their health. Breathing with the diaphragm, deep breathing, increases blood return back to heart, and results in increased oxygenated blood circulating to the body. Breathing practice increases chi, which is the leader of blood, and flows as the blood flows. If chi stops, blood flow stops. As chi circulates faster, oxygenated blood circulates more efficiently to the organs, delivering oxygen and nutrients. With respect to the gastrointestinal tract, better absorption of nutrients results, improving overall health. Increased blood flow can also improve the clearance of toxins, such as cholesterol, from veins and arteries, thus reducing the burden on the heart. In general, the health rewards of Chi Kung practice include beneficial effects on the heart, lungs, vasculature, blood cells, and endocrine (hormone) system.

Recognition that certain foods, such as meats, require the body to expend more energy for digestion than foods such as fruits and vegetables, allows the topic of diet to be a consideration in the art of Chi Kung. Nurturing chi is, essentially, the building up of chi within the body. Expending more energy to digest foods, such as meats, relative to fruits and vegetables, leaves less energy to be devoted to nurturing chi. In an effort to maximize nurturing of chi, energy expenditure must be minimized. Diet is one mechanism, through which, energy expenditure can be minimized effectively.

The above concepts rely on the body remaining in a stationary, or quiet, position when practicing. Through practicing chi, the internal organs are primarily exercised, but body tissues, such as muscles and tendons, receive little exercise. Adding external exercise to practicing chi provides an extended dimension to Chi Kung. Tai Chi Chuan is considered both an internal and external exercise, since it combines Chi Kung with external movement. For maximum results, stationary Chi Kung should be practiced prior to practicing Tai Chi Chuan, so that sufficient chi is generated and available.

Conceptually, the external and internal environments are connected. With the human being positioned between heaven and earth, evil chi (factors in the external environment) can influence the body. Evil Chi (Sick Chi) is considered wind, cold, heat, wet (dampness), fire, or dry heat. Too much, or too little, of these can cause illness. If the extent of these lies in the middle, or neutral position, then the chi is referred to as natural chi. Many people, who observe and study longevity, watch natural weather changes closely to avoid sick chi. Daoists watched these patterns also, and taught students methods to deal with sick chi. They also discovered that, "bad material" in the body must be cleared, such as bacteria, fat, etc. The methods taught to accomplish this goal, included exercise. They stressed the use of exercise, for both the internal and the external body. Exercise must be done, in such a manner, as to increase energy, not to decrease energy. The best exercise to accomplish this purpose is considered Tai Chi Chuan. This type of exercise increases internal chi to defend against the evil chi.

Methods

When beginning to practice Chi Kung, several suggestions are helpful. One should practice in a place where there will be no disturbances. It is recommended for beginners, to keep external influences and disturbances to a minimum. Therefore, a quiet and peaceful place should be chosen without noise or potential for distraction. There should be an adequate supply of fresh air in the practice area. The location should be well ventilated. The room temperature should be comfortable, not too hot or too cold. If the area is too warm, excess body sweat will cause internal chi to dissipate. If the area is too cold, the body may become susceptible to this low temperature, which is unhealthy. When practicing in the sitting position, a blanket may be placed over the knees to protect against cool or cold temperatures. One should not practice during inclement weather, since storms will disturb concentration. Similarly, practice in the wind or rain should be avoided.

Before starting the practice, be certain to relieve the bladder and bowels. Clothing should be loose fitting. If necessary, the belt and pants can be loosened. The sitting position can be assumed on the floor or in a chair. If sitting on the ground, pillows can be placed to soften the sitting area. Breathing should be natural, very smooth, slow and gentle. The abdomen and diaphragm should be used for breathing in order to create a strong foundation for future practice. Before beginning actual practice, a few slow, comfortable breaths can be taken, allowing the mind to relax.

Chi Kung practice trains the mind to direct the flow of chi. When practicing, the mind should not attend to extraneous thoughts, for example, about the past or future events, or problems in life. Beginners must first learn to quiet the mind and concentrate in order to focus attention on the exercises at hand. It must be remembered, the mind will never become devoid of all thought, nor is it expected to do so. The body can live for many weeks without food, for a few days without water, and only a few seconds without air. The mind will not properly function without thought. Therefore, the goal of practice is not to silence the mind of all thought. The mind must always have thought of some type. Practice involves not giving attention to these thoughts.

There is a difference, between allowing a thought to pass through the mind and following that thought, by giving it attention. While practicing a Chi Kung exercise, as thoughts arise about work, or relationships, or various things happening in life, allow them to pass through the mind. Do not follow or add to them. The ultimate goal in practice is to maintain focus, awareness, and concentration on the exercise. Thoughts will arise and dissipate like waves on the ocean, unattached, if attention is not given to them. As thoughts arise they will naturally dissipate, if not dwelled upon or followed. Another thought may arise in its place. If left alone, it too, will disappear. Do not become anxious or concerned if thoughts arise and dissipate. Simply, do not follow or give attention to them. In other words, do not progress to the next thought in the logical sequence of the thought process. The initial thought will, then, dissipate. Because thought is always active in the mind, one thought will always arise after another. However, it is the lack of attention, in relation to these thoughts, which allows for a successful development of practice. During the practice, attempt to maintain the focus of attention solely upon the exercise. Let thoughts come and go freely, not attaching any attention to them.

It may be difficult to ignore thoughts that arise in the mind. If this occurs, light a candle, and focus attention upon the flame. Alternatively, as thoughts arise, rather than think further about them, open the eyes and re-establish focus on the moment, the practice. It may be helpful to take a deep breath, then return the focus to the practice. Another method for maintaining concentration on the moment is to be keenly aware of the surroundings. To accomplish this, sense the weight of the body, feel the air on the skin, and sense the sounds in the environment. If the senses become dull to these stimuli, it is usually because a thought has been followed. Again, do not become anxious. Simply, return attention and focus to the practice at hand. It is most important to be gentle and relaxed about the process of taming the mind's attention. At first, the mind behaves like a child, picking up one toy, then another. Bringing the mind's attention under control to maturity, is a delicate process. Curiously, any form of "effort" or "will power" will only serve to increase the potency of distractions. If thoughts grab the mind's attention, simply let go of the thought. Do not make any judgments about the fact that, a thought came up, or recriminate over having followed it for a while. Judgement and recrimination are simply following thoughts of another type. Allow these thoughts to go away, and gently return focus and attention to the practice. Over time, with patience, returning focus, again and again, to the practice will cause the mind to naturally grow attentive. It will become progressively easier to maintain concentration and awareness during the exercises.

Table 1. Important points before starting practice

1. Be certain that the mind and emotions are calm and controlled.
2. Choose an area that has good ventilation but is not drafty. The area should be quiet and conducive to tranquility, free from obnoxious odors or loud noises, and pleasant.
3. Relieve the bladder and bowels, if necessary, prior to practice.
4. Wear loose-fitting, soft and comfortable clothing.
5. The body should be clean and relaxed. If tense, perform self-massage to relieve muscle tension.

6. Be certain that the area to be seated is of a suitable height, hardness, and comfortable for the body.
7. In cases of inclement weather, such as thunder storms, rain, high wind, etc., temporarily suspend practice and choose a better time or place for practice.

Table 2. Important points for practice

1. Choose a direction for practice and assume a sitting posture.
2. Take several slow, deep breaths to relax the body; quiet the mind and allow stray thoughts to subside. Focus the attention on the dan tien.
3. Once the body is relaxed and a few deep breaths have been taken, return to natural breathing. The breath should be natural, light, free, easy, and unhindered. There are many kinds of breathing techniques, which can be used. Beginners should simply breath naturally.
4. During deep meditation, hallucinations may be experienced. Do not be alarmed by them. Do not become attentive to them either. Notice that they have occurred and allow them to pass naturally.
5. If the posture becomes uncomfortable, move the body to again regain comfort. It is important to remember that, in Chi Kung practice, muscles should be relaxed. If one is not relaxed, chi flow can become blocked, leading to the side effects. Therefore, relax, and move the body if needed.
6. Sometimes salivary production will increase during meditation. If this occurs, rinse the saliva around the mouth, then swallow.
7. If the body tires during practice, spend a few minutes concentrating on the dan tien, rest, breathing relaxed and freely.

8. Do not stop practice suddenly. Direct the chi to return to the dan tien before stopping practice. Then determine if there is a real need to stop practice. If not, continue with the practice. If there is a problem that must be attended to, stop the practice.

Table 3. Important points when ending practice

1. Focus the mind on the dan tien to re-gather chi in that area. If a lot of saliva has accumulated in the mouth, circulate it around the mouth several times, then swallow. Take several deep breaths, as at the beginning, and then slowly open the eyes.
2. Massage and limber up. If the practice entailed active movement (as in Tai Chi), walk about naturally, take several deep breaths, stretch the back and arms, and then remain quiet for a while before doing anything else.

Foundational Exercise

A mental visualization of blue water, flowing into the top of the head through the body and down into the earth, is a first step of Chi Kung practice. This creates a complete relaxation of the body. Three paths of relaxation exist along the body. The first path begins at the top of the head. Visualize blue water flowing down both sides of the neck and into the shoulders. From the shoulders, the mind directs the image of water and relaxation into the upper arms, to the elbows, forearms, wrists, and hands, and then out the ends of each finger. Repeat the deep breath and imagine relaxation spreading like clear blue water from the top of the head down through the neck, into the shoulders and arms, and out the fingers. Continue to breathe in and out, feeling the relaxation deepening, visualizing the blue water flowing over and through the body.

During the next cycle of gentle, slow breaths, imagine blue water passing along the second path, which begins at the face and goes down the front of the body, first to the neck, then to the chest and abdomen, spreading throughout the pelvis and into the two thighs, down past the knees, shins, ankles, into the feet, then out through the tips of the toes. Visualize the blue water traveling along this route, beginning at the top of the head going down the front of the body and out the ends of the toes. Imagine the water is drawing all tension and stress with it. Breathe for a few moments and feel the relaxation deepening in the front of the body.

The third path begins at the back of the head and travels down the spine into the buttocks, then into the back of the thighs, knees, calves, ankles, then into the feet, and out through the soles of the feet, into the ground. Take slow, full, comfortable breaths, and send the water down the body into the ground. Feel the relaxation deepening along the backside of the body.

Rather than utilizing the three paths, simply imagine the entire body being filled and cleansed, by the image of blue water cascading down through it, then into the ground. Focus on this image of blue water cleansing and purifying the body of all tension and stress.

With these exercises, beginners should practice for fifteen minutes, then work up to a half-hour practice each day. Keep in mind that, throughout this practice, one should be relaxed and breathe easily, with no effort or strain to the body or muscles.

Some people are more visually inclined than others. The image of blue water may be easily visualized. Others may be more inclined with respect to sound. In this case, sense the sound of water, rather than visualize the water. Some are more touch oriented, therefore utilize the feeling of water flowing in the body during this practice. A combined approach may be taken, seeing, hearing, and feeling the water in varying degrees.

During this first level of relaxation exercises, one may find places in the body, where the water does not easily flow. This may indicate a blockage of chi flow. Spend some time visualizing the water slowly penetrating into these areas of the body. It may take more than one practice session until the water flows freely through these areas. Keep working on the image until water flows easily throughout the entire body. Imagine the water penetrating deeply into the muscles, tendons, and bones, carrying away any dark or clogged energy, visualizing its flow out of the body into the earth. It is important to maintain the image of the water not only flowing throughout the body, but also into the earth, as this completes the cleansing circuit.

If stiffness in the joints or muscles occur, one can use the image of water to flow through those areas, until the joints loosen and the muscles relax. Martial artists may acquire greater flexibility with this exercise.

The mind is a powerful tool in healing and developing the body. Breaking and dissolving blocks to the flow of chi will greatly benefit health, in general. These exercises can also be of therapeutic value in the self-healing of diseases. The three paths of relaxation, using the image of blue water flowing through the body and down into the earth, is the first level of Chi Kung practice.

Breathing Exercise

Once the body is completely relaxed and open to the flow of chi, it is time to begin accumulating chi in the dan tien (sea of chi). The dan tien is located in the lower abdomen, approximately three finger widths below the navel. The second level of Chi Kung practice serves to develop and store chi. This practice utilizes a faint focus of the mind on the area of the dan tien. Using the sitting posture, keeping the back straight, the head upright, neck straight, mouth and lips lightly closed, with the tongue touching the hard palate (inside of the upper mandible at the base of the front teeth). The shoulders should be relaxed. Place the hands on the thighs or cross them over the dan tien. When crossed, the right is placed over the left for men; for women, the left hand is placed on top of the right. If a standing posture is chosen, the double-weighted stance is suitable. Stand with legs shoulder-width apart. Slightly bend the knees and lower the body, while bringing the pelvis forward to achieve a balanced stance. Relax the entire upper body. At chest level, form a circle with the arms, as if hugging a tree with the palms facing inward. The fingers should lightly touch, with the arms, wrists, and hands completely relaxed. Specific points regarding posture, direction, breathing, and precautions are outlined below.

Posture (Sitting, Crossing-Leg)

With the left leg bending at the knee, the foreleg is placed on the top of the right leg (inner thigh). With the right leg bending at the knee the foreleg is placed on top of the left leg (inner thigh). The souls of the feet face upward. Both arms are relaxed with hands on top of the respective knees. The principle applied for this position is that of water and fire melting and functioning together. Fire is associated with the heart; water is associated with the kidneys. The heart and kidneys work together to produce longevity. Jing from the kidneys is pumped through the heart via the blood throughout the body and organs. Thus, these two organs work together to produce a long and healthy life.

The whole body should be relaxed, yet upright. The eyes should be slightly closed, looking toward and concentrating on the dan tien. The mouth should be naturally closed, with the teeth lightly touching. The tongue gently touches the upper mandible at the base of front teeth, as mentioned above. The practitioner should face in a southerly direction for best results.

Breathing

For natural breathing, the dan tien extends outward with inhalation. The dan tien contracts with exhalation. Everything follows with the natural, maintaining quiet within. To maintain quiet, do not listen to anything, not even your own breathing. Breathing must be slow, soft, balanced, smooth, and quiet, to the point that one cannot sense the breathing. The sense of the body can dissipate with this type of breathing. At that time, Jing, Chi and Shen melt together. If a person is truly having difficulty emptying or quieting the mind, concentrate on one thing, such as the dan tien. If stomach pain or dizziness occurs, then too much air has been exchanged because of excessive breathing, either too deep or rapid. To correct this problem, it is advised to stand then walk around for a period of time. Walking allows this bad reaction to dissipate. Once this reaction has subsided, restart the breathing process.

Breathing is used to nurture, prepare, recruit, and increase chi. At a basic level, when chi is present, a person is alive; when chi is gone, then life cannot be supported. The lungs are considered the house of the chi. Chi is the main source or king of power and strength. People with good lungs become strong and have power. Those with poor lungs become weak in terms of health. An increase in chi will increase life. Two methods of breathing are relied upon in Chi Kung to increase chi. These include natural breathing and reverse breathing. Both methods are discussed below.

Natural breathing is the normal manner in which people breathe from the point of birth and beyond. Several important points must be adhered to, and include: 1) breathe in and out from the nose, keeping the mouth closed; 2) the upper and lower teeth come together in a gentle bite; 3) the tip of the tongue touches the inside of the mandible at the base of the upper front teeth; 4) breathe in as the dan tien extends outward, breath out as the dan tien contracts inward or shrinks (the full lung capacity is made available by dropping the diaphragm down with inhalation); 5) practice 30 minutes per day (benefits should be observed in 3 months, as lung capacity should be increased and one should feel more energy and tire less easily); 6) both inhalation and exhalation must be slow, light, natural, deep, smooth, and not forceful.

To begin practice, spend a few minutes relaxing the body with the foundational level one practice. After the body has relaxed, begin the second level of practice by focusing the mind lightly on the dan tien. Feel the abdomen expand while inhaling and contract while exhaling. Gradually deepen respiration until it is full, gentle, even and deep. When this foundation is strong, change to reverse abdominal breathing (see *The Principles and Practice Methods of Sitting Chi Kung*). During reverse abdominal breathing, the abdomen contracts during inhalation and expands on exhalation. This form of breathing will serve to collect and renew chi in the dan tien. Continue to focus the mind on the dan tien. Do not attempt to circulate chi. The sole purpose of this exercise is to accumulate chi in the dan tien. Begin with fifteen to twenty minutes of practice per day and work up to one half- hour per day. Further levels of Chi Kung practice are built upon the foundations established in the first and second levels of practice. These first two foundational levels are critical to the development of the whole practice. It would be useless to attempt any of additional levels of Chi Kung practice, until the body is open to the flow of chi and chi has begun to accumulate in the dan tien. Generally, one can expect to practice the first two levels for three months each, before enough chi has been gathered to support further levels of exercise.

When beginning to perform deep breathing practice, avoid making the mistake of breathing too much initially, which can cause dizziness. Therefore, limit the number of breaths to 49 initially (never over 100); then work up to an increased number over time. The environment within the home must be considered, especially during the winter season. Open the windows for a period of time before practice to bring in fresh air from the outside. The environment should also be quiet to improve concentration. Never use the mouth to breathe out. Exhale through the nose. One must concentrate, not allowing the mind to wander, thus avoiding chi blockages in the body. When the breathing exercises are performed for a period of time, the body may feel hot or cool. The muscles may twitch or jump; numbness may occur; or a person may feel very comfortable. White light may also be visualized. Do not allow the mind to wander, focusing on these occurrences.

Further levels of practice require the attention and guidance of a qualified instructor. However, considerable benefit to health and longevity may be achieved through the practice of the above exercises.

Western Perspectives on Deep Breathing and Health

In contrast to the long history of breathing practice, including its progressive development over generations of Chinese history, deep breathing has only recently received attention as an intervention to improve health and treat disease in western society. According to a study in the British Medical Journal, activities that promote deep breathing can alter several of the body's vital signs in a positive manner (225). Dr. Herbert Benson, president of the Mind/Body Medical Institute in Boston points to a formidable body of evidence, indicating breathing exercises are very important to health and well being (220). The results of the study showed that, slow deep breathing was associated with synchronized cardiovascular rhythms, leading to positive body and mind effects. The leading author of the study indicated that, slow, deep breathing leads to more oxygen being in the blood. The well-known stress response, which has been associated with the cause of many diseases and worsening of others, can be alleviated by the relaxation response. Dr. Benson indicated that, the relaxation response could be harnessed, through a two-step process, similar to the practice of prayer or meditation; and that such techniques, throughout history, have been associated with breathing practices. The first step is the repetition of a word, phrase or muscular activity; the second step involves ignoring other thoughts that pass through the mind.

The effects of relaxation may also extend to reducing artery blockages and the risk of heart attacks and strokes, according to an article published in Stroke (222). Meditation was shown to be associated with a significant reduction in artery wall thickness, when two similar groups of patients were studied. One group practiced meditation, while the other group did not. Several programs are available throughout the United States, which assist patients taking better care of themselves through relaxation (223). These programs assist those, who have various underlying diseases including, heart disease, anxiety, panic disorders, job or family related stress issues, chronic pain, cancer, AIDS, headaches, sleep disturbances, behavior issues, high blood pressure, fatigue, and skin diseases. Research also points to higher levels of a chemical in the body, Interleukin-6, in people who are under considerable stress, as compared to individuals who are not (221). Interleukin-6 has been associated with several diseases, such as heart disease, arthritis, osteoporosis, type-2 diabetes, and some types of cancer. Various factors can increase Interleukin-6 levels, including smoking. Interleukin-6 is secreted by fat cells, suggesting those who are overweight and obese may be at higher risk for increased levels of this chemical in the body. Positive health behaviors, such as exercise and normal amounts of sleep, reduce and regulate Interleukin-6 levels in the body. This observation suggests Interleukin-6 levels may be higher and not regulated properly in those who do not exercise or receive proper sleep.

Weak support exists in the medical literature for the effectiveness of breathing techniques and relaxation in helping to reduce acute pain (226). More widely accepted, and recommended, is the use of patterned breathing as an intervention for women in active labor. However, this practice may increase fatigue level, if begun too early in the course of labor (227).

Tai Chi Chuan has shown promise as an adjunct to cardiac rehabilitation exercise training, with reported improvement in cardiorespiratory function, balance and postural stability, fall prevention, and stress reduction (228). Breathing and coughing exercises have also been shown to prevent pulmonary complications after coronary artery surgery (229). Patients with chronic heart failure have also been evaluated, with respect to the average saturation of oxygen in the blood, and its relationship with the degree of instability in breathing pattern (230). In these evaluations, some patients were taught to practice coordinated deep diaphragmatic and chest breathing, while others did not practice these techniques. Those that practiced had improved average oxygenation throughout the month of "training" and for a month after the end of the program, compared to those that did not practice. The breathing techniques led to small, but useful, improvements in exercise tolerance, with a reduced sensation of shortness of breath.

The practice of Tai Chi Chuan can also increase the function of the immune system. The chickenpox virus, which rests in a dormant state, can become active, when immune function dips and results in painful blisters, shingles. This can be a devastating condition, especially for elderly patients. People over 60 years of age were studied to determine if a fifteen-week exercise program of Tai Chi Chuan is effective in improving shingles immunity (231). The study demonstrated that, those who practiced Tai Chi Chuan had a fifty percent increase in immune function, compared to those who did not. This represented an increase, thought to prevent outbreaks of shingles. Since the test actually assesses overall immune memory and function, it is thought that, general immunity to viruses can be increased by this practice. A reduction in stress may also provide a basis for improved immune response, in that stress can reduce immunity to viruses, such as Epstein-Barr (232).

Respiratory diseases, such as cystic fibrosis, are associated with significant problems in clearing secretions from the lung. Several methods have been used to help patients clear these secretions, including relaxed breathing in combination with pulmonary therapy techniques, breathing with chest expansion, and active cycle of breathing methods. These breathing methods have demonstrated promise in clearing secretions in patients with this disease (233-238). Breathing techniques have also shown promise in the treatment of asthma. The Buteyko breathing technique was shown, in one study, to provide benefit in some outcome measurements, at a three-month evaluation period (239). In this study, patients using the breathing technique reported decreased medication use and a trend toward increased quality of life, compared to those patients, who did not use the technique. Limited benefits were demonstrated on subjective and objective measures of asthma control using a yoga breathing technique in patients with severe asthma (240). Larger reviews on the subject, without controlling for the specific breathing techniques employed, could form no conclusions as to the benefits of breathing, in general, on asthma control measures (241). No benefit was seen in severe asthma (242). The use of diaphragmatic breathing, as an adjunct treatment for individuals with chronic obstructive pulmonary disease (COPD), is held in question. While certain subpopulations of patients with COPD may benefit (243,244), other subgroups of patients with COPD may experience worsening of this condition, when using deep breathing techniques (245,246).

In summary, scientific research is emerging showing at least some benefit of deep breathing, as an adjunct in the treatment of a limited number of diseases. It appears that little benefit, and possible worsening of the condition, may result, if the disease is severe or in advanced stages. This concept supports the idea that, the greatest benefit from deep breathing is preventative in nature and some benefit may be derived when applied in the early stages of illness. The state-of-the-art of breathing, as reported in this research, does not address the level of sophistication found in Chi Kung practice. However, this research is beginning to address the role breathing plays in health.

Conclusions

In light of the principles and basic methods outlined in this chapter, it can be appreciated that, breathing, from the perspective of the legacy left by the great kung fu masters for modern men and women, is much more than the inhalation and exhalation of air. Breathing incorporates the manner in which deep breathing is performed, as well as its function in nurturing and building energy. This perspective is based upon generations of independent practitioners, who have achieved and reported similar results, when using similar practices. Currently, these practices do not readily lend themselves to the research method. Until such time as this type of research is possible, the potential benefits to health and longevity can only be experienced through participation in the practice of breathing, with these principles and basic practice methods in mind.

Chapter 6

Exercise and Rest

Introduction

The young are naturally active. Often, adults find amazement in the level of energy and activity of young children. As people grow older, however, the level of physical activity normally decreases. Modern conveniences only add to the trend of becoming sedentary with age. The type of work, available to employees in modern society, trends toward more sedentary activities, compared with the physical labor common during the previous two centuries. Routine activities, such as shopping, often necessitate driving a car to the store, rather than walking, most likely as a result of time constraints imposed by the fast pace of life. Rather than park a distance from the entrance to a shopping maul, shoppers often search for the nearest parking space. Rather than walking up a few flights of stairs, elevators and escalators are preferred.

Unfortunately, if the choice is made to exercise, the environment in which exercise occurs is often unhealthy. For example, walking along the roadside to a store, rather than though a park, allows exposure to higher concentrations of carbon monoxide and other noxious fumes; swimming in pool water, rather than a lake or pond exposes the swimmer to the potential absorption of chlorine; exercising in a cold air conditioned gym, rather than exercising out-of doors at dawn, precludes taking advantage of nature's cool early morning temperatures.

For most, the tendency is to become sedentary, where sitting or lying down excessively becomes the norm. As a result, weight is gained. In combination with other habits associated with a sedentary life style, such as consuming unhealthy foods, the risk of atherosclerosis, heart disease, diabetes, and obesity become more likely. With exercise, the risk of these problems can be reduced.

Exercise is one of the cornerstones of building a healthy body. With the increased breathing and blood circulation associated with physical activity, in general, the internal organs can better be supported, and cell turnover can become more robust; the immune system can become more responsive, leading to fewer common infectious illnesses; and, in combination with a healthy diet, weight reduction can be achieved. The risk of illnesses, such as diabetes and cardiovascular diseases, can thus, be reduced. Many have recognized the need for physical fitness, giving rise to a multitude of products and programs to accomplish this goal. While many advocate the need for lengthy and vigorous exercise routines, even a moderate amount of physical activity can produce significant benefits. While daily exercise is optimal, considerable benefit may be achieved from only thirty to forty-five minutes of walking, three times per week. For those, who have not exercised and have been mostly sedentary, starting slow in an exercise routine, then working up to even a minimum of thirty minutes of physical activity, three times per week, has been advocated (247-249). The cardiovascular and pulmonary systems must slowly become accustomed to even minimal physical activity, therefore starting slow is recommended. For those with medical problems, a physician should always be consulted before embarking upon any physical activity program. When exercising, choose a good environment, for example, one that minimizes exposure to pollutants, such as a park. Wooded areas provide the advantage of the normal oxygen content found in fresh air, and the abundance of negative ions. Avoid walking near roadsides, swimming in chemically treated water, or exercising in cool air-conditioned rooms.

General Benefits of Physical Activity

According to recently updated information, provided by the Centers for Disease Control and Prevention (249,250), "more than sixty percent of adults do not achieve the recommended amount of regular physical activity" and twenty five percent are not physically active. Physical inactivity is more common in women, lower income earners, and the less educated. A pattern of becoming less active with age is also apparent. Of equal concern is the lack of regular and vigorous activity in almost fifty percent of young people, between twelve and twenty-one years of age. As with adults, activity decreases with age during the adolescent period; and females are much less active than males. Among high school students, enrollment in daily physical education classes was noted to have fallen to a low of twenty-five percent in 1995, from forty-two percent in 1991. Furthermore, a minority of students is active for more than twenty minutes in physical education classes every day, during the school week (249).

This information indicates that, the lack of physical activity is now considered a nationwide problem in the United States. A lack of activity promotes unnecessary illness and premature death (249-253). In contrast, regular physical activity, occurring most days of the week, reduces the risk of premature death and death from a number of diseases, including heart disease. Regular physical activity also reduces the risk of developing various other diseases, including diabetes, high blood pressure, colon and breast cancer (254-257). Regular activity has been shown to help reduce blood pressure in patients with hypertension; promotes psychological wellbeing and reduces feelings of depression and anxiety; helps control weight; maintain healthy bones, muscles and joints; and assists the elderly by increasing strength and mobility without falling.

The association between physical activity and health has been recognized for thousands of years. In addition to the benefits of exercise outlined by government agencies, many believe physical activity can improve immune system function. This may be a direct effect, or secondary to other benefits, such as improved emotional status (249,255,258,259). Moderate amounts of regular physical activity, such as walking for 30 minutes, can improve health and wellbeing, thus affecting emotional status. Greater health benefits can be realized with increased duration, frequency, or intensity of physical activity.

The belief that only vigorous exercise can benefit health appears to be unfounded. Often exercising to the point of pain can cause more harm than benefit. Exercising in such a manner may tax the heart, lungs, muscles, and bones, thus, risking injury. Strong evidence exists indicating, moderate activity can produce important health improvements, and also add to an appealing appearance and self-confidence (250). In combination with a well controlled and balanced diet, physical activity can provide significant assistance in weight control efforts. To achieve a moderate level of physical activity, changes in the daily routine need not be burdensome. For example, to achieve the level of physical activity provided by a brisk 30 minute walk, one can walk up stairs rather than use an elevator or escalator; walk instead of drive for short errands; garden, rake leaves, or perform other daily chores. Separating physical activity into shorter periods per day, which total 30 minutes, is also beneficial.

Several other myths surround the subject of exercise, in addition to those that call for long, strenuous, and arduous physical programs. One of these myths is the notion that diet need not be a concern, when participating in a vigorous exercise program (248). The health consequences of consuming refined sugar, foods high in fat, and over-eating remain unchanged, despite the level of intensity, frequency, and duration of physical activity. In addition, there are no easy, magic, quick fix solutions that can replace physical activity.

Attempts at participating in regular physical activity often fail. One key to maintaining a daily routine of physical activity is to participate in something enjoyable. Several activities can be tried in an attempt to identify which are fun to do. Including friends and/or immediate family members, and changing locations in which activities are performed, may help to maintain the routine of physical activity. Overall, establishing personal goals helps maintain the effort, over time. The greatest benefit from any physical activity is achieved over the long term, and therefore, should be considered a lifestyle change.

The benefits of regular physical activity have been recognized by government; individually, among a small percentage of the nations population; and by small and large businesses alike. Private businesses have begun to promote exercise among their employees. Company wellness programs have reduced the rise in health care costs, reduced employee turnover, and reduced compensation costs for businesses that participate in these programs (260,261). Wellness programs offer educational services covering a variety of topics, including nutrition and weight control. Some offer exercise facilities and coordinate physical activities, such as aerobic exercise classes. Research is underway to identify methods effective in promoting regular exercise to a majority of the adults in the United States (262). These examples clearly indicate that, the benefits of physical activity are being recognized as a major contributor to fitness and health in modern society.

The benefits of physical activity, both vigorous and slow motion, have been long recognized within the Chinese martial arts community. In addition to the benefits identified above, the breathing methods incorporated into these exercises offer additional benefits to the internal organs. The breathing methods used in the Chinese martial arts and Chi Kung practices represent the general mechanism through which health maintenance is given to the internal organ. As a result of improved oxygenation, the health of internal organs can be maintained, while the external tissues, such muscles and tendons, are strengthened. This can be accomplished through both vigorous and slow motion physical activity.

Recent studied are supportive of the view recognized within the martial arts community, in particular, that, breathing assists the capacity for exercise (external tissues) as well as benefiting the internal organs (reduce disease risk). For example, studies have demonstrated the advantages to improved lung capacity and oxygenation in women who participate in recreational running (263). For patients suffering from chronic obstructive pulmonary disease (COPD), pulmonary rehabilitation has been shown to improve exercise capacity in the elderly (264) and maximal exercise tolerance, oxygen uptake, exercise endurance, self-efficacy for walking, and reductions in perceived breathlessness, muscle fatigue, and shortness of breath (265). Improvement was shown as a reduction in anxiety and distress levels, associated with shortness of breath, in patients with COPD (266). Benefit has also been demonstrated in some aspects of age-associated baroreflex sensitivity, with improvement following a non-aerobic exercise, yoga, as well as aerobic exercise (267). In combination with dietary modification, an increase in physical activity may shortly be scientifically proven to represent the foundation for successful weight reduction and maintenance. This concept is currently being studied (268). In fact, physical activity of any kind is more effective in producing weight loss, than controlling diet alone. Increased physical activity, even moderate activity, not only promotes weight loss, but also reduces the risk of breast cancer in women (254).

Physical activity appears to reduce the severity of symptoms in depressed patients (258). Substantial mood improvement may be gained following aerobic exercise, even a single bout. Other literature points to an improved self-image, with greater levels of self-esteem, occurring as improvement in body shape is achieved. Exercising with others may also provide a means of social interaction, contributing to a sense of well-being.

Some have pointed to the anti-aging effect of exercise (247), where it is believed, exercise is one of the most effective anti-aging methods available. Exercise can increase blood flow to the brain, reducing the risk of stroke and improve thinking. Regular exercise appears to slow down degeneration of the brain, thus reducing the development of slower reaction time and poor coordination. In addition to improving lung function, reducing body fat, and increasing muscle strength, blood pressure can be reduced for several hours following exercise (253). The biochemical effects of vigorous exercise appear to include production of IL-6, which counteracts the inflammatory effects of TNFa, a substance in the body associated with inflammation (257)). IL-6 is thought to bring balance to the effects of TNFa, and could be helpful against atherosclerosis, diabetes, and obesity. Further experiments are underway, testing the role of exercise in increasing the levels of not only IL-6, but also, IL-1, as well as their role in enhancing immune function. Funding for this research has been made available through the NIH (256).

Type of Physical Activity

Activities that promote the strength and shape of external muscles, and increase cardio-vascular endurance, such as weight lifting, aerobics, running, boxing, and the martial arts, are examples of exercises practiced in Western society. As a general category of exercise, these are often referred to as body-oriented, in that they focus on the development of the physical body. Most who participate in this type of exercise intend to get "in shape" from a cardiovascular standpoint, and firm the tough-to-tone body parts, in addition to any other sport related benefit. The tough-to-tone areas include the legs, butt, chest, arms, back and abdominal muscles. Exercises performed to this end can include squats, push-ups, and abdominal crunches. Many myths surround participating in such exercise routines, including the idea that, more is better; specific exercises can selectively reduce fatty tissue, in particular, specific body areas; women will develop bulky muscles when lifting weights; and long hours at the gym are required to shape-up. Despite the interest and good intent of many who wish to get in shape, less than 25% of people in the United States regularly engage in exercise, especially long-term exercise programs (269).

Another general category of exercises adds a component of mental focus, as well as breathing, to muscular activity. These types of exercises can be referred to as mind-body exercises, and include disciplines such as yoga, Tai Chi Chuan, Chi Kung, and some martial arts. These exercises emerged from the traditions of Eastern cultures. In contrast to body-oriented exercises, where attention is seldom given to breathing technique or mental focusing, mind-body exercises promote calmness; increase energy, and a sense of wellbeing, in addition to producing physical strength, endurance and muscular flexibility. Considerable attention has recently been given to the health promoting benefits of practicing Tai Chi Chuan and other types of slow motion exercises (270).

The external benefits of body-oriented exercise routines may be achieved at the expense of the internal organs, if the practices associated with mind-body exercises are not applied. Proper breathing and mental focus minimize the stress response, and are thought to be responsible for several health benefits related to the internal organs, including lowering blood pressure, mental tension, fatigue, and negative emotions, such as anger (271). Greater aerobic capacity, balance, flexibility, muscle endurance, and strength, as well as a decrease in body fat (30.8% to 19%) have been reported, when individuals participate, for example, in martial arts that specifically incorporate mind-body exercises, compared to sedentary participants (272).

The postures assumed, breathing methods employed, and mental focusing techniques associated with the mind-body disciplines, contribute to promoting the health of the internal organs. Herein lies the main difference between the traditional concept of Western exercise, and that of the Chinese martial arts, as well as other mind-body disciplines. The benefits associated with the mind-body disciplines can be applied, both in terms of health improvement, as well as therapeutically. For example, yoga has been applied in the management of various health conditions, such as pregnancy and childbirth (273,274). Appropriate stretching techniques can be used to prepare the muscles of the lower body for childbirth, while the breathing methods can assist with the shortness of breath, associated with pregnancy. Assistance is also provided, through these exercises, for the physical challenges encountered during the delivery process, post partum period, and stresses of child rearing. In addition, anecdotal reports describe the health benefits of yoga practice in the context of several diseases, including menopause, premenstrual syndrome, musculoskeletal pain, cardiovascular diseases, and respiratory diseases such as asthma.

In combination with dietary modification, the impact of yoga and meditation was studied as a method to change cardiovascular risk (275). In this report, body mass index, total and LDL, serum cholesterol, fibrinogen, and blood pressure were significantly reduced in those with elevated levels. Urinary excretion of adrenaline, noradrenaline, dopamine, aldosterone, as well as serum testosterone and luteinizing hormone levels were reduced; all of which are thought to be beneficial. Despite the potential health benefits of mind-body disciplines, reports indicate that, many, who practice such exercises in the United States, prefer to exclude the mental portion, retaining only the body-oriented exercises of the yoga disciple (276). This exclusion is unfortunate since much of the benefit to health and longevity may be lost as a result.

Rest and Sleep

While exercise is an important component of health, excessive activity can damage the body. It has been appreciated for centuries, within Chinese Medicine, that, excessive walking can damage ligaments; standing for lengthy periods can damage bones; and excessive physical work can damage chi. Excess in weight lifting routines can damage the kidneys, as can partaking in excessive sexual activity. Other activities are believed to damage internal organs and tissues, when in excess. For example, reading too much can damage the blood; worrying and thinking too much can damage the heart and spleen function. Therefore, an appropriate balance between activity and rest is considered good for health. Not only is rest necessary, but also, the timing of rest is equally significant. Rest following consumption of a meal, for example, prevents depleting the body of energy, at a time when increased energy is necessary for digestion. This pattern is evident in animals, where rest is taken following feeding times. Energy is conserved in this manner. Humans, on the other hand, often override the impulse to rest following meals, due to work and family related pressures. Sometimes the urge to sleep also arises during the course of the day, for no apparent reason. In most circumstances, people do not yield to the desire for rest. The body must, therefore, expend more energy to stay awake under these conditions, taxing the system. In contrast, excessive relaxation, such as sitting or lying down in excess of normal rest requirements, can damage the muscles and chi, respectively.

As important as exercise is to health, is obtaining the proper amount of rest and sleep. Sleep is a natural process to restore energy. It is the foundation of the body and fundamental to refresh the nervous system, including the brain, the muscles, bones, and joints. The human body can survive approximately forty days without food, but cannot survive for that length of time without sleep. Infants require approximately twelve to fourteen hours of sleep per night, while the elderly require approximately eight hours per night of sleep. Over-exercise, over-work, insomnia, stress, anxiety, lack of attention to differing sleep requirements based on age, may all result in the ill effects of improper or insufficient rest and sleep. Sleep related breathing disorders might also be associated with an increased risk of coronary artery disease, stroke, hypertension, and mortality due to all causes (277). A lack of sleep can affect mood, concentration, and alertness, as well as increase the risk for diabetes, obesity, and impair immune system function. Some have postulated that, hypertension and compromise of the immune system are the result of the body becoming slightly acidic, resulting from long-term reductions in sleep duration.

A discussion of rest must include the subject of fatigue (278). Fatigue can be described in many ways, including being tired, weak, and exhausted. Excessive physical activity, including insufficient resting time to allow for recovery when exercising, and a lack of sleep, can both lead to fatigue. Fatigue may be due to psychological reasons, in addition to being physical in origin. A lack of control over emotion, or the occurrence of excessive emotion resulting from stress, for example, can lead to the feelings of fatigue. In the case of fatigue due to physical reasons, rest and sleep are necessary to alleviate the symptoms. On the other hand, addressing the psychological source can usually relieve mental fatigue. People can also feel fatigue due to illnesses, such as anemia, heart or lung disease, cancer, diabetes, and other diseases of the hormone system. Whatever is the cause that underlies fatigue, when persisting beyond a few days, medical advice should be sought.

Specifically, exercising can cause fatigue, directly from either over-exertion of the muscles or from the inability of the nerves to properly transmit impulses, or both. Muscle fatigue can be due to dehydration, overheating, and/or accumulation of metabolic byproducts, such as lactic acid. Changes, which occur in the nervous system during exercise can cause fatigue. This type may involve the build up neuro-chemical levels in the brain, such as serotonin. Serotonin can cause sleepiness and fatigue. In either case, the fatigue tells the body to rest and sleep, when necessary. While drinking liquids to compensate for a loss of fluids is essential to compensate for dehydration, other measures, which have been promoted, such as taking stimulants, including caffeine and ephedrine, are not advised.

Too much sleep, as well as too little sleep, has been shown to be associated with an increased risk of coronary heart disease in women (279). Sleeping five hours or less per night was associated with a thirty percent increase in the risk for coronary heart disease. Sleeping six hours per night was associated with an eighteen percent increase in risk. This is somewhat alarming, since one-third of Americans sleep six hours or less per night. Those, who slept eight hours per night, had the lowest risk. In contrast, those, who slept greater than nine hours per night, actually had a thirty-eight percent increase in the risk of developing coronary heart disease. Long-term decreases in sleep duration may soon be considered an additional risk factor for heart disease, in part, based on this evidence. Other important risk factors for heart disease include: smoking, lack of exercise, and diets high in fats.

Short-term decreases in sleep duration is associated with several symptoms including, increased blood pressure, variability in heart rate, decreased tolerance of glucose, and increased cortisol levels. Reduced or disrupted sleep may also increase the risk of obesity and diabetes (280), compounding risk. Sleep loss appears to affect the body's ability to metabolized sugar. Restricting sleep in an adult to four hours per night, for one week can induce a pre-diabetic state, and increase hunger and appetite, which is also a risk factor for obesity (277). Cortisol (a stress hormone), leptin (a hormone which controls appetite), and thyroid hormone (helps control metabolism), are all affected by lack of sleep. The immune system can also be affected by a lack of sleep. It has been shown that, a lack of sleep can reduce the immune response to the flu vaccine by as much as fifty percent.

Several factors play a role in the trend to sleep less in the American society. These include: working to late hours, staying up late to watch television or use the Internet, and over-involvement in multiple activities, such as dance, soccer, gymnastics, arts and crafts, leaving little time for rest and sleep. Children may be particularly impacted by over-involvement, in that, up to twenty-five percent of children suffer from the effects of sleep related problems, ranging from sleep walking to hormonal problems that slow growth (281). Shifting the sleep schedule beyond two hours, even on weekends, can significantly disrupt the body's clock and therefore, sleep. Sleep-deprived children perform poorly in school, and some may be misdiagnosed with attention deficit disorder (ADHD). Statistics indicate that twenty-seven percent of school-age children resist going to bed, and eleven percent cannot fall asleep. Many children are becoming deprived of the positive effects of deep sleep. Deep sleep triggers the release of growth hormone, which stimulates the growth of muscles and bones. Poor sleep and reduced sleep duration may possibly result in children becoming underweight for their age. As mentioned above, other hormones, which can be affected by a lack of sleep include, thyroid hormone and cortisol. Both hormones affect energy levels and control sugar, respectively. A lack of sufficient sleep in children also can cause crankiness, decreased attention span, and irritability, which in turn, impact upon socialization. Teenage children are as impacted as younger children. Often, part-time jobs, extra-curricular activities, and peer pressures limit sleep to an average of seven hours per night. Teenagers require approximately nine hours of sleep per night. Of course, many other factors can affect sleep, and medical advice should always be sought if a problem exists in this area.

In many cases, people continue to feel tired, even after obtaining the proper amount of sleep. This can be due to sleeping at an incorrect time, according to Chinese Medical theory. Chinese Medicine outlines the optimal time to sleep, according to the body clock. In short, when sleep is obtained from 9 p.m. to 11 p.m., the immune system becomes rejuvenated. Similarly, the liver becomes recharged from 1 a.m. to 3 a.m., allowing the individual to have more energy available throughout the day. Blood is also produced during this time period. Blood is also produced between 11 p.m. and 1 a.m. and from 11 a.m. to 1 p.m. This concept suggests that, the amount of sleep may not be as important as the timing of sleep. At a minimum, sleeping between 11 p.m. and 3 a.m. is necessary. During this time, blood is produced and the liver is rejuvenated. The liver is the most important organ of the body, in this regard. Liver problems can result in problems for all other organs including the heart, spleen/pancreas, lungs, kidneys, intestines and stomach. Short-term lack of sleep, during these important times is not at issue. It must be recognized on the other hand, that, long term disregard for appropriate sleep times, according to this concept, can be problematic. Consider the ill health of those who frequently stay out all night, not sleeping at the appropriate times, as well as participating in other activities that damage the liver, including over-consumption of alcohol. These individuals frequently suffer from upper respiratory infection, poor healing, and tire easily, despite obtaining at least eight hours of sleep per day. Working the third shift may be problematic for individuals, as well, due to suboptimal sleep times despite obtaining the proper amount of sleep. With improper sleep or sleep times, the body will be deficient, despite having excellent nutrition and practicing other healthy activities and disciplines.

The body clock dictates times of optimal organ function. As mentioned, 11 p.m. to 1 a.m. is associated with blood cell production; 1 a.m. to 3 a.m., with recharging the liver; 3 a.m. to 5 a.m., with lung function. The period between 3 a.m. and 5 a.m. is optimal to perform breathing exercises for this reason. The large intestine is addressed between 5 a.m. and 7 a.m., while the stomach is addressed between 7 a.m. and 9 a.m. This time is therefore optimal for consuming the breakfast meal. From 9 a.m. to 11 a.m. the spleen/pancreas functions optimally, and is, therefore, the best time for extracting nutrition from the food eaten at breakfast. With the processing of nutrients, the body is poised to produce blood cells between 11 a.m. to 1 p.m. Resting at this time also assists in recharging the blood, especially after eating lunch. From 1 p.m. to 3 p.m. the small intestine functions optimally. Therefore, the best time to eat lunch is before 1 p.m. In doing so, food is available to the small intestine, for the absorption of nutrients. From 3 p.m. to 5 p.m. the bladder functions optimally; and from 5 p.m. to 7 p.m. the kidneys receive the predominant flow of chi; these are the best times to drink the majority of fluids. From 7 p.m. to 9 p.m. the heart and nervous system receive predominant chi flow; and is therefore, the best time for exercise. Recent research points to the evening, as being the best time for optimal exercise and athletic performance (282). From 9 p.m. to 11 p.m. cellular immune function is rejuvenated.

Several recommendations regarding sleep are made within the Chinese martial arts. These include, avoiding excessive thought and worry prior to sleeping. Deep breathing exercises can be used to assist in relieving anxiety and stress, if performed prior to anticipated sleep times. Bathing in water, containing a few pieces of rock salt, which increases negative ion content, is also believed to relieve muscle tension, allowing for better sleep quality. Making a list of concerns, which can be dealt with the following day, can also assist with falling asleep, by removing the need to think about such issues at bedtime. Sleeping in the dark is considered optimal, therefore night-lights are not recommended. Eating, within two hours of sleeping, can interfere with proper sleep, and is, therefore, not recommended. Sleeping in a natural state, without night clothing, is considered best for a restful sleep, because the skin is allowed to "breathe" more easily. The room temperature should be comfortable, not too hot or cold. One can assess the quality of sleep by noting whether or not dreams are remembered. With a good quality of sleep, dreams are seldom remembered. Excessive sleep has long been recognized to be a contributor to body weakness, according to Chinese Medicine. However with illness, longer durations of sleep are necessary for proper recovery and healing.

Specific Exercises within Chinese Martial Arts

The subject of exercise, within the Chinese martial arts, cannot be fully appreciated without consideration of deep breathing exercises (Sitting Chi Kung). With Sitting Chi Kung, the mind directs chi, and the individual remains in a stationary position during the practice. With Sitting Chi Kung practices, in general, blood circulation only results from the action of the heart, since no physical activity is involved, other than breathing. The circulation of the whole body, therefore, slows. This allows chi and/or blood blockages to easily occur. In contrast, external exercise allows the body to move. Relative to Sitting Chi Kung, an increase in blood circulation occurs, while the internal environment remains quiet. External movement helps prevent and eliminate both blood and chi blockage. In this sense, the external exercise is used to assist the internal practice of Sitting Chi Kung. Once internal practice is accomplished, external practice is usually initiated. The internal aspect of Sitting Chi Kung and the external practice using physical exercise are like two sides of one coin, akin to yin and yang. The advantage of the internal exercise of Sitting Chi Kung is the circulation of chi, while the disadvantage is a slow blood circulation. In contrast, the advantage of external exercise includes both movement and blood circulation, while the internal aspects of practice are maintained, such as gaining quietness. Therefore, one type of practice assists the other. These are considered twin exercises. Moving Chi Kung, external exercise, is the basis of Sitting Chi Kung, and visa versa. With Moving Chi Kung, internal quietness is required, as well as a relaxed and soft body. The requirements are the same as Sitting Chi Kung but the body is moving.

Requirements for Internal Moving Chi Kung:

1. Keep the body soft, offering no resistance, like an infant, using no force, thus avoiding improper practice. If force is used, chi will travel externally, representing

incorrect practice. This will result in practicing an external martial art chi kung, out of sequence.

2. Concentrate on the Dan Tien when practicing. Do not force chi to the Dan Tien. Follow with the natural way, not using force; simply concentrate on the Dan Tien. This will avoid problems in practice in the future.

3. Allow the breathing to follow the body movement. Movement is up, down, opening and closing, i.e. four different ways. For example, the hands go upward, downward, open to the left and right, and close. Breathing follows the movement. As one opens the arms, breathe out. As one closes, breathe in. Similarly, as one moves the arms upward, breathe in; downward, breathe out.

The process is divided into two parts: hand movement with breathing, and mental concentration on the Dan Tien. All concentration is on the Dan Tien. This applies to exercises that assist the organs, such as the lungs, heart, and kidneys. The home base is the Dan Tien, the point of utmost importance. As pointed out above, do not force the chi, but allow the chi to follow with the movements.

4 Breathing must be soft and continuous, without stopping. The breathing can be either regular or reverse breathing. Breathing should be light and soft, going to the home base, the Dan Tien. This type of breathing is analogous to the silk worm, which produces silk continuously. Silk is light and soft. Breathing to the Dan Tien is light and soft, yet is designed to build a strong home base. Soft and continuous breathing is basis for building chi.

A spider's web is built in four directions; up, down, left, and right (open, close). Once these four main directions are built, the remainder of web is finished. Once the web is completed, insects can be caught at any time; the spider can consume the insect at will. If practice builds the web of chi correctly, then chi automatically travels to the proper place. Issuing chi can then be accomplished appropriately, at will.

5. When moving, each connected section of muscle, joint, and ligament must follow the other, in sequence, like a caterpillar moving. These body parts should all be coordinated in movement, as a snake moves smoothly, not fragmented. The fingers, wrists, elbow, and spine should move fluidly, connected like a snake or caterpillar. Each section is separate but connected, and reliant on the other, as one section pushes to the next, and so on.

6. The nervous system becomes trained, as each type of movement addresses a different channel. However, the internal and external must work together. Each of the external movements is designed to address a specific internal organ area. The external movement combines with the internal breathing, thus all the body channels are connected together. If anything enters the body to attack an organ, such as evil chi (wind, cold, etc), the nervous system senses the attack. The whole body, then, becomes involved in moving the chi, like water, to any area that needs it. This can occur as the body becomes trained, through these exercises. For example, as a certain area of the body is touched (external), the entire chi travels to that area (internal). When cold attacks a certain part of the body (external), both the internal (chi) and external (covering) aspects of defense travel to the exposed area. The same pattern applies to addressing problems with an internal organ. Both the external and internal aspects travel to the same area to assist. Chi and blood (internal), water and air (external) work together in this manner. This process is like a wave, where the internal energy of the wave, plus the water itself, crash against the shore. Blood and chi travel to the location of a weak organ to provide healing, just like water hitting the shore. This process applies to any internal organ. That is, chi and blood

travel to open the blockage, and repair the injured organ or tissue.
7. Breathe in through the nose and out through the mouth.

Classification of Moving Chi Kung

Several types of Moving Chi Kung exist and can be classified into two major categories, including Internal Moving and External Moving Chi Kung. The Eight Pieces of the Brocade and Five Organ Chi Kung represent the Internal Moving type. Health Dancing Chi Kung is an example of a transitional form of Moving Chi Kung, from Internal to External. Tai Chi Chuan is considered the best and most complete type of Internal Moving Chi Kung, and is also an internal martial art. An example of an External Moving Chi Kung is the Five Animals Chi Kung. External forms of martial arts also possess their own Chi Kung exercises, and are specific to each style or system. In these forms of Chi Kung, chi is directed to the muscles, ligaments, and skin.

The internal, or soft, forms of Chi Kung must be practiced prior to practicing external forms. The internal forms build chi, step by step, until it is strong. Chi can then be directed to the outside. If the external forms are practiced first, extreme difficulty is encountered practicing the internal forms. Some would say that, internal practice could never be accomplished, if the external forms are practiced first, out of sequence. If the internal forms are practiced first, the external aspect will eventually be included. The necessity for this sequence is similar to playing with a ball, either filled with air or empty. Air is pumped into the ball first, making the surface of the ball hard and able to bounce. If one tries to bounce an empty ball, without first being filled with air, the ball will not bounce, and the surface of the ball may become damaged. Similarly, to protect the internal organs, one must build chi internally, first. Once enough internal exercise has been accomplished, to protect the internal organs, then the external can be exercised, without injuring the internal organs. Injury can occur when the muscles become tight, blocking chi circulation. Blocking chi circulation, in this manner, causes blood circulation to slow, leading to blood blockages. Blood blockages cause stokes and heart attacks. Anecdotally, many martial artists, known to me, have suffered heart attacks at a young age. In my opinion, these incidents have resulted from practicing external exercises out of sequence, with respect to internal exercises, in their training. If a martial artist builds the internal first, then the external is automatically addressed, as chi goes outward to strengthen the external.

When practicing Moving Chi Kung, concentration and maintaining a soft body are most important. Each movement involves the head, neck, shoulders, arms, elbows, wrists, palms, fingers, spinal cord, waste, pelvis, muscles, knees, ankles, feet, toes, chest, abdomen, etc., together, such that each part of the body includes the flow of chi. When the movement is fast then all parts of the body move fast; when slow, all is slow. The amount of chi, yin and yang change, and change of the channels are adjusted with the movement.

When following these requirements, chi, which is internal, combines and works together with the external movements, just like a spider web. The straight lines are constructed first, vertical and horizontal. The four points are then connected. Further construction of the web allows addition threads to combine eight points, or directions. The spider then waits in the center. The Dan Tien is the center of the eight directions. The internal channel lines and external direction lines become joined together with the exercises. Internal chi lines and external directions become aligned and support each other. When an insect becomes caught in the web, the spider senses the movement. The spider then devours the insect at will. Herein lies the key to martial arts technique. When the hands touch in self-defense, it is like the insect attaching to the web. From the center, the Dan Tien, power is directed outward automatically, since it goes along the chi lines; the outside touches the inside, creating an automatic reaction. Practicing internal martial arts produces the same connection of organs and channels; the internal and external become combined together. The internal breathing and circulation to organs depends on the outside movements. Internally, one is using the chi; externally, one is using movement.

Many different feelings occur as chi begins to flow. Finally, chi flow feels like power and heat. When the feeling elicited by chi flow and movement are joined together, then the internal is combined with the external. Once the internal chi is built, external factors cannot impact the person. For example, the immune system begins to function at a high level.

When performing the movement, one may not feel the power in a certain area. This is due to a blockage. One can then concentrate on freeing the blockage. When practicing, one must concentrate to correct chi blockages when power in not sensed in the movement. Internal visualization is applied not only in Sitting Chi Kung, but also to Moving Chi Kung, for this purpose. First, the mind is used to direct the chi. Later the mind merely observed the flow of chi, since chi "knows" where it is going. When chi flows with the movement, then the internal and external are combined and free to flow together, without blockages. The chi and blood circulation become smooth; the body changes and heals. Both Moving and Sitting Chi Kung are the basis for healing Chi Kung and involve self-healing, as well as transferring energy to help others. In the process of learning to control chi flow more efficiently, self-control of human emotion can result. This is an added benefit of practice.

Five Organ Chi Kung

The five organs included in this form of Chi Kung include the lungs, kidneys, liver, heart, and spleen. Not only are the organs a focus of the exercise, but also the organ channels are included, as an integral aspect for proper practice. Various movements are practiced in addressing each specific organ. The series of movements are complex and best learned through personal instruction by a qualified teacher. However, the warm-up exercise, gate opening exercise, and lung exercise are easily described, and serve as a good introduction to this type of Chi Kung.

Hanging Hands and Legs Warp Up Exercise

The first portion of this exercise begins with the feet positioned shoulder width and parallel to one another, double weighted stance. The arms swing forward and upward in front of the body to shoulder level; this is considered the yin aspect of the movement. The arms then swing downward and backward behind the body; this is considered the yang aspect of the movement. The exercise benefits the yin and yang channels of the hands. As these channels are exercised, the associated organs of the body are strengthened. With their strengthening, a mechanism for healing illnesses can be achieved for those organs.

When positioned in the double weighted stance, inhale, extending the abdomen fully, while the arms swing forward and upward, straight in front of the body. As the arms swing back, behind the body, exhale, collapsing the abdomen downward into the lower perineum. Continue swinging arms back and forth, with inhaling and exhaling, at a pace that is comfortable. The abdomen should have time to expand and contract without forcing the process. Continue the repetition at least fifty times at first. Try to work up to one hundred and fifty times, or more, as competence is gained in this exercise.

Those who suffer from digestive problems and irregularity will benefit from this exercise. The swinging exercises the stomach, small and large intestine, urinary bladder, and gall bladder. Those organs are used by the body to get rid of waste and bad chi. Also, when the arms are swinging repeatedly, the nerves and chi channels in the shoulder area are stimulated. A number of these channels are connected in this area to the different organs, ultimately terminating in the hands. In addition, swinging the arms increases the circulation in the hands.

Natural breathing is used when performing the exercise. With natural breathing the abdomen expands with inhalation, and contracts with exhalation. Natural breathing causes a heat sensation to rise up the spinal column, via the Governing meridian, located along the centerline of the back, to the Bai Hui area, which is located at the top of the cranium. With exhalation, the mind is used to guide the chi down the Conception Vessel, which is located along the centerline of the front of the body. The anal sphincter is tightened and the tongue is placed on the palate connecting the Zen and Du meridian as in Sitting Chi Kung practice. Breathe in as the hands go up (yin channel), breathe out as hands go down (yang channel).

The knees should bend as the hands move downward. The knees should straighten, while raising the body upward, as the hands rise upward.

To similarly exercise the legs, one leg should swing up and down, akin to the arm movement, while the other leg supports the body in a standing position. Each leg should be exercised twenty-five times to begin. Then, one should work up to seventy-five repetitions, for each leg. Older individuals should set a goal of one-half this number. When moving the legs forward, inhale, since this movement addresses the yin channels. When swinging the leg backward, exhale, since this movement addresses the yang channels. The elderly, who cannot balance and move the legs in such a manner, may simply concentrate from the perineum (Hui Yin) to the center of the sole of the feet (acupuncture point, Kidney 1), along the yin channel of the inside of the legs, while inhaling. Then focus attention along the yang channel, from Kidney 1 to the tailbone, while exhaling. The Spleen, Liver, and Kidney channels (yin meridians) are located along the inside of the legs. The Stomach, Gall Bladder, and Urinary Bladder channels (yang meridians) are located along the outside of the legs. Each of the hand and leg exercises is designed to open a path for chi to travel freely to the organs.

Open the Four Chi Gates Exercise

The "Open the Four Gates" exercise is to be performed after the "Swinging the Hands" exercise. This exercise is designed to stretch and loosen the spine, to facilitate the flow of chi through the Governing Vessel, which runs along the back from the tailbone to the top of the head.

Begin with the hands hanging by your side, after the last swing of the hands. Raise the arms up to each side, then over the head. Starting with the head, bend forward to feel cervical vertebrae stretch. The hands will then feel very heavy. This heaviness pulls the hands forward. The hands, then, slowly start to pull your body over, beginning with the first thoracic vertebra. Do not bend at the waist at this point. The goal is to bend in a fashion, similar to the manner in which a small thin tree would bend, if the top is grabbed and pulled to the ground. Allow your hands to pull your arms, which in turn pull the shoulders, which pull your torso, then, finally, bend at the waist. The idea is to feel each vertebrae of the spine stretch sequentially, such that a rippling effect occurs down the spine. This will facilitate maximum stretch of the spine. The legs remain straight.

When bent forward, with the arms hanging downward, the two thumbs press on the Tai Chong (acupuncture point, Liver 3). The Tai Chong is located on the top of the foot, at the fleshy point, located just below the area where the bones aligned with the Large and second toes meet. As the thumbs press on this point the palms of the hands are touching the ground. The large toe of each foot interlocks with the respective hand, in such a manner as to press on the fleshy area of the back of the hand, located between the thumb and index finger, the He Gu point. This is known as the Heaven and Earth Harmony. When in this position correctly, the thumbs can press on the Tai Chong, as the large toe presses downward on the He Gu. Remain in this position for three minutes, concentrating on these two points, on each side of the body; four points total. These four points are used in acupuncture to treat chi deficiency, and control chi flow for the entire body. Breathe in and out naturally.

When the time period is completed, stand up. Beginning, when in the bent over position, envision picking up a ball with your hands, bringing the ball up to the Dan Tien when inhaling, then along the chest to over the head as you exhale. With this movement bring the torso upright, to the starting position. At this point, the hands are over the head, and the knees are bent slightly. When the hands are over the head, concentrate on the He Gu.

Repeat the sequence to a total of three times, then, end the exercise. To end the exercise, drop the hands to each side when in the upright position.

Lung Exercise

The lungs are considered the mother of the kidney, according to Chinese Medicine. That is, the lungs control the chi of the entire body, because the lungs control post-birth chi. The lungs are the starting point in the flow of chi from organ to organ. The lungs act as mother to the kidneys; the kidneys in turn act as mother to liver; the liver serves as mother to heart; and the heart to the spleen. The lung meridian, therefore, controls energy and breathing. The kidneys control pre-birth chi. In practice, the lungs are used, through breathing exercises, to entice pre-birth chi from the kidneys. The Ming Men, which is the area between the kidneys, is the center for pre-birth chi, and holds prominence in this process, as well.

When consulting acupuncture channel diagrams, to identify the path of chi flow along the lung meridian, the dotted line represents the path of core chi flow; whereas, the solid line identifies the path of surface chi flow. The lungs are associated with the emotions of grief and sadness. The lung element is metal; and the associated color is brilliant white. The chi associated with the lung is "greater yin". The chi is strongest in the lungs from 3 a.m. to 5 a.m. daily. Seasonally, chi is strongest in the lungs during August and September. The lungs are most vulnerable to illness in late autumn, as changes in the weather occur. They are primarily susceptible to cold and dry heat.

The lung exercise is designed to address the lung meridian breathing system. Since the lung controls the skin and circulation of chi in the body, as the vital chi of the lungs move, the individual will feel an itching and prickling sensation, particularly, on the face.

Following the "Open the Four Chi Gates" exercise, the feet remain shoulder width apart, and the hands usually rise upward over the head, then, drop down to side when finishing. However, when continuing directly to this exercise, the hands rise up above head while inhaling then; exhale as the hands drop down to the sides. The hands then circle in to the chest, with inhalation; then push the hands out, in a forward direction, while exhaling. The thumbs and fingers are bent; the thumb is directed straight forward, and the fingers point upward. When chi is sensed from the Dan Tien, use the mind to direct the chi, by concentrating on the tip of the thumb. The chi will automatically be connected, when concentrating on this point, and travel up and out to the thumb. Inhale through the nose, and exhale through the mouth. The teeth must lightly touch. The tongue tip is positioned at the intersection of the top front teeth touching the inner gum.

When exhaling, the sound, "SHONG," should be made, if chi is weak or deficient. The "SHONG" sound vibrates with the lungs and increases strength. If the body is considered in excess or overheated, on the other hand, breathe in through the nose, as usual, but open the mouth, not touching the teeth or top gums with the tongue, and make a "HE" sound when exhaling. The sound should be whispered. No vibration is produced in the lungs. The sound emanates directly from the Dan Tien, outward. The "HE" sound increases strength, even when chi is in balance. Either sound, depending on whether the body is deficient or excessive with regard to chi, will improve the lungs. If chi is deficient, use the "SHONG" sound first; then, once strengthened, switch to the "HE" sound to attain further strengthening. With chi deficiency the person is always tired, weak, and fatigues easily. With excess, the person is overly energetic, extremely active, and overheated in appearance.

The hands should then drop to the waist, while continuing to breathe out slightly. The exercise should be repeated to a total of nine times, initially. With enough practice, the exercise can be increased by nine repetitions periodically, to a total of thirty-six repetitions. When finishing the last repetition, the hands should follow a path upward, rather than forward; then, drop to each side, ending at the right and left hips, respectively.

Ending Movement Following Completion of the Exercises

Separate the legs a little wider than shoulder width; raise the hands fully over the head while inhaling. Then, allow the hands to drop down in front of the body, while sitting into a horse stance position. When in this position, the knees are bent as in riding a horse. Then bend the body forward, moving both hands forward; the chest is knee high and breathing is continued. Turn the hands so that, the Lau Gung, center of the palms, point toward your face, when making a fist. Then, hit toward the ground, breathing out as much as possible when ending the exhalation. The Lau Gung now faces the legs. Turn the palms upward, to open palms, as you raise the body upward. Continue to raise the hands above the head while inhaling. Finally, direct the hands downward to each side, as you bring the feet together, while exhaling. Bring the left foot into center, first; then the right foot. The hands end in front of Dan Tien, with the thumbs interlocked and palms facing the body. Maintain this position for one or two minutes, until body cools down. At this time, the tongue should massage around the inside of the mouth thirty-six times; then, swallow the saliva in three separate portions. If saliva is not produced, the body is considered too hot (yang excess or yin deficiency). If saliva production is excessive, the body is considered too wet and cold (yang deficiency). In this is the case, rub the hands back and forth to heat them up; then, place the palms on the face and walk thirty-six steps.

Summary

The entire series of exercises includes an exercise for each organ. The series is designed to either maintain the health of the organs, or to reinstate health, if sickness is present. The remainder of the exercises in this series requires the instruction of a qualified teacher.

Tai Chi Chuan

Tai Chi Chuan holds many similarities with other mind-body exercises. As an art, distinct from other mind-body disciplines, Tai Chi Chuan is considered the most complete and best moving form of Chi Kung. Sequences of graceful movements, performed in a continuous and contiguous fashion, incorporate breathing techniques to allow chi, life energy, to flow smoothly through the chi channels, acupuncture meridians. Tai Chi Chuan offers a mechanism for health improvement, as well as self-healing, as chi flow is promoted throughout the spectrum of chi channels. The learning and practice of Tai Chi Chuan is somewhat complex, and requires direct instruction from a qualified teacher, not only for proper learning of the movements and postures, but also for learning breathing technique and appropriate mental focusing methods. While complex and often requiring several months to years to learn, benefit can be achieved within a few months of practice. Range of motion, balance, improved muscle tone, and muscle and skeletal fitness are some of the initial benefits realized.

Improved mental concentration and unrestricted circulation of chi develop, with time and practice.

Many styles of Tai Chi Chuan are practiced today, but historical records indicate its origins lie with the Chen family, founder of Chen Style Tai Chi Chuan, approximately 1100 A.D. Silk tomb paintings, circa 400 B.C., however, depict people positioned in many Tai Chi Chuan postures, suggesting the origins of this discipline, in part, date back much earlier.

The slow movements, and slow, natural diaphragmatic breathing techniques employed, are thought to provide many of the health benefits of this art. In the practice of Tai Chi Chuan, stress is reduced. Stress is known to initiate many hormonal responses. If these responses persist, both mental and physical health can adversely be affected. This is primarily due to the effects of the stress hormones, epinephrine (adrenaline) and cortisol, which affect the cardiovascular and immune systems. For example, adrenaline is released into the bloodstream, as a result of stress, causing an increase in blood pressure and heart rate. The chronic or long-term effects of prolonged stress and adrenaline release include: high blood pressure (hypertension), anxiety, difficulty sleeping, and irritability. The increased levels of cortisol, produced by stress, can contribute to hypertension by causing the body to retain sodium and water. Cortisol also reduces the ability of the immune system to function, thus, increasing susceptibility to diseases, such as those caused by infection. Through release of these and other hormones, glycogen is converted to glucose, raising blood sugar and cholesterol levels; muscle tension increases, raising lactic acid levels, producing muscle aches, headaches, and pain. Gastric acid secretion, digestive enzyme excretion, and intestinal peristalsis are affected, causing indigestion, ulcers, and constipation. Perspiration increases. Emotional control declines, leading to outbursts and depression.

As a result of practicing Tai Chi Chuan, many of the ill effects of chronic stress can be avoided, thus, promoting and improving health. The practice of Tai Chi Chuan has also been shown to provide therapeutic benefit for many diseases. For example, to decrease morbidity and mortality, and improve the quality of life, Tai Chi Chuan has been studied as an adjunct to cardiac rehabilitation exercise training, following a cardiac event (228). Improved cardio-respiratory function, balance and postural stability, fall prevention, and stress reduction are some of the benefits demonstrated by this research. In addition, Tai Chi Chuan practice is associated with other health-related behaviors. A recent review suggests that the practice of Tai Chi Chuan is safe, and possibly beneficial, for older adults with heart failure, high blood pressure, arthritis, and multiple sclerosis (283). The health benefits noted include: improved balance and strength, cardiovascular and respiratory function, flexibility, immune function, and improvement in the symptoms of arthritis (284). Reduced stress and anxiety were also noted as health benefits. The researchers conclude that, the problem of insufficient information still exists, to definitively recommend Tai Chi Chuan to patients with chronic conditions. However, other research has demonstrated that, the practice of Tai Chi Chuan improves the immune response to the virus that causes shingles, varicella zoster virus (231). In an interview with the researcher of this study (285), it was pointed out that the general enhancement of immune memory is likely generalizable to other infections.

Health Dancing Chi Kung

This series of exercises are considered transitional, in that, they offer a bridge from the Internal to the External types of Moving Chi Kung.

Basic Footwork

Starting with the feet together, step back and diagonally to the right with the right foot. The left foot follows the right foot, with the toes touching the ground, and the heel raised next to the right foot (combined stance). The left foot then returns to the original position, with the toes pointing straight forward. The right foot follows the left foot to the original position, but in the combined stance. The step may be initiated with the left foot first, stepping back and diagonally to the left, and so on.

Basic Whole Body Adjustment

1. Adjusting the Yin and Yang

    Press the palm of both hands together in front of the chest area with the fingers pointing upward, as if praying. Starting with the feet together, begin the above-described basic footwork, with the hands in this position. Breathe normally, inhaling when stepping back diagonally, and exhaling when returning forward. The mind does not direct the chi in this series. The mind does not focus; simply perform the breathing and the movements. This type of Chi Kung is more external, rather than internal, therefore, there is no mental directing of chi. The hands are simply positioned and Chi Kung breathing is exercised. Each movement affects many organs.

    Repeat the movement, stepping back and forth nine times, initially; then, increase in intervals of nine repetitions, to a total of thirty-six. Once this number of repetitions has been achieved, the next position can be initiated.

2. Holding the Heaven (Breathe the Heaven Chi)

    Continuing from Step 1, Adjusting the Yin and Yang, finish in position with the forward movement, then begin Step 2. In this step, both hands are raised above the head, with the palms facing the sky and the fingers pointing toward each other. Continue the stepping pattern and breathing with the hands in this position.

3. Breathe the Plant Chi

   Continuing from Step 2 above, start Step 3 in the same manner. In this step, the hands drop, with the palms facing to each respective side, East and West, for example, if the body is facing to the North. With the palms facing outward, the fingers point upward. Continue the stepping pattern and breathing with the hands in this position.

4. Breathe the Earth Chi

   Continuing from Step 3 above, start Step 4 in the same manner. In this step, the hands drop down to each side of the body, with the palms facing downward toward the ground and the fingers pointing forward. Continue the stepping pattern and breathing with the hands in this position.

5. Chi into the Bai Hui (Dragon Head)

   Continuing from Step 4 above, start Step 5 in the same manner. In this step, the hands are raised above the head. The thumbs and all the fingers point to the Bai Hui (center of the top of the head); the palms are, therefore, facing downward. Continue the stepping pattern and breathing with the hands in this position.

6. Chi into the Dragon Heart

   Continuing from Step 5 above, start Step 6 in the same manner. In this step, both hands drop down in front of the body, with the thumbs and fingers pointing inward toward the heart, through the sternum. The palms are, therefore, facing the chest. Continue the stepping pattern and breathing with the hands in this position.

7. Chi into the Dragon Belly (Dan Tien)

   Continuing from Step 6 above, start Step 7 in the same manner. In this step, both hands drop down to the lower abdomen, with the fingers pointing inward, toward the Dan Tien. The palms, therefore, face the abdomen. Continue the stepping pattern and breathing with the hands in this position.

8. Chi into the Dragon Kidney

   Continuing from Step 7 above, start Step 8 in the same manner. In this step, place the hands behind the back over the area of the kidneys, with the palms touching the back. Continue the stepping pattern and breathing with the hands in this position.

9. Chi into the Dragon Ball (Breathing the Chi from the Earth to Dragon Ball)

   Continuing from Step 8 above, start Step 9 in the same manner. In this step, the hands return to a position in front of the chest, with the palms together and fingers pointing upward, as in Step 1. Continue the stepping pattern and breathing, with the hands in this position. In this step, however, one must concentrate on directing chi to the acupuncture point at the bottom center of the foot, Kidney 1, as the stepping is continued. Kidney 1 draws chi from the earth.

10. Finish

    Both hands are raised upward, above the head; then, drop to each side, respectively, standing with the feet together.

Summary

In this exercise, two points are utilized, the Lau Gong, located at the center of each palm, which receives chi. The hands then point, successively, to the Bai Hui, then the Heart (ocean of chi), then the Dan Tien, then the Kidneys, then concentration is directed to the Yong Chuen (Kidney 1 point). This is referred to as nursing the chi, from the outside to the inside. This exercise represents the basic Moving Chi Kung exercise. Once sufficient chi is developed, this exercise then uses chi, circulating chi from the inside to the outside; then again, outside to inside. The exercise can be used as a self-healing method, pointing to the part of the body that needs healing, thus, delivering the necessary energy, chi, for this purpose.

External Forms of Moving Chi Kung

External forms of Moving Chi Kung are, in general, specific to each of the martial art systems. A specific description of Moving Chi Kung forms would, therefore, be beyond the scope of this book. An important consideration, however, is the requirement for practicing Internal forms of Chi Kung, prior to embarking on a serious schedule of External Chi Kung training. The primary reason for this is to avoid the deleterious consequences of practicing out of sequence. As mentioned earlier in this chapter, practicing out of sequence may be responsible for chi and blood blockages, which can result in stroke and myocardial infarction. An experienced and qualified instructor, with knowledge related to these issues, should always be engaged when considering this type of training.

Chapter 7

The Spirit and Religion

Introduction

The intent of this chapter is not to present a review of comparative religions or attempt to persuade one to participate in a particular religious belief. Rather, the general spiritual aspect of the human being, along with the relationship to health and longevity, will be explored. Thus far, attention has been given to several aspects of health and longevity, focusing on the physical and, in part, the mental components of the overall subject. The third general component impacting health is spiritual, in particular, the spirit itself. The spirit will herein be considered an aspect of a person that is distinctly different from the body and mind, yet interwoven and integrated to such an extent, particularly with the mind, that it is often considered one and the same.

The brain is responsible for thought; and is linked to the body. Similarly, the spirit can be viewed to have a similar relationship. As a progression occurs, conceptually, from the body, to the mind, then to the spirit, the degree in lack of understanding, definition, attention, appreciation, and tangibility, can also progressively occur. Basic human need and the normal senses provide the desire and ability to appreciate, understand, and define almost any aspect of the physical nature of the human being. However, when progressing further, to the mental and spiritual aspects of life, a similar degree of understanding and ability to sense even the most obvious elements, are often not found. This is likely due to the lack of physical tangibility with regard to thought and the spirit. Within the more advanced levels of Chinese martial arts practice, little difference exists with regard to the tangibility between the physical, mental, and spiritual components. To achieve a high level of practice, the understanding, definition, attention, and appreciation of the mind and spirit must be, and are, similar to that of the body. All three are of similar tangibility and exercised in the course of daily practice. In this context, the tangibility of the spirit is indistinguishable to the tangibility described by those who sincerely participate in religious beliefs. In point of fact, high-level practitioners of the martial arts are, often, also sincere practitioners of their chosen religion. High-level Chinese martial arts practice requires exercise of the entire human being, inclusive of the body, mind, and spirit. The spirit is exercised to a degree, similar to that of the mind and body. Maintenance of health and the pursuit of longevity require attention to all three of these basic human elements.

The contrary to this position is instructive. Consider the outcomes resulting from little attention to proper care of the body. Overeating, while one of a variety of physical excesses resulting from a lack of attention and discipline to proper care of the body, can give way to becoming overweight, possibly obese. The resultant health related problems include heart disease; joint problems, such as osteoarthritis; diabetes; and diseases related to poor immune function. A similar scenario can be envisioned with regard to a lack of attention to the mind. Consider the state of human existence if the discipline of a structured education were not required. Giving the choice to attend elementary school and study to each child would likely result in a disastrous social quagmire. At the very least, the personal and social discipline derived from attending school, completing the required assignments, interacting with peers and authority figures, during youth, which often provides a mechanism to develop emotional maturity, would be lacking. The level of emotional immaturity, inability to maintain emotional control during interpersonal interactions, or offer appropriate emotional responses to life circumstances would be much different from what we are currently accustomed. The benefits to proper disciple of the body and the mind become obvious, when the consequences to the lack of such discipline are considered. This line of though can be extended to spiritual considerations as well. The spirit, being the least tangible component of the human being, can easily be, and often is, ignored. The spirit, therefore, often suffers from a lack of attention and exercise, resulting in an immaturity.

Proper attention to, and exercise of, the spirit is as necessary as exercise of the mind and the body. Proper attention to the spirit, as that given to the mind and body, is necessary in providing for a holistic approach to human health. The manner in which the exercise occurs is of a personal nature, and therefore, left to the discretion of each individual. However, health and longevity require holistic attention. Addressing merely the body, or the body and mind only, exposes the individual to the possibility of failing to achieve the goals of good health and long life, despite years of mental and/or physical discipline. The spirit, the aspect of the human being that is distinct, yet inherently integrated to the body and mind, without which, life would cease, must be given attention and exercise to optimize health and longevity. Often, in exercising the spirit, the mind is also exercised. For example, the practice of Immortal Chi Kung involves the Jing-Chi-Shen transformation process. In this practice, the mind is intimately involved in circulating chi through meditation. Here, breathing and diet assist in producing post-birth chi, which in turn is directed by the mind, resulting in the production of post-birth jing. The spirit, a component of pre-birth jing, is drawn out in the process, from a position of dormancy to one that is active within the individual. The result is the tangible activity of the spirit, in the life of the individual. Another example of exercising the mind, in addition to the spirit, can be found in the Christian faith, whereby, through prayer and faith in Jesus Christ (mental aspect), the individual receives salvation, redemption, and new life through the Holy Spirit (spiritual aspect). The result is the active role of the Holy Spirit in the life of the individual. The mental component (meditation) predominates initially in Chi Kung practice, followed by the activity of the spirit. The mental component (prayer) predominates following the spiritual activity involved with salvation in the Christian faith. In both cases, the mind and spirit are exercised, when practice is sincere. As a result of this exercise, spiritual maturity develops; emotions can be brought under control, and health and longevity can be affected in a positive manner. The health and longevity effects of exercising the mind and spirit can be viewed as indirect (passive) or direct (active) in nature.

Religious Belief and Indirect (Passively Acquired) Health Effects

Within Chinese martial arts the practice of Sitting Chi Kung, including Health and Longevity Chi Kung, and Moving Chi Kung, including the practice of Tai Chi Chuan, provide indirect or passive health benefits. These include control over emotion, opening of acupuncture channels, and allowing free flow of chi, with the resultant benefit to the organs. The abdominal breathing exercises incorporated into Chi Kung practice assist in this process by increasing oxygenation and circulation of the blood. This results in better oxygenation of the organs, including the brain. Many lifestyle conformations are required to optimize practice. For example, smoking cigarettes, excessive consumption of alcoholic beverages, lack of proper sleep, rest, exercise, and an improper diet must all be modified to conform to proper Chi Kung practice. The health benefits of abandoning such lifestyle characteristics are associated with better health. These practices, therefore, offer an indirect or passive mechanism to achieve the end result of improved health and longevity.

The indirect effects on health of similar practices are beginning to receive some degree of attention within Western culture. Businesses, hospitals, community centers, and an increasing number of physicians and other health care providers in the United States offer meditation as a mechanism to reduce stress, cope with pain, heart disease, and HIV infection. Programs in meditation based stress reduction are offered at major medical centers and universities across America, including the Center for Integrative Medicine at Duke University and the University of Massachusetts Medical School (223). Patients are referred to these centers for a variety of illnesses, including heart disease, anxiety, stress due to family and job related issues, chronic pain, caner, HIV infection, AIDS, headaches, sleep disturbances, high blood pressure, and fatigue. Specific research has recently delineated the effects of meditation on specific regions of the brain. These effects are associated with attention and control of the autonomic nervous system, such as control of heart rate and respiratory rate (286). This research suggests that, meditation acts to quiet the body, evoking a relaxation response, reducing the harmful effects of stress. Other experts have suggested that, the response to meditation may be similar to practices such as reciting the rosary. These activities appear to promote deep and slow breathing, which in turn synchronize cardiovascular rhythms, leading to positive mental and physical effects (287).

Some researchers point out that, while the practice of meditation has secular benefits with respect to health and health care, in general, meditation also serves as a tool for inner transformation. This non-secular attribute appears to hold significant health benefit as well. For example, impatience and hostility represent two hallmarks of the "type A" personality pattern. Interestingly, impatience and hostility are characteristics that may be addressed, through exercise of the mind and spirit, via mediation and prayer. According to recent research (288), impatience and hostility specifically increase the long-term risk of high blood pressure in young adults, with greater risk as these behaviors intensify. Young adulthood and middle age are critical periods for developing high blood pressure. Other "type A" behaviors, such as competitiveness, depression, and anxiety, do not appear to increase high blood pressure. High blood pressure is a major risk factor for heart disease, kidney disease, congestive heart failure, and a major risk factor for stroke. This information suggests that, modification of behavior, through exercise of the mind and spirit in adhering to one's religious beliefs, may modify behaviors such as impatience and hostility, thus reducing risk for high blood pressure and related diseases.

Since emotions impact several diseases, the indirect effects of religious belief on modifying emotion can have a significant impact on health and longevity. For instance, other diseases related to the cardiovascular system are affected by emotion. Emotional disturbance is considered a significant risk factor for coronary artery disease, especially those with pre-existing disease (289). In particular, "type A" behavior, depression, and lower levels of well-being and quality of life were found to be significant features of acute myocardial infarction (290). In patients with a fragile heart, anger can trigger sudden death (224,291,292). Anger and hostility also predict the development of atrial fibrillation in men (293). Higher depression scores are associated with an increased risk of stroke. In contrast, high levels of positive affect appear to protect against stroke (294). Emerging evidence is beginning to elucidate the role emotion, in particular stress related emotion, plays on the immune system. Chronic stress increases IL-6, which is a chemical involved with producing inflammation in the body, as well as accelerating many age-related diseases by prematurely aging the immune system (221). Stress can reduce the cellular immune response to viral infection and responsiveness in general (295, 296). Emotion also appears to play a role in cancer survival in patients with metastatic melanoma (297). In patients with sleep apnea, anger plays a role in decreasing oxygen (298). Religious practices such as prayer and meditation can impact emotion and stress, thus reducing their influence on health and longevity (223,299-301).

With regard to mental health, in general, more than 200 studies have demonstrated benefits of adherence to religious beliefs and practices. These studies largely identify a correlation between religiosity and mental health, with most showing positive effects (302). In an effort to understand the relationship between the practice of religion and psychological benefit, religiously motivated social interaction and intrapsychic regulation of emotions appear to provide a model to interpret the interactions between religiosity and subjective wellbeing.

Overall, according to researchers in the area of spirituality and health, approximately twelve hundred studies have been conducted on the healing power of faith and the health effects of spirituality (303). In addition, more than seventy of the one hundred and twenty five medical schools in the United States offer courses in spirituality, or incorporate this theme into the curriculum (304). One of the largest of the studies (305) reported the association between religious attendance and longevity for 5286 individuals over a 28-year period. The findings of the study indicate, frequent religious attendees had lower mortality rates, when compared to infrequent attendees. The results were stronger for females. Lower mortality rates were partly explained by indirect effects, such as improved health practices, increased social contacts, and more stable marriages, occurring in conjunction with attendance. A follow-up to this study evaluated 6545 individuals over a 31-year period (306). After adjusting for age and sex, infrequent religious attendees (never or less than weekly) had significantly higher rates of circulatory, cancer, digestive, and respiratory mortality, compared to individuals described as frequent attendees at religious services. When adjusting for other factors, infrequent attendees had higher death rates due to circulatory and respiratory causes. The authors conclude, these results are consistent with the view that, religious involvement is a general protective factor that promotes health through a variety of pathways. In an effort to identify these pathways, further analysis of the data revealed that, those individuals reporting at least weekly religious attendance were more likely to both improve health behaviors and maintain these good health behaviors, over a 29-year period of time. Weekly attendance was also associated with improving and maintaining good mental health, increased social relationships, and marital stability (307). Increases in leisure time physical activity was also associated with a decrease in all-cause mortality and cardiovascular mortality, over a 28-year period, in the individuals studied (308).

Further supporting the concept of indirect or passive health effects of exercising the mind and spirit is evidence indicating that, exercising faith, through prayer or meditation, can have a positive impact on attitude toward ones illness. Religious meaning appears to provide a source of resilience, late in life, bolstering health in the face of adversity (309-311). In addition, a positive impact of forgiveness on health and psychological well being, in general, was supported. Researchers have demonstrated that, people, who forgive others easily, tend to suffer from less aversive emotions and have lower stress responses, than those who hold grudges (312).

Overall, this research supports the idea that, some health benefits of religious adherence are acquired passively. In other words, through meditation or prayer, for example, stress can be reduced, which, in turn, provides a health benefit; either returning a person to good health or maintaining health in a otherwise, healthy individual. The health benefit may be evaluated subjectively, as psychological well being, or objectively, as reduced stress, resulting in lower blood pressure (313). On the other hand, adherence to religious belief may provide an active mechanism to cure illness and maintain health.

Religious Belief and Direct (Actively Acquired) Health Benefits

The direct benefit of exercising the mind and spirit on health involves healing of disease. Within the spectrum of Chinese medicine lie Traditional Chinese Medicine (TCM) and Abimoxi, a branch of Chinese Medicine taught at the more advanced levels of learning within the Chinese martial arts. While several differences exist between TCM and Abimoxi, one of the greatest is the application of Chi Kung therapy within Abimoxi. The reason for this may be due to the necessary reliance of Chinese martial artists on the personal development of internal power, chi. Practice and exercise of chi, in part, involves the practice and exercise of the mind and spirit. The end result is the development of chi, to the extent where it can be directed to the surface of the body for protection. This form of practice is referred to as External Moving Chi Kung. For use in the treatment of disease, rather than directing chi in this manner for martial art goals, chi is transferred to the patient to assist in the healing process. The practitioner's chi harmonizes with that of the patient. That is, the practitioner focuses on transferring chi to the patient's area of illness, while the patient focuses on directing the transferred chi to the same area. In addition, within the practice of Health and Longevity Chi Kung, the practitioner may direct chi to an area of illness, within his or her own body, for the purpose of self-healing.

Other major religions adhere to practices through which disease can be cured by adherence to specific beliefs. For example, following salvation through Christ, the Christian receives power provided through the Holy Spirit. Through this power healing can be delivered by placing hands on the patient. This is referred to as the "laying-on-of-hands." Christians are instructed by Christ to heal the sick through this means. Through prayer, healing of self, as well as others, may be sought. The application of Christian principles to the martial arts and related issues, such as healing, has extensively been reviewed (314).

Healing has been defined on several levels. For instance, patients may find comfort from caregivers who, at a minimum, acknowledge the role of belief or faith in the treatment of disease. This acknowledgement may offer a means of dealing with terminal illness and a sense of peace with end of life issues (315). Supporting this notion is a poll indicating that seventy-two percent of Americans would welcome a conversation with their health care provider about faith (316). A similar proportion indicate, they believe praying to God can cure illness, referring to a different level of healing. Here, the role of belief or faith may offer a direct interventional effect. Major religions, including diverse faiths within Judeo-Christianity, Buddhism, and Daoism, possess specific series of beliefs, addressing both self-healing and healing of others, through exercise of the mind and spirit, as mentioned above.

Scientific support for this notion involves a report of a diverse group of randomized clinical trials, fifty-nine in all, comparing healing through faith or prayer, with a control intervention (317). In twenty-two published trials, this type of healing was used for existing diseases or symptoms, with ten trials reporting a significant effect on outcome, compared with the control. Two of the studies reviewed were sound, from both a methodological and sample size standpoint. Both studies demonstrated a significant impact of intercessory prayer on the clinical progress of cardiac patients. One study evaluated the effect of remote intercessory prayer on the medical course of almost one thousand patients, who were admitted to a coronary care unit. Remote intercessory prayer refers to an individual praying from a location, different from the location of the patient; that is, the person praying is not in contact or communication with the patient. Approximately one-half of the patients were randomized to receive intercessory prayer remotely, while the other half were assigned to receive usual care, the control group (318). Remote intercessory prayer was associated with lower coronary care unit course scores, suggesting that, prayer may be an effective adjunct to standard medical care. A similar intervention was tested following discharge to assess the effect of prayer on cardiovascular disease progression (319). No significant effect was observed for the outcome variables evaluated, as a result of intercessory prayer, in this study. Due to the controversial nature of this type of research and conflicting results, a large scale, well-controlled study was conducted and has enrolled over eighteen hundred patients, who were undergoing coronary artery by-pass surgery. The intent of the study is to evaluate the effects of intercessory prayer, and the effects of awareness of intercessory prayer, on outcome (320). Methodological rigor, such as performing a complete and blinded audit of medical records to insure study accuracy, and an independent monitoring process, is incorporated into the study design. The final data analysis is not available at the time of this writing, yet will hopefully resolve some of the controversy, associated with this type of research.

Prayer has also been shown to be of benefit as an adjunct to standard medical care for certain patients with rheumatoid arthritis when offered in person as opposed to prayer, offered remotely, from a distance (321). Prayer, in addition to standard medical care, was randomly assigned to approximately one half of thirty-three hundred patients with infection of the blood, and resulted in a shorter length of hospitalization and duration of fever (322). No effect was observed on survival. The effect of intercessory prayer was also studied on pregnancy rates in women treated with in vitro fertilization-embryo transfer (323). As an adjunct to medical care, pregnancy rate was 50% in the group receiving intercessory prayer, compared to 26% in the group not receiving prayer, in a double-blind, prospective, randomized fashion. These results were statistically significant.

Multimodality approaches, incorporating diet, exercise, herbal food supplementation, and stress reduction meditation, was shown to attenuate atherosclerosis in older patients, in particular, those with coronary artery disease (324). The effects of this type of meditation, alone, have preliminarily been shown to reduce carotid atherosclerosis, compared with a control group (325).

Summary

The exercise of the mind and spirit, either through the practice of religious faith, Chi Kung, or martial arts, has been at the foundation of healing practices for centuries, in some form, among most cultures of the world. It has only been within the recent few decades, Western medicine has attempted to address this subject from a scientific basis, and not without significant controversy. The trend of attempting to include the scientific method in understanding the role of the spirit in health, healing and longevity, supports the findings of surveys, indicating a large majority, at least of the population in the United States, acknowledging the role of the spirit in health and healing. Despite the presence or absence of evidence, modern men and women appear to accept an innate spiritual heritage, particularly in times of ill health. The great martial arts masters viewed the subject of health and longevity from a holistic framework, recognizing the need to exercise the spirit, as well as the body and mind. Holistic attention to the entire spectrum of factors, affecting the human health, including the environment, diet, exercise, rest, breathing, the mind, and spirit, provides the most favorable conditions for success, in terms of good health and longevity. It is, therefore, from this perspective, that exercise of the mind and spirit are emphasized. With a holistic approach, the optimal conditions for success, in the pursuit of health and longevity, can be established.

Chapter 8

History and Conclusions

History

Since the principles and practices related to health and longevity presented in this book arose through the lineage of Eight Step Preying Mantis Kung Fu, the history of this system is noteworthy. The spelling of Eight Step Preying Mantis using an "e" rather than "a" in the word praying was revised to more clearly depict the character of the insect, upon which the martial art arose. The Praying Mantis System of Kung Fu (Tang Lang Chuan) began in Gimore County, located in the Shantung Province of China during the Ming Dynasty (1368-1644). Wang Lang is considered to be the founder of this system. The lineage of Eight Step Preying Mantis includes five other grandmasters, succeeding Wang Lang, in a branch of the original system, Plum Flower Praying Mantis. This lineage progressed to Chiang Hua Long, who founded the next lineage branch of Eight Step Preying Mantis, specifically. By this time, the art of Praying Mantis became very famous and many sought to learn the system, but it was kept secret over these centuries. It was not until the 1800's that documentation of the history became clearer. During this time, Chiang Hua Long, who gained the love and admiration of the Chinese people, not only because of his martial art skill but also for his moral character, became a prominent figure in Chinese history. To uphold his responsibilities as Grandmaster of the system, he was compelled to consider the very energetic jumping style of the monkey footwork contained within the system. While extremely effective from a martial art standpoint, it required a great deal of energy. In order to perform to the expected abilities of the system into the decades of advanced age of those who practiced, he realized that a new system of footwork would have to be created. Being highly respected, Chiang Hua Long consulted with masters of many kung fu systems. Recognizing this as an honor, masters of several of the most effective systems openly shared their techniques and secrets with Chiang Hua Long. He studied the footwork of other systems, such as Ba Gua and Tom Pei. He spent much time studying and experimenting with each movement. After ten years of careful study and development, intended to improve the system, he distilled the stepping into eight long and eight short steps. While maintaining and even improving on this aspect of the technique, the changes addressed the ability to practice into longevity. The Eight Step System of Preying Mantis was born. Chiang Hua Long lived to be 106 years of age.

    The system of Eight Step Preying Mantis Chuan was passed to Feng Huan Yi, who became the Second-generation grandmaster. While he was noted to have lived to an advanced age, and born in 1800's, documents do not record the exact date of his death. Through a series of events, the father of Wei Hsiao Tang, who helped Feng Huan Yi during a challenging time, requested that he teach his son. There could have been no better teacher-student match, since Wei Hsiao Tang was destined to become the Third-generation Grandmaster of the system. Born in 1888, Grandmaster Wei lived to be 96 years of age.

In the early 1950's the youngest of the Shyun family, Shyun Kwong Long, became very ill. Despite consultation with the best Chinese and western physicians, none could be found to help their son. Faced with the possibility of the most grim of outcomes, a moment of hope sprouted into their lives, as well as the destiny of the Eight Step system, as Mr. Shyun heard of a healer, who could possibly help. Friends of the Shyun family spoke to him of Grandmaster Wei, who the Shyun family later met, and trusted their son into his care. Wei Hsiao Tang transported the young boy to the fresh air of a forest environment at the foot of a mountain range and treated the young boy for one year. As detailed in Chapter 2, he prepared a special diet for the boy daily, gathered herbs to prepare medicines, instructed him to perform certain breathing and healing exercises (Chi Kung Therapy); and administered other treatments, which remain part of the heritage of this kung fu system. Within one year Shyun Kwong Long was back to full health, and was to begin formal training in the martial arts under Wei Hsiao Tang. Beginning early mornings, he would start his days with stretching and Chi Kung exercises, some of which he practiced during the period of his healing. After a normal day of school and completion of homework, several more hours were spent training in the techniques of the system. It was during this period that Grandmaster Wei came to live in the Shyun family home, and the decision was made by the Grandmaster to pass the system down to his young disciple. At eleven years of age, Shyun Kwong Long began learning the medical aspects of the system. The term, Abimoxi, was coined in the latter part of the twentieth century to capture the spectrum of health and healing knowledge contained within the system, inclusive of, but not limited to environmental factors, diet and dietary therapy, exercise and rest, Chinese herbal medicine, the fundamentals of Chinese Medicine, acupuncture and acupressure, massage (Tui Na), and Chi Kung therapy (Sitting and Moving Chi Kung).

After twelve years of martial arts training, having grown into a strong young man, eager to compete, Shyun Kwong Long entered himself into the International Full Contact Martial Arts Championships. The competitions were intense, and at times, proved to be fatal. While losing the first match, following the tradition of the competitions, Shyun Kwong Long was able to challenge others, who lost as well. Competing in up to twelve matches per day, he climbed his way to the top, winning first place. He continued his success for five consecutive years and then retired from competition. Once he completed his training under Wei Hsiao Tang, he inherited the Eight Step Preying Mantis system at 26 years of age. Beginning in his third decade of life, Grandmaster Shyun began studying Traditional Chinese Medicine, gaining a better understanding and more complete knowledge of the vast spectrum of Chinese Medicine.

After considering many offers and having traveled to many countries, including Japan, Singapore, Australia, France, and West Germany, he decided to travel to the United States, taking the name James Sun. Since he had seen many styles of authentic kung fu dissipate and become lost, Grandmaster Shyun resolved in 1984 to take steps to preserve the system of Eight Step Preying Mantis Kung Fu and its integrity. This system of famous fighting techniques and healing arts had been passed down from generation to generation, master to disciple, for over 350 years. It is and will hopefully remain one of the notably pure and authentic systems in existence, for those who wish to participate as martial artists and/or as a means of developing and maintaining health, fitness, and a foundation for longevity. With his background in Eight Step Preying Mantis Kung Fu, including Abimoxi and Traditional Chinese Medicine, Grandmaster Shyun provides a unique ability to compare and contrast the various aspects of Chinese Medicine, as he lectures and teaches throughout the United States, and in many cities, worldwide, on these subject.

Today many systems and styles of kung fu are in existence, with various degrees of completeness. The Eight Step Preying Mantis system includes the entire spectrum of fighting methods mentioned above, Shyun Style Tai Chi Chuan, Cultural principles, and Abimoxi, a branch of Chinese Medicine specific to the Chinese martial arts. Together these are the practices associated with health, fitness, and a foundation for longevity. Grandmaster Shyun Kwong Long, James Sun, introduced this system to western culture in 1984. Grandmaster Shyun and instructors of his program are certified to teach through the American-Chinese Martial Arts Federation. Over fifteen schools, in as many states within the United States, are available to provide instruction related to the benefits of these arts for health, fitness, longevity, self-defense, and the preservation of the art. While much of the information presented in this book can be effectively applied in our daily lives, many of the methods mentioned require the expert instruction and guidance of certified teachers. It is, therefore, advisable to seek such instruction when attempting to learn these practices.

It is recognized, that a similar body of knowledge may exist within other kung fu systems. Interested individuals are advised to seek out instructors within any system qualified to provide this type of information. Many may ask, "How will I know if a particular school, which does not have this type of certification process, is capable of addressing the issue of health and fitness?" Clarification regarding this issue is necessary. The contents of this book should provide a fairly clear picture of the principles and methods, which form the basis for achieving health, fitness, and potential for longevity through the martial arts. Considerable variability may exist beyond the basics, and is acceptable. Other characteristics of schools or instructors that should be considered for quality purposes, include a definable lineage. For example, a qualified instructor should be able to provide the name of his or her instructor, with a document indicating the status of that instructor within the system. In addition, a document indicating the lineage of grandmasters culminating with that instructor's teacher, should be available. Ideally, a grandmaster of the system exists, who can be contacted to verify these details. The curriculum offered should include many of the aspects covered in this book, with respect to health, fitness, and longevity. Any instructor should be able to adequately discuss questions that you may have, regarding the health, fitness, and longevity aspects of kung fu. While the answers to these questions may not be exactly the same as provided within this book, they should be consistent.

With respect to Eight Step Preying Mantis Kung Fu and Shyun Style Tai Chi Chuan, a certification process has been established through Grandmaster James Shyun, via the American-Chinese Martial Arts Federation, to verify the competence of instructors within this system. These instructors are posted on the system website, 8step.com, as to their status to teach. Questions regarding authenticity can be addressed to Grandmaster James Shyun or the United States representative of the American-Chinese Martial Arts Federation, via 8step.com. All documents pertaining to lineage and authenticity are posted on the website. As the sole inheritor of Eight Step Preying Mantis, James Shyun has also taken the rigorous step to insure the fidelity, authenticity, and integrity of the system, through trademark of its name, Eight Step Preying Mantis. In doing so, only those trained in this kung fu system, according to the curriculum outlined by Grandmaster Shyun, succeed in passing the requirements for certification as a Sifu (teacher) of the system, and remain in good standing, are authorized to teach. These steps will assist in promoting the appropriate instruction of all elements of the system to the general public.

Conclusions

The childhood experience of Shyun Kwong Long, the treatment of a life-threatening illness, exemplifies several paths used toward achieving the prize of good health and longevity. These paths include managing interactions with the environment, in such a manner as to minimize exposure to the many substances and factors that negatively impact health. In addition, proper diet, food preparation, and meal times play a significant role in health and longevity, by supplying the body with necessary nutrients, as well as other ingredients that assist the body in coping with environmental insults, such as polluted air, food, and water. The sophisticated art of breathing, Chi Kung, was discussed, relative to its ability to impact health by increasing the level of body energy, as well as energy flow. The union of physical exercise with this type of breathing, Moving Chi Kung, was presented, offering additional insight into this path to good health and longevity. The role of the spirit and function of religion in fostering the spirit was discussed, stressing the holistic nature of health and longevity, relative to the entire human being. Finally, the probability of achieving the goal of health and longevity was presented as being dependent not on one or two paths, but on all paths, working in unison. For instance, to be physically fit, while eating poorly, or perform breathing exercises in a polluted environment are not optimal for achieving success in this regard. It is the adoption of a combination of paths, united together in one practice, which is likely to result in success. These are the ancient ways regarding health and longevity, passed down, generation to generation, to men and women of these modern times.

Contacts

For further information on health, fitness, and longevity; additional books and publications on these subjects; location of schools; seminars, seminar locations, and dates; the website, 8step.com, has been made available.

References

1. *Subtle Energy: Awakening to the Unseen Forces in Our Lives* by William Collinge, Ph.D., Warner Books, Inc., 1998. Kruger AP, Sheelah S. Ions in the air. Human Nature, July 1978:46-52
2. Author unknown. Healthy ions, healthy air. Liberty Times, Health Section October 10, 1998. Available at www.beautyu.com.tw/information15_e.htm
3. Garmon L. Something in the air. Science News 1981;120:364-365.
4. Rosenberg BL. A Study of atmospheric ionization. Federal Aviation Administration. Atlantic City, New Jersey; 1972.
5. Bond, NA Jr. Negative ions and positive vibes. Technology Review (Trends Section) Jan 1983:74.
6. Clarke DJ. Ions in Nature; 1996. Available at www.djclarke.co.uk/file03.html
7. National Institute for Occupational Safety and Health: a report on electromagnetic radiation surveys of video display terminals. Cincinnati. DHEW (NIOSH) Publication No. 78-129, 1977.
8. Ott JN. The TV radiation storey. Health and light pocket book publications: New York, 1976:125.
9. Radiation emissions from video display terminals. Australian Radiation Protection Agency. Available at www.arpansa.gov.au/is_vdtrd.htm
10. Kruger AP, Reed EJ. Biological impact of small air ions. Science 1976;4259:1209-13.
11. Sugahara A, Sugiyama. A survey of worldwide agriculture systems in the 21st century utilizing negative ion technology. Report on negative ion cultivation experiment with strawberries. Sugahara research institute Co., Ltd, June 30, 2003.
12. Assael M, Pfeifer Y, Sulman FG. Influence of artificial air ionization on the human electroencephalogram. Int J Biometeorol 1974;18(4):306-372.
13. Sulman FG, Levy D, Lunkan L, Pfeifer Y, Tal E. New methods in the treatment of weather sensitivity. Fortschr Med 1977;95(11):746-752.
14. Sulman FG. The impact of weather on human health. Rev Environ Health 1984;4(2):83-119.
15. Tal E, Pfeifer Y, Sulman FG. Effect of air ionization on blood serotonin in vitro. Experientia 1976;32(3):326-327.
16. Kruger AP. Influence of air ions on certain physiological functions. Medical Biometeorology 1963:351-369.

17. Schwartz E. Ill winds that make you sick. The Saturday Evening Post 1982:12-16.
18. Nazzaro JR, Jackson DE, Perkins LE, et al. Effects of ionized air on stress behavior. Medical Research Engineering 1967:25-28.
19. Levy D, Lunkan L, Sulman FG. Weather sensitivity and atmospheric electricity. Harefuah 1978;95(12):414-417.
20. Inbar O, Rotstein A, Dlin R, Dotan R, Sulman FG. The effects of negative ions on various physiologic functions during work in a hot environment. Int J Biometeorol 1982;26(2):153-163.
21. Armijo VM. Biological and therapeutic significance of atmospheric ions. Anals de la Real Academia Nacional de Medicina 1983;100(4):635-668.
22. Osterballe O, Weeke B, Albrechsten O. Influence of small atmospheric ions on the airways in patients with bronchial asthma. Allergy 1979;34(3):187-194.
23. Albrechsten O, Clausen V, Christensen FG, Jensen JG, Moller T. The influence of small atmospheric ions on human well-being and mental performance. International Journal of Biometeorology 1978;22(4):249-262.
24. Friedrich H. Production and measurement of small atmospheric ions for medical studies and their effect on the reaction time and specific muscle reflex in man. Elektromedizin, Biomedizin und Technik 1967;12(5):188-193.
25. Badre R, Guillerm R, Hee J, Razouls C. Study in vitro of the action of light atmospheric ions on ciliary activity of the tracheal epithelium. Annales Pharmaceutiques Francaises 1966;24(6):469-78.
26. Palti Y, DeNour E, Abrahamov A. The effect of atmospheric ions on the respiratory system on infants. Pediatrics 1966;38(3):405-411.
27. Olivereau JM. Psychophysiological incidences of climactic factors o the environment. Bulletin de Psychologie 1971;24:597-606.
28. Chiles ED, Fox RE, Rush JH, Stilson DW. Effects of ionized air on decision making and vigilance performance. United States Air Force Medical Research Laboratory Technical Documentary Report. No. 62-51, 1962, iii, 10.
29. Frey AH, Human behavior and atmospheric ions. Psychological Review 1961;68:225-228.
30. San Gil Martin J, Gonzalez de Rivera J, Gonzalez Gonzalez J. Weather and psychiatry: Meteorotropism and psychopathology. Psiquis 1988;9:11-18.
31. Gualtierotti R, Solimene U, Tonoli D. Ionized air respiratory rehabilitation techniques. Minerva Medica 1977;68:3383-3389.

32. Jones DP, O'Connor SA, Collins JV, et al. Effect of long-term ionized air treatment on patients with bronchial asthma. Thorax 1976;31(4):428-432.
33. Eliz P. Amazing number of pollutants found in humans. Associated Press. 2003.
34. Scientists begin measuring pollution in humans. Available at www.cnn.health.printthis.clickability.com
35. Saving our watersheds, Effects of water pollutants on human health. National Wildlife Federation. Available at www.nwf.org/watersheds/wildlife.htlm
36. Saving our watersheds, Toxic buildup in the food chain. National Wildlife Federation. Available at www.nwf.org/watersheds/fertility/part1.htlm
37. Saving our watersheds, The ways of hormones, natural and unnatural. National Wildlife Federation. Available at www.nwf.org/watersheds/part1_2.htlm
38. Ecobichon D. Organophosphorus ester insecticides. In: Pesticides and Neurological Diseases (Ecobichon Dj, Joy RM, eds). Boca Raton, FL:CRC Press, 1994:171-250.
39. Eskenazi B, Bradman A, Castoria R. Exposures of children to organophosphate pesticides and their potential adverse health effects. Environ Health Perspect 1999;107(S-3):409-419.
40. Weiss B. Pesticides as a source of development disabilities. MRDD Research Reviews 1997;3:246-256.
41. Liess JK, Savitz DA. Home pesticide use and childhood cancer: a case-control study. Am J Public Health 1995;85:249-252.
42. Davis JR, et al. Family pesticide use and childhood brain cancer. Arch Environ Contam Toxicol 1993;24:87-92.
43. Ries LAG, et al. Cancer incidence and survival among children and adolescents: United States SEER program 1975-1995. National Cancer Institute, SEER Program. NIH Pub. No. 99-4649. Bethesda, MD, 1999.
44. Shaw GM, Wasserman CR, O'Malley CD. Maternal pesticide exposures as risk factors for orofacial clefts and neuronal tube defects. Am J Epidemiol 1995;14(suppl 11):S3.
45. Blatter DM, et al. Paternal occupational exposure around conception and spins bifida in offspring. Am J Ind Med 1997;32:283-291.
46. National Research Council. Pesticides in the diets of infants and children. Washington: National Academy Press, 1993.
47. Hill RH, et al. Pesticide residues in urine of adults living in the Unites States: reference range concentrations. Environ Res 1995;71:99-108.

48. Gurunathan S, et al. Accumulation of chlorpyrifos on residential surfaces and toys accessible to children. Environ Health Perspect 1998; 106:1-6.
49. Addiss SS, Alderman NO, Brown DR, Each CN, and Wargo J. Pest control practices in Connecticut public schools. Environment and Human Health, Inc., North Haven, CT, 1999.
50. Kaplan J, Marquardt S, Barber W. Failing health: pesticide use in California schools. CALPIRG Charitable Trust. San Francisco: 1998.
51. Volberg DI, Surgan MH, Jaffe S, Hamer D, Sevinsky JA. Pesticides in schools: Reducing the risks. New York Office of the Attorney General. New York:1993.
52. Solar Radiation and Human Health, Too much sun is dangerous. WHO Fact Sheet No. 227, 1999. Available at www.who.int/inf-fs/en/fact227.html
53. Health effects of overexposure to the sun. US Environmental Protection Agency. Available at www.epa.gov/sunwise/uvandhealth.htlm
54. Understanding the ozone layer? Meteorological Service of Canada. Available at www.msc-smc.ec.gc.ca/cd/brochures/understandozonelayer_e.cfm
55. Far infrared therapy technology comes of age. Far Infrared Technology. Available at www.electricalbody.com/far-infrared-therapy.htm
56. Food that may be making you fat. Today in MSNBC News. Available at www.msnbc.com/news/970123.asp?vts=092420031005
57. Hart RW, et al. Adaptive role of caloric intake on the degenerative disease processes. Toxicological Sciences 1999;52 (2 Suppl):2-12.
58. Frame LT, Hart RW, Leakey JE. Caloric restriction as a mechanism mediating resistance to environmental disease. Environmental Health Perspectives 1998; 106 (Suppl1):31-324.
59. Samaras TT, Elrick H. Less is better. Journal of the National Medical Association 2002;94(2):88-99.
60. Lee IM, et al. Epidemiologic data on the relationships of caloric intake, energy balance, and weight gain over the life span with longevity and morbidity. Journals of Gerentology Series A- Biological Sciences & Medical Sciences 2001 ;56(Spec No1):7-19.
61. Masoro EJ. Influence of Toxicology & Environmental Health Part B: Critical Reviews 1998; 1(3):243-257.
62. Masoro EJ. Possible mechanisms underlying the antiaging actions of caloric restriction. Toxicologic Pathology 1996;24(6):738-741.

63. Yu BP, Chung HY. Stress resistance by caloric restriction for longevity. Annals of New York Academy of Sciences 2001;928:39-47.
64. Wanagat J, Allison DB, Weindruch R. Toxicological Sciences 1999;52 (2 Suppl):35-40.
65. Sohal RS, Weindruch R. Oxidative stress, caloric restriction, and aging. Science 1996;273(5271):59-63.
66. Dubey A, Forster MJ, Lal H, Sohal RS. Effect of age and caloric intake on protein oxidation in different brain regions and on behavioral functions of the mouse. Archives of Biochemistry & Biophysics 1996; 333(1):189-197.
67. Lane MA, et al. Calorie restriction lowers body temperature in rhesus monkeys, consistent with postulated anti-aging mechanism in rodents. Proceedings of the National Academy of Sciences of the United States of America 1996;93(9):4159-4164.
68. Lipman RD, Smith DE, Blumberg JB, Bronson RT. Effects of caloric restriction or augmentation in adult rats: longevity and lesion biomarkers of aging. Aging-Clinical & Experimental Research 1998;10(6):463-70.
69. Forster MJ, Morris P, Sohal RS. Genotype and age influence the effect of caloric intake on mortality in mice. FASEB Journal 2003;17(6):690-692.
70. High cholesterol level (hypercholesterolaemia) – Available at www.netdoctor.co.uk/diseases/facts/hypercholesterolemia.htm
71. Hypercholesterolemia. eCureMe 11/7/03 – Available at www.ecureme.com/emyhealth/data/Hypercholesterolemia.asp
72. Hypercholesterolemia. Complementary Medicine 2001 – Available at www.ivillagehealth.com/library/onemed/content/0,,241012_245634,00.html
73. Schaefer E. Risky red meat: Big beef on the run. Available at www.renewalresearch.com/book/risky_red_meat.html
74. Food-pesticides and other chemicals. BetterHealthChannel – Available in www.betterhealth.vic.gov.au/bhcv2/bhcarticles.nsf/pages/Food_pesticides_and_other_chemicals?OpenDocument
75. Putzkoff IH, Cho BH, Oh JH. Animal stress results in meat causing disease – Available at www.scn.org/~bk269/fear.html
76. Mercola J. Is meat from diseased animals safe for consumption? Available at www.mercola.com/2000/jul/23/diseased_meat.htm
77. The real dope on beef hormones. Canadian Health Coalition. Available at www.healthcoalition.ca/hormones.html

78. The meat we eat. Capitalnewsonline 2002 11(3). Available at http://temagami.carleton.ca/jmc/cnews/01112002/c2.shtml
79. Eating – Making sense of food safety issues. Health Resources Wild Oats Monthly Feature – Available at www.wildoats.com/app/cda/oat_cda.html?pt=HealthArticle
80. Toxins in food and the environment. Sandra Cabot MD The Liver Doctor – Available at www.liverdoctor.com/05_toxins.asp
81. Is your meat safe. FRONTLINE – Available at www.pbs.org/wgbh/pages/frontline/shows/meat/safe/
82. Interview: Dr. Glenn Morris. FRONTLINE – Available at www.pbs.org/wgbh/pages/frontline/shows/meat/interviews/morris.html
83. Mad Cow Disease: Are you at risk? – Available at http://64.225.56/2_Animal%20World/A_MadCow.htm
84. Microbes, not chemicals, are the major source of foodborne illness. American Council on Science and Health Press Release – Available at www.acsh.org/press/releases/eatsaf0699.html
85. Mercury in fish: Cause for concern? FDA Consumer 1994. Available at www.fda.gov/fdac/reprints/mercury.html
86. Toxicological Effects of Methylmercury, National Academies Press 2000 in chapter Executive Summary – Available at http:/books.nap.edu/books/0309071402/html/4.html
87. Smith JC, Farris FF. Methyl mercury pharmacokinetics in man: a reevaluation. Toxicology & Applied Pharmacology 1996;137(2):245-252.
88. Mercury toxicity and diseases. Available at www.curezone.com/dental/dental_alzheimer.asp
89. Rosenberg D. in MVI Pediatric, MVA –12 Communication – Our Questions. Aluminum toxicity.
90. DeNoon DIs your salmon safe – Farm raised salmon may harbor unsafe levels of toxins. WebMD 2003. Available at http://webmd.com/content/Article/71/81477.htm
91. Mentor2006@aol.com. Milk – the hidden toxins. Available at www.curezone.com/foods/milk.asp
92. Bovine Growth Hormone (rBGH). Shirley's Wellness Café. Available at www.shirleys-wellness-café.com/bgh.htm
93. Midgley JP, Matthew AG, Greenwood CM, Logan AG. Effect of reduced dietary sodium on blood pressure: a meta-analysis of randomized controlled trials. JAMA 1996;275(20):1590-1597.
94. Graudal NA, Galloe AM, Garred P. Effects of sodium restriction on blood pressure, rennin, aldosterone, catecholamines, cholesterols, and triglyceride: a meta-analysis. JAMA 1998;279(17):1383-1391.

95. Cohen AJ, Roe FJ. Evaluation of the aetiological role of dietary salt exposure in gastric and other cancers in humans. Food Chem Toxicol 1997;35(2):271-293.
96. Cohen AJ, Roe FJ. Review of risk factors for osteoporosis with particular reference to a possible aetiological role of dietary salt. Food Chem Toxicol 200; 38(2-3):237-253.
97. Devine A, Criddle RA, Dick IM, Kerr DA, Prince RL. A longitudinal study of the effect of sodium and calcium intakes on regional bone density in postmenopausal women. Am J Clin Nutr 1995;62(4):740-745.
98. Tobian L. Dietary sodium chloride and potassium have effects on the pathophysiology of hypertension in humans and animals. Am J Clin Nutr 1997;65(2 Suppl):606S-611S.
99. High-normal blood pressure bad for the heart. Available at www.health.harvard.edu/fhg/Harchive/healthy.1201.shtml
100. Salt restriction more potent than exercise. Available at www.health.harvard.edu/fhg/Harchive/healthy.1201.shtml
101. Chrysant SG, et al. There are no racial, age, sex, or weight differences in the effect of salt on blood pressure in salt-sensitive hypertensive patients. Arch Intern Med 1997;157(21):2407-2408.
102. Safar ME, Thuilliez C, Richard V, Benetos A. Pressure-independent contribution of sodium to large artery structure and function in hypertension. Cardiovasc Res 2000;46(2):269-276.
103. MSG Adverse Health Effects. Available in www.curezone.com/foods/msg.asp
104. Millichap JG, Yee MM. The diet factor in pediatric and adolescent migraine. Pediatric Neurology 2003;28(1):9-15.
105. Yang WH, Drouin MA, Herbert M, Mao Y, Karsh J. The monosodium glutamate symptom complex: assessment in a double-blind, placebo-controlled, randomized study. Journal of Allergy & Immunology 1997;99(6 Pt 1):757-762.
106. Reif-Lehrer L. Possible significance of adverse reactions to glutamate in humans. Federation Proceedings 1976:35(11):2205-2211.
107. Walker R, Lupien JR. The safety evaluation of monosodium glutamate. Journal of Nutrition 2000;130 (4S Suppl):1049S-1052S.
108. Smith JD, Terpening CM, Schmidt SO, Gums JG. Relief of fibromyalgia symptoms following discontinuation of dietary excitotoxins. Annals of Pharmacotherapy 2001;35(6):702-206.
109. Hermanussen M, Treguerres JA. Does high glutamate intake cause obesity? Journal oif Pediatric Endocrinology & Metabolism 2003;16(7):965-968.

110. Oliver AJ, et al. Monosodium glutamate-related orofacial granulomatosis. Review and case report. Oral Surgery, Oral Medicine, Oral Pathology 1991;71(5):560-564.
111. Simon RA. Additive-induced urticaria: experience with monosodium glutamate (MSG). Journal of Nutrition 2000;13(4S Suppl):1063S-1066S.
112. Prandota J. Possible pathomechanism of autoimmune hepatitis. American Journal of Therapeutics 2003;10(1):51-57.
113. Mourtzakis M, Graham TE. Glutamate ingestion and its effects at rest and during exercise in humans. Journal of Applied Physiology 2002;93(4):1251-1259.
114. Scopp AL. MSG and hydrolyzed vegetable protein induced headache: review and case studies. Headache 1991;31(2):107-110.
115. Gold MD. The bitter truth about artificial sweeteners. Blazing Tattles 1995; 4(Nos. 4,5,6) – Available at www.blazingtattles.com
116. Blaylock RL, MD. Excitotoxins: The taste that kills. See www.curezone.com/foods/aspartame.asp
117. Wurtman and Walker. Dietary phenylalanine and brain function. Proceedings of the First Meeting on Dietary Phenylalanine and Brain Function, Washington, DC, May 8, 1987. See www.curezone.com/foods/aspartame.asp
118. Camfield PR, et al. Aspartame exacerbates EEG spike-wave discharge in children with generalized absence epilepsy: a double-blind controlled study. Neurology 1992;42(5):1000-1003.
119. Ven den Eeden SK, et al. Aspartame ingestion and headaches: a randomized crossover trial. Neurology 1994;44(10):1787-1793.
120. Koehler SM, Glaros A. The effect of aspartame on migraine headache. Headache 1988;28(1):10-14.
121. Walton RG, Hudak R, Green-Waite RJ. Adverse reactions to aspartame: a double-blind challenge in patients from a vulnerable population. Biological Psychiatry 1993;34(1-2):13-17.
122. Lapierre KA, et al. The neuropsychiatric effects of asparttame in normal volunteers. Journal of Clinical Pharmacology 1990;30(5):454-60.
123. National Cancer Institute SEER Program Data. See www.curezone.com/foods/aspartame.asp
124. Olney JW, Farber NB, Spitznagel E, Robins LN. Increasing brain tumor rates: is there a link to aspartame? J Neuropathology & Experimental Neurology 1996;55(11):1115-1123.
125. Gurney JG, et al. Aspartame consumption in relation to childhood brain tumor risk: results from a case-control study. Journal of the National Cancer Institute 1997;89(14):1072-1074.

126. Sugar, diabetes and incurable diseases. Available in www.curezone.com/foods/sugarpage.asp
127. Warren JM, Henry CJ, Simonite V. Low glycemic index breakfast and reduced food intake in preadolescent children. Pediatrics 2003;112(5):414-419.
128. Jumping for java. Healthoughts USC Health Magazine. Available at www.usc.edu/hsc/info/pr/hmm/sp98/healthoughts.html
129. Heliovaara M, et al. Coffee consumption, rheumatoid factor, and the risk of rheumatoid arthritis. Annals of the Rheumatic Diseases 2000;59(8):631-635.
130. Karlson E, et al. Coffee consumption and risk of rheumatoid arthritis. Arthritis and Rheumatism 2003;48(11):3055-3060.
131. Cirrhosis of the liver. National Digestive Diseases Information Clearinghouse, NIH. Available at http:/digestive.niddk.nih.gov/ddiseases/pubs/cirrhosis/
132. Kenney JJ. 10 Steps to healthy barbecuing. Sun Integrative Health. Available at www.sunintegrativehealth.com/main_pages2/maindisplayarticle.asp
133. Murtaugh MA, et al. Meat consumption patterns and preparation, genetic variants of metabolic enzymes, and their association with rectal cancer in men and women. Journal of Nutrition 2004;134(4):776-784.
134. Microwave ovens. The hidden hazards. Available in www.curezone.com/foods/microwave_oven_risk.asp
135. Cardinal F, 2003 Sleep in America poll highlights. From the National Sleep Foundation. Available at www.sleepdisorders.about.com/cs/sleepdeprivation/a/sleeppoll.htm
136. Suter PM, Sierro C, Vetter W. Nutritional factors in the control of blood pressure and hypertension. Nutrition in Clinical Care 2002;5(1):9-19.
137. Miller ER 3rd, et al. Results of the diet, exercise, and weight loss intervention trial (DEW-IT). Hypertension 2002;40(5):612-618.
138. Lopes HF, et al. DASH diet lowers blood pressure and lipid-induced oxidative stress in obesity. Hypertension 2003;41(3):422-430.
139. Appel LJ, et al. Effects of comprehensive lifestyle modification on blood pressure control: main results of the PREMIER clinical trial. JAMA 2003;289(16):2083-2093.
140. Appel LJ. Lifestyle modification as a means to prevent and treat high blood pressure. Journal of the American Society of Nephrology 2003;14(7 Suppl 2):S99-S102.

141. Svetkey LP, et al. Premier: a clinical trial of comprehensive lifestyle modification for blood pressure control: rationale, design and baseline characteristics. Annals of Epidemiology 2003;13(6):462-471.
142. NHLBI Communications Office. NHLBI Study finds all-in-one approach to lifestyle changes effectively lowers blood pressure. Available at www.nhlbi.nih.gov/hbp/index.html
143. Darnton-Hill I, Nishida C, James WP. A life course approach to diet, nutrition and the prevention of chronic diseases. Public Health Nutrition 2004;7(1A):101-121.
144. Bray GA. Risks of obesity. Primary Care; Clinics in Office Practice 2003;30(2):281-299.
145. DeJong G, Sheppard L, Lieber M, Chenoweth D. The costs of being a couch potato. Michigan Health & Hospitals 2003;38(4):24-27.
146. Brand-Miller JC. Glycemic load and chronic disease. Nutrition Reviews 2003;61 (5 Pt 2):S49-S55.
147. Michels KB. Early life predictors of chronic disease. Journal of Women's Health 2003;12(2):157-161.
148. Centers for Disease Control, National Center for Chronic Disease Prevention and Health promotion. Physical activity and good nutrition; essential elements to prevent chronic diseases and obesity 2003. Nutrition in Clinical Care 2003;6(3):135-138.
149. Steppan CM, et al. The hormone resistin links obesity to diabetes. Nature 2001;409(6818):307-312.
150. Sauvaget C, Nagano J, Allen N, Kodama K. Vegetable and fruit intake and stroke mortality in the Hiroshima/Nagasaki Life Span Study. Stroke 2003;34(10):2355-2360.
151. Lampe J. Health effects of vegetables and fruit: assessing mechanisms of action in human experimental studies. The American Journal of Clinical Nutrition 1999;70 (suppl):475S-90S.
152. Davis JL. Recipe for preventing stroke. Available at www.webmd.com/content/Article/74/89066.htm
153. Acid/Base balance. Available at www.tuberose/Acid_Base_Balance.html
154. The pH equation & health. Available at www.niomedx.com/microscopes/rrintro/rr4.html
155. Approximate pH of foods and food products. Available at www.phlife.com/coralcalcium/ph-of-foods.htm
156. Hogg N. Free radicals in disease. Seminars in Reproductive Endocrinology 1998;16(4):241-248.
157. Southorn PA, Powis G. Free radicals in medicine. II. Involvement in human disease. Mayo Clinic Proceedings 1988;63(4):390-408.

158. Bagchi D, et al. Free radicals and grape seed proanthocyanidin extract : importance in human health and disease prevention. Toxicology 2000;148(2-3):187-197.
159. Bonnefoy M, Drai J, Kostka T. Antioxidants to slow aging, facts and perspectives. Presse Medicale 2002;31(25):1174-1184.
160. Ames BN. Dietary carcinogens and anticarcinogens. Oxygen radicals and degenerative diseases. Science 1983;221(4617):1256-1264.
161. Babbs CF. Free radicals and the etiology of colon cancer. Free Radical Biology & Medicine 1990;8(2):191-200.
162. Chen C. Factors influencing mutagen formation during frying of ground beef. Dissertation Abstracts International: Section B: the Sciences & Engineering 1989;49(9).
163. Foods causing cancer. Available at www.alternativehealthtalk.com/Living-Foods-mutagenics-in-cooked-food.htm
164. Inflammation: a new link to disease by the American Institute for Cancer Research. Available at www.pioneerthinking.com/aicr_inflammation.html
165. Laimer M, et al. Marker of chronic inflammation and obesity : a prospective study on the reversibility of this association in middle-aged women undergoing weight loss by surgical intervention. Int J Obes Relat Metab Disord 2002 ;26(5) :659-662.
166. Morrison HI, Ellison LF, Taylor GW. Periodontal disease and risk of fatal coronary heart and cerebrovascula diseases. J Cardiovascular Risk 1999;6(1):7-11.
167. Mattila KJ. Dental infections as a risk factor for acute myocardial infacrtion. European Heart Journal 1993;14(Suppl K):51-53.
168. Slots J. Casual or causal relationship between eriodontal infection and non-oral disease? J Dent Res 1998;77(10):1764-1765.
169. Back J, et al. Periodontal disease and cardiovascular disease. Journal of Periodontology 1996;67(10 Suppl S):1123-1137.
170. Mendez MV, et al. An association between periodontal and peripheral vascular disease. Am J Surg 1998;176(2):153-157.
171. DeStefano F, et al. Dental disease and risk of coronary heart disease and mortality. British Medical Journal 1993;306(6879):688-691.
172. Boyles S. Can broccoli prevent lupus? Available at www.webmd.com/content/Article/76/90169.htm
173. Park EJ, Pezzuto JM. Botanicals in cancer chemoprevention. Cancer Metastasis Reviews 2002;21(3-4):231-255.
174. Weisburger JH. Lifestyle, health and disease prevention: the underlying mechanisms. European Journal of Cancer Prevention 2002;11 Suppl 2:S1-S7.

175. Huang MT, Osawa T, Ho CT, Rosen RT. Food phytochemicals for cancer prevention I: fruits and vegetables. Available at CANCERLIT data base abstract number ICDB/96616418.
176. Shikany JM, White GL Jr. Dietary guidelines for chronic disease prevention. Southern Medical Journal 2000;93(12):1138-1151.
177. Anonymous. Micronutrients in health and disease prevention. CANCERLIT data base number 93688895.
178. Mayne ST. Beta-carotene, carotenoids, and disease prevention in humans. FASEB Journal 1996;10(7):690-701.
179. Willett WC. Diet and health: what should we eat? Science 1994;264(5158):532-537.
180. Weisburger JH. Approaches for chronic disease prevention based on current understanding of underlying mechanisms. American Journal of Clinical Nutrition 2000;71(6 Suppl):1710S-1714S.
181. Terao J. Dietary flavinoids as antioxidants in vivo: conjugated metabolites of (-)-epicatechin and quercetin participate in antioxidative defense in blood plasma. Journal of Medical Investigation 1999;46(3-4):159-168.
182. Peck P. Dark beer may be better for the heart. Flavinoids in dark beer may help prevent blood clots. Available at www.webmd.com/content/Article/76/90285.htm
183. Warner J. New healthy ingredient found in red wine. Saponins may be another reason why your heart prefers red wine. Available in www.webmd.com/content/Article/73/88896.htm
184. Sorgen C. The benefits of flaxseed. Available at www.webmd.com/content/Article/62/71499.htm
185. Kirchheimer S. Vitamin E, exercise prevent aging damage. Available at www.webmd.com/content/Article/71/81479.htm
186. Ritchie LD, Ivey SL, Woodward-Lopez G, Crawford PB. Alarming trends in pediatric overweight in the United States. Sozial-und Praventivmedizin 2003;48(3):168-177.
187. Kolbe L, et al. Enabling the nation's schools to help prevent heart disease, stroke, cancer, COPD, diabetes, and other serious health problems. Public Health Reports 2004;119(3):286-302.
188. Meydani M. Nutrition interventions in aging and age-associated disease. Annals of the New York Academy of Sciences 2001;928:226-235.
189. Brown WV. Dietary recommendations to prevent coronary heart disease. Annals of the New York Academy of Sciences 1990;598:376-388.
190. Warner J. Broccoli sprouts may protect heart. Available at www.webmd.com/content/Article/86/98988.htm

191. Cutler RG. Genetic stability and oxidative stress: common mechanisms in aging and cancer. EXS 1992;62:31-46.
192. Yu BP, Lim BO, Sugano M. Dietary restriction downregulates free radical and lipid peroxide production: plausible mechanisms for elongation of life span. Journal of Nutritional Science & Vitaminology 2002;48(4):257-264.
193. Hursting SD, et al. Calorie restriction, aging, and cancer prevention: mechanisms of action and applicability to humans. Annual Review of Medicine 2003;54:131-152.
194. Spiteller G. Linoleic acid peroxidation – the dominant lipid peroxidation process in low density lipoprotein and its relationship to chronic diseases. Chemistry & Physics of Lipids 1998;9(2):105-162.
195. Barnard ND, Nicholson A, Howard JL. The medical costs attributable to meat consumption. Preventive Medicine 1995;24(6):646-655.
196. Roth E. Oxygen free radicals and their clinical implications. Acta Chirurgica Hungarica 1997;36(1-4):302-305.
197. Floyd RA, West M, Hensley K. Oxidative biochemical markers; clues to understanding aging in long-lived species. Experimental Gerontology 2001;36(4-6):619-640.
198. Pryor WA. Free radical biology: xenobiotics, cancer, and aging. Annals of the New York Academy of Sciences 1982;393:1-22.
199. Warner J. Whole-grain cereal saves lives. Available at www.webmd.com/content/Article/61/67445.htm
200. Ridker PM. Clinical application of C-reactive protein for cardiovascular disease detection and prevention. Circulation 2003;107(3):363-369.
201. Jialal I, Devaraj S. Role of C-reactive protein in the assessment of cardiovascular risk. American Journal of Cardiology 2002:91(2):200-202.
202. Zimmerman M. Phytochemicals: Nutrients of the future. Available in www.realtime.net/anr/phytonu.html
203. Barrett DM. Overview of endogenous fruit and vegetable enzymes. 2003 IFT Annual Meeting. Available at www.ift.confex.com/ift/2003/techprogram/paper_15811.htm
204. Enzymes and their activity in fruits and vegetables. Available at www.saps.plantsci.cam.ac.uk/osmoweb/nzymmenu.htm
205. Dietary fiber. Available at www.jhbmc.jhu.edu/cardiology/rehab/fiber.html
206. Dietary fiber. Available at www.hoptechno.com/book29q.htm
207. Dietary fiber. Available at www.acsh.org/publications/reports/fiber.html

208. New report evaluates health effects of dietary fiber. American Council on Science and Health Press Release. Available at www.acsh.org/press/releases/fiber.html

209. Second most common cause of caner death may be 80 percent preventable, says panel of scientists. American Council on Science and Health Press Release. Available at www.acsh.org/press/releases/colorectal.html

210. Importance of nuts and seeds. Available at www.indiangyan.com/books/healthbooks/foods_that_heal/home5.shtml

211. Seeds and beans. Available at www.acne-advice.com/diet/seeds/shtml

212. Oxygenated water. Tools for Wellness. Available at www.toolsfor-wellness.com/oxygenated-water.html

213. The stabilized oxygen answer. Angel Woman Miracle II Products. Available at www.angel-oracles.com/oxygen.html

214. Oxygen enriched drinking water. Aqua Technology Water Stores, 21st Century Water Products. Available at www.aquatechnology.net/frame86001.html

215. Activities of living systems. In Fruit and Vegetable Processing, Chapter 2 General properties of fruit and vegetables. Available at www.fao.org/docrep/V5030E/V5030E07.htm

216. Shyun J, Cimino MA. Abimoxi Fundamentals, The Way of Martial Arts Healing. American-Chinese Martial Arts Publications. Hacienda Heights, CA 2004.

217. McCaffrey R, Fowler NL. Qigong practice: A pathway to health and healing. Holistic Nursing Practice 2003;17(2):110-116.

218. Trieschmann RB. Energy medicine for long-term disabilities. Disability & Rehabilitation 1999;21(5-6):269-276.

219. Chen, Y-L D. Conformity with nature: A theory of Chinese American elders' health promotion and illness prevention process. Advances in Nursing Science 1996;19(2):17-26.

220. Carpenter J. Take a deep breath. Available at www.abcnews.go.com/sections/living/DailyNews/Deepbreath011221.html

221. Kiecolt-Glaser JK, et al. Chronic stress and age-related increases in the proinflammatory cytokine IL-6. Proceedings of the National Academy of Sciences of the United States of America 2003;100(15):9090-9095.

222. Costillo-Richmond A, et al. Effects of stress reduction on carotid atherosclerosis in hypertensive African Americans. Stroke 2000;31:568.

223. Livni, E. Mindfulness medication. Available at www.abcnews.go.com/sections/living/DailyNews/mindfulness0705.html
224. Chang PP, et al. Anger in young men and subsequent premature cardiovascular disease : the precursors study. Archives of Medicine 2002;162(8):901-906.
225. Bernardi L, et al. Effects of rosary prayer and yoga mantras on autonomic cardiovascular rhythms: comparative study. British Medical Journal 2001;323:1446-1449.
226. Seers K, Carroll D. Relaxation techniques for acute pain management: a systematic review. Journal of Advanced Nursing 1998;27(3):466-475.
227. Pugh LC. First stage labor management: An examination of patterned breathing and fatigue. Birth 1998;25(4):241-245.
228. Taylor-Piliae, RE. Tai chi as an adjunct to cardiac rehabilitation. Journal of Cardiopulmonary Rehabilitation 2003;23(2):90-96.
229. Stiller K, Jenkins S, Hall B. Efficacy of breathing and coughing exercises in the prevention of pulmonary complications after coronary artery surgery. Chest 1994;105:741-747.
230. Coats AJS. Teaching heart-failure patients how to breathe. The Lancet 1998;351(9112):1299-1300.
231. Irwin MR, Pike JL, Cole JC, Oxman MN. Effects of a behavioral intervention, tai chi, on varicella-zoster virus specific immunity and health functioning in older adults. Psychosomatic Medicine 2003:65(5):824-830.
232. Glaser R. Stress and the memory T-cell response to the Epstein-Barr virus in healthy medical students. Health Psychology 1993;12(6):435-442.
233. Stiller K. Are thoracic expansion exercises necessary during the active cycle of breathing techniques for adult cystic fibrosis patients? 12th International Cystic Fibrosis Conference 1996. Cochrane Central Register of Controlled Trials CN-00291608.
234. Miller S, Hall DO, Clayton CB, Nelson R. Chest physiotherapy in cystic fibrosis: a comparative study of autogenic drainage and the active cycle of breathing techniques with postural drainage. Thorax 1995;50(2):165-169.
235. Pryor JA, Webber BA, Hodson ME, Warner JO. The flutter VRPI as an adjunct to chest physiotherapy in cystic fibrosis. Respiratory Medicine 1994;88(9):677-681.
236. Steven MH, Pryor JA, Webber BA, Hodson MR. Physiotherapy versus cough alone in the treatment of cystic fibrosis. New Zealand Journal of Physiotherapy 1992;August:31-37.

237. Cecins NM, Jenkins SC, Pengelley J, Ryan G. The active cycle of breathing techniques—to tip or not to tip? Respiratory Medicine 1999;93(9):660-665.
238. Kofler AM, et al. PEP-mask and active cycle of breathing techniques. What is better in children with cystic fibrosis? 19th European Cystic Fibrosis Conference 1994. . Cochrane Central Register of Controlled Trials CN-00291401.
239. Bowler SD, Green A, Mitchell CA. Buteyko breathing techniques in asthma: a blinded randomized controlled trial. Medical Journal of Australia 1998;169(11-12):575-578.
240. Manocha R, et al. Sahaja yoga in the management of moderate to severe asthma: a randomized controlled trial. Thorax 2002;57(2):110-115.
241. Holloway E, Ram FSF. Breathing exercises for asthma. Cochrane Database of Systematic Reviews. 1,2003. Accession Number 00075320-100000000-01057.
242. Ernst E. Breathing techniques – adjunctive modalities for asthma: a systematic review. European Respiratory Journal 2000;15(5):969-972.
243. Savci S, Ince DI, Arikan H. A comparison of autogenic drainage and the active cycle of breathing techniques in patients with chronic obstructive pulmonary diseases. Journal of Cardiopulmonary Rehabilitation 2000;20(1):37-43.
244. Dunn NA. Keeping COPD patients out of the ED. RN 2001;64(2):33-38.
245. Lacasse Y, Guyatt G, Goldstein RS. The components of a respiratory rehabilitation program: A systematic overview. Chest 1997;111(4):1077-1088.
246. Cahalin LP, Braga M, Matsuo Y, Hernandez ED. Efficacy of diaphragmatic breathing in persons with chronic obstructive pulmonary disease. A review of the literature. Journal of Cardiopulmonary Rehabilitation 2002;22(1):7-21.
247. Anti-aging effects of exercise. Health 24, October 7, 2002. Available at www.q.co.za/2001/2001/10/07-health.html
248. Lerche Davis J. Busting health and fitness myths. Available at www.content.health.msn.com/content/article/64/72532.htm
249. Physical activity and health. A report of the Surgeon General. National Center for Chronic Disease Prevention and Health Promotion. CDC. Available at www.cdc.gov/nccdphp/sgr/ataglan.htm
250. Physical activity. BUPA's Health Information Team. Available at www.hcd2.bupa.co.uk/fact_sheets/html/exercise.html

251. Carnethon MR, et al. Cardiorespiratory fitness in young adulthood and the development of cardiovascular disease risk factors. Journal of the American Medical Association 2003;290:3092-3100.
252. Whelton PK, et al. Primary prevention of hypertension. Journal of the American Medical Association 2002;288:1882-1888.
253. Even leisurely exercise has health benefits, Says researcher. Advance on the web. Available at www.advance.uconn.edu/01022607.htm
254. McTiernan A, et al. Recreational physical activity and the risk of breast cancer in postmenopausal women. Journal of the American Medical Association 2003;290:1331-1336.
255. The benefits of exercise. Department of Kinesiology and Health, Georgia State University. Available at www.gsu.edu/~wwwfit/benefits.html
256. Johnson Rowsey P. Beneficial effects of exercise on health and disease. Carolina School of Nursing. Available at www.nursing.unc.edu/research/current/rowsey.html
257. Febbraio MA, Pedersen BK. FASEB Journal 2002;16:1335-1347.
258. Dimeo F, et al. Benefits from aerobic exercise in patients with major depression: a pilot study. British Journal of Sports Medicine 2001;35(2):114-117.
259. The psychological effects and mechanisms of exercise. Available at www.btinternet.com~diptone/arp/psyylo1.html
260. Harper P. Shap up your company with a wellness program. Available at www.bentral.com/articles/msnfeature/jun03_01.asp?LID=34245
261. Ness P. Understanding of health. How individual perceptions of health affect health promotion needs in organizations. AAOHN Journal 1997;45(7):330-336.
262. Dunn AL, Andersen RE, Jakicic JM. Lifestyle physical activity interventions. History, short- and long-term effects, and recommendations. American Journal of Preventive Medicine 1998;15(4):398-412.
263. Marti B. Health effects of recreational running in women. Some epidemiological and preventive aspects. Sports Medicine 1991;11(1):20-51.
264. Couser JI Jr, et al. Pulmonary rehabilitation improved exercise capacity in older elderly patients with COPD. Chest 1995;107(3):730-734.

265. Ries Al, et al. Effects of pulmonary rehabilitation on physiologic and psychological outcomes in patients with Chronic Obstructive Pulmonary Disease. Annals of Internal Medicine 1995;122(11):823-832.

266. Carrieri-Kohlman V, et al. Exercise training decreases dyspnea and the distress and anxiety associated with it. Monitoring alone may be as effective as coaching. Chest 1996;110(6):1526-1535.

267. Bowman AJ, et al. Effects of aerobic exercise training and yoga on the baroreflex in healthy elderly persons. European Journal of Clinical Investigation 1997;27(5):443-449.

268. NHBLI Study tests novel ways to help Americans keep weight off. Available at NHLBINetwork@AIR.org

269. LaForge R. Encouraging prospects for primary and secondary prevention. Journal of Cardiovascular Nursing 1997;11(3):53-65.

270. Slow motion fitness. Available at www.msnbc.com/news/860363.asp

271. Berger BG, Owen DR. Mood alteration with yoga and swimming. Aerobic exercise may not be necessary. Perceptual and Motor Skills 1992;75:1331-1343.

272. Douris P. Martial arts for middle-age health. British Journal of Sports Medicine 2004;38:143-147.

273. Jordan S. *Yoga for pregnancy*. New York. St. Martin's Press 1988.

274. Lasater J. *Relax and renew: Restful yoga for stressful times*. Berkley, CA. Rodmell Press 1995.

275. Schmidt TI, et al. Changes in cardiovascular risk factors and hormones during a comprehensive residential three month kriya yoga training and vegetarian nutrition. Acta Physiologica Scandanavica 1997;161 (Suppl 640):158-162.

276. Capouya J. Real men do yoga. Available at www.msnbc.com/news/923331.asp

277. Sleep for your health. Available at www.abcnews.go.com/sections/living/Healthology/HO_sleep-health.html

278. DiPasquale M. Fatigue and exercise. Available at www.qfac.com/articles/fatigue.html

279. Ayas NT, et al. A prospective study of sleep duration and coronary heart disease in women. Archives of Internal Medicine 2003;163:205-209.

280. First national sleep conference March 29-30 explores sleep's role in public health. Available at NHLBINetwork@AIR.org

281. Levine S. Up too late. Hectic lives rob kids of sleep and health. Available at www.usnews.com/usnews/nycu/health/articles/020909/9sleep.htm
282. Exercise effects dependent on time of day. The University of Chicago Hospitals. Available at www.uchospitals.edu/news/2001/20010620-timing.html
283. Wang C, Collet JP, Lau J. The effect of tai chi on health outcomes in patients with chronic conditions. Archives of Internal Medicine 2004;164:493-501.
284. Carney K. Tai chi may aid in arthritis treatment. Available at www.cnn.health.printthis.clickability.com/pt/cpt?action=cpt&title=CNN.com+-+Tai+Chi+
285. DeNoon D. Tai chi each day keeps shingles away. Available at www.webmd.com/content/Article/74/89134.htm
286. Lazar SW, et al. Functional brain mapping of the relaxation response and meditation. Neuroreport 2000;11(7):1581-1585.
287. Carpenter J. Take a deep breath. Available at www.abcnews.go.com/sections/living/DailyNews/Deepbreath011221.html
288. Yan LL, et al. Psychosocial factors and risk of hypertension. Journal of the American Medical Association 2003;290:2138-2148.
289. Tennant C, McLean L. The impact of emotions on coronary heart disease risk. Journal of Cardiovascular Risk 2001;8(3):175-183.
290. Coelho R, et al. Acute myocardial infarction: psychological and cardiovascular risk factors in men. Journal of Cardiovascular Risk 1999;6(3):157-162.
291. Lampert R, et al. Emotional and physical precipitants of ventricular arrhythmia. Circulation 2002;106(14):1800-1805.
292. Williams JE, et al. Anger proneness predicts coronary heart disease risk: prospective analysis from the atherosclerosis risk in communities (ARIC) study. Circulation 2000;101(17):2034-2039.
293. Eaker ED, et al. Anger and hostility predict the development of atrial fibrillation in men in the Framingham offspring study. Circulation 2004;109(10):1267-1271.
294. Ostir GV, et al. The association between emotional well-being and the incidence of stroke in older adults. Psychosomatic Medicine 2001;63(2):210-215.
295. Glaser R, et al. Stress and the memory of T-cell response to the Epstein-Barr virus in healthy medical students. Health Psychology 1993;12(6):435-442.

296. Yu BH, Dimsdale JE, Mills PJ. Psychological states and lymphocyte beta-adrenergic receptor responsiveness. Neuropsychopharmacology 1999;21(1):147-152.
297. Butow PN, Coates AS, Dunn SM. Psychosocial predictors of survival in metastatic melanoma. Journal of Clinical Oncology 1999;17(7):2256-2263.
298. Bardwell WA, Berry CC, Ancoli-Israel S, Dimsdale JE. Psychological correlates of sleep apnea. Journal of Psychosomatic Research 1999;47(6):583-596.
299. Kermode S, MacLean D. A study of the relationship between quality of life, health and self-esteem. Australian Journal of Advanced Nursing 2001;19(2):33-40.
300. Greenwood M. Energetics and transformation: insights on the paradoxical opportunity presented by chronic illness and pain—Part IV. American Journal of Acupuncture 1999;27(3-4):201-205.
301. Stress: It's all in your head. Available at www.msnbc.com/news/934327.asp
302. Grom B. Religiosity and subjective well-being. Psychotherapie, Psychosomatik, Medizinische Psychologie 2000;50(3-4):187-192.
303. Livni E. Science meets spirituality. Available at www.abcnews.go.com/sections/living/DailyNews/prayer-power001214.html
304. Faith & healing. Available at www.msnbc.com/news/988071.asp
305. Strawbridge WJ. et al. Frequent attendance at religious services and mortality over 28 years. American Journal of Public Health 1997;87(6):957-961.
306. Oman D, Kurata JH, Strawbridge WJ, Cohen RD. Religious attendance and cause of death over 31 years. International Journal of Psychiatry in Medicine 2002;32(1):69-89.
307. Strawbridge WJ, Shema SJ, Cohen RD, Kaplan GA. Religious attendance increases survival by improving and maintaining good health behaviors, mental health, and social relationships. Annals of Behavioral Medicine 2001;23(1):68-74.
308. Kaplan GA, Strawbridge WJ, Cohen RD, Hungerford LR. Natural history of leisure-time physical activity and its correlates: associations with mortality from all causes and cardiovascular disease over 28 years. American Journal of Epidemiology 1996;144(8):793-797.
309. Strawbridge WJ, et al. Religiosity buffers effects of some strssors on depression but exacerbates others. Journals of Gerentology Series B-Psychological Sciences & Social Sciences 1998;53(3):S118-S126.

310. Krause N. Religious meaning and subjective well-being in late life. Journals of Gerentology Series B-Psychological Sciences & Social Sciences 2003;58(3):S160-S170.

311. Krause N, et al. Religion, death of a loved one, and hypertension among older adults in Japan. Journals of Gerentology Series B-Psychological Sciences & Social Sciences 2002;57(2):S96-S107.

312. vanOyen Witvliet C, Ludwig TE, Vander Laan KL. Granting forgiveness or harboring grudges: implications for emotion, physiology, and health. Psychological Science 2001;12(2):117-123.

313. Harmon RL, Myers MA. Prayer and meditation as medical therapies. Physical Medicine & Rehabilitation Clinics of North America 1999;10(3):651-662.

314. Chen M. *Christianity and Martial Arts Power: Basic Concepts and Methods*, 2002. Dorrance Publishing.

315. Taylor EJ, Outlaw FH. Use of prayer among persons with cancer. Holistic Nursing Practice 2002;16(3):46-60.

316. Kalb C. Faith & healing. Available at www.msnbc.com/news/987695.asp

317. Abbot NC. Healing as a therapy for human disease: a systematic review. Journal of Alternative & Complementary Medicine 2000;6(2):159-169.

318. Harris WS, et al. A randomized, controlled trial of the effects of remote, intercessory prayer on outcomes in patients admitted to the coronary care unit. Archives of Internal Medicine 1999:159(19):2273-2278.

319. Aviles JM, et al. Intercessory prayer and cardiovascular disease progression in a coronary care unit population: A randomized controlled trial. Mayo Clinic Proceedings 2001;76(12):1192-1198.

320. Dusek JA, et al. Study of the therapeutic effects of intercessory prayer (STEP): Study design and research methods. American Heart Journal 2002;143(4):577-584.

321. Matthews DA, Marlowe SM, MacNutt FS. Effects of intercessory prayer on patients with rheumatoid arthritis. Southern Medical Association Journal 2000;93(12):1177-1186.

322. Leibovici L. Effects of remote, retroactive intercessory prayer on outcomes in patients with bloodstream infection: randomized controlled trial. British Medical Journal 2001;323(7327):1450-1451.

323. Cha KY, Wirth DP, Lobo RA. Does prayer influence the success of in vitro fertilization-embryo transfer? Report of masked, randomized trial. Journal of Reproductive Medicine 2001;46(9):781-787.

324. Fields JZ, et al. Effect of a multimodality natural medicine program on carotid atherosclerosis in older subjects: A pilot trial of Maharishi Vedic Medicine. The American Journal of Cardiology 2002;89(8):952-958.
325. Castillo-Richmond A, et al. Effects of stress reduction on carotid atherosclerosis in hypertensive African Americans. Stroke 2000;31(3):568-573.